ORIOLE PARK BRANCH
DATE DUE   7/02

DEMCO 38-296

SOUTH AMERICA REVEALED

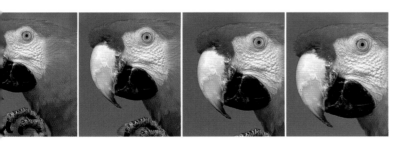

south america revealed

a wildlife guide from andes to amazon

MICHAEL BRIGHT

With gazetteer compiled by Dan Tapster & Jessica Auty

London, New York, Sydney, Delhi, Paris,
Munich, and Johannesburg

Publisher Sean Moore
Editorial director LaVonne Carlson
Art director Tina Vaughan
Project editor Barbara Minton
Editor Jane Perlmutter
Art editors Gus Yoo, Michelle Baxter
Production editor David Proffit

First US edition published in 2000 by
Dorling Kindersley Publishing, Inc.
95 Madison Avenue
New York, New York 10016

This book is published to accompany the television series
Andes to Amazon, produced by the BBC Natural History Unit,
first broadcast in the UK on BBC2 in 2000.
Series producer: Karen Bass
Producers: Huw Cordey, Ian Gray and Tim Scoones

Published by BBC Worldwide Ltd,
80 Wood Lane, London W12 0TT

First published in 2000
Text © Michael Bright 2000
Gazetteer © Dan Tapster and Jessica Auty 2000

Library of Congress Cataloging-in-Publication Data
Bright, Michael.
    South America Revealed/by Michael Bright.--1st American ed.
    p. cm.
    ISBN 0-7894-7498-0 (alk. paper)
    1. Zoolpgy--South America. I. Title.

QL235 .B75 2001
508.8--dc21   00-0058934

Commissioning editors: Rosamund Kidman Cox and Anne Gatti
Project editor: Sarah Lavelle
Text editor: Caroline Taggart
Art director: Linda Blakemore
Designers: Andrew Barron & Collis Clements Associates
Picture researcher: Laura Goodchild
Maps: Cedric Knight

Set in Gill Sans and Imprint
Printed and bound in the UK by Butler & Tanner Ltd, Frome
Colour separations by Radstock Reproductions Ltd, Midsomer Norton
Jacket printed by Lawrence Allen Ltd, Weston-super-Mare
Frontispiece: Brown pelican and volcanic eruption, Galápagos

See our complete catalog at
www.dk.com

CONTENTS

ACKNOWLEDGMENTS

This book has been written to accompany a series of BBC television programs, and all those who worked on the films contributed directly or indirectly to the book. I am grateful to the production team – Karen Bass (series producer), Huw Cordey, Ian Gray, and Tim Scoones (producers), Chris Cole, Laureen MacEwen, and Rhonda Klevansky (researchers), Sue Loder (production manager), Katie Hall, Gaynor Scattergood, and Miranda Sturgess (production co-ordinators) and Clare Bennett (production secretary) – for sharing with me their research and experiences in the field. I would also like to thank Rob Collis in the Natural History Unit Library for digging out a clutch of factual gems.

Individual sections of the book have been read by leading authorities on South American wildlife and geology, including, in alphabetical order, Jim and Teresa Clare, Will Crampton, David Day, Nigel Dunstone, Lucas Leuzinger, John Loder, Ricardo Matus, Gordon Paterson, James Patton, Ian Strange, Monica Swartz, and Yerko Vilina. I am indebted to them for helping me through the maze of latest research findings and deflecting me from too many errors. Roz Kidman Cox, Anne Gatti, Sarah Lavelle, and Caroline Taggart have worked tirelessly to refine the text; Andrew Barron has blended words and pictures to bring the pages alive; and Laura Goodchild has unearthed the most stunning photographs. Dan Tapster and Jessica Auty compiled the extensive gazetteer. Lastly, but not least, I'd like to thank the Bright family not only for their support but also their tolerance of an absentee father.

GALAPAGOS

Caracas

VENEZUELA

Orinoco

Georgetown

Paramaribo

FRENCH
GUIANA

GUYANA

Cayenne

Bogotá

LLANOS

SURINAME

COLOMBIA

Essequibo

Guaviare

Branco

Quito

Japurá

Amazon

ECUADOR

AMAZON RAINFOREST

Amazon

Marañón

Gurupi

Amazon

Jurud

Purus

Medeira

Xingu

B R A Z I L

Parnaiba

Jaguaribe

PERU

Tapajós

Araguaia

São Francisco

Lima

CERRADO

Tocantins

La Paz

Brasília

BOLIVIA

Cuiabá

ALTIPLANO

PANTANAL

PACIFIC
DESERT

Pacific Ocean

PARAGUAY

Paraná

Pilcomayo

Asunción

ATLANTIC
RAINFOREST

CHILE

Bermejo

A N D E S

Salado

Uruguay

Atlantic Ocean

Colorado

Buenos Aires

URUGUAY

Santiago

Montevideo

ARGENTINA

PAMPAS

PATAGONIAN
STEPPE

Negro

B R A Z I L
Political state

ALTIPLANO
Major habitat

State boundary

CHILEAN FJORDS

FALKLANDS

0   500   1000   1500   2000   2500km

foreword

As a wildlife television producer, I've been fortunate to have had the opportunity to travel in many parts of the world, but nowhere has surprised me more than the continent of South America. I could never have imagined just how spectacular it is. A continent of natural superlatives, it contains the world's longest mountain chain, mightiest river system, largest rainforest, driest hot desert, tallest waterfalls, and some of the greatest wetlands.

If you are even remotely interested in wildlife, South America is one of the best places in the world to visit. And it's not just the scale that makes it such an extraordinary place for wildlife. South America also has an incredible variety of unusual locations, landscapes, and habitats. There are vast, shimmering salt lakes dotted with cactus-covered islands home to hummingbirds, eagles, and viscachas. Steaming high-altitude hot springs surround thousands of courting flamingoes. Huge ice sheets spill into dramatic fjords. Towering Patagonian peaks form a spectacular backdrop for condors soaring in search of the latest puma kill. Glowing termite mounds light up the vast Brazilian grasslands at night with the bioluminescent beetles that live inside them. There are endless plains, across which strange maned wolves hunt in grass taller than a man. Misty desert beaches provide home to penguins nesting beneath giant cacti. Hidden jungle clay-licks attract spider monkeys, parrots, and tapirs. In a maze of flooded forests swim giant otters, stingrays, and pink dolphins.

Despite this astonishing variety, there has never been a book or television series surveying the wildlife of the entire continent. This is the first natural history guide covering the whole of South America. Of course, there's always a reason why things have not been done before, as I soon discovered when I traveled there. It's a continent of great extremes that often make it very difficult to work in – burning deserts, icy wastes, steaming jungles, high-altitude plains with incredibly thin air, and coasts swept almost constantly by howling

gales. The various ways that animals survive and actually thrive in these harsh conditions are truly remarkable. These unique conditions have led to the evolution of some very strange animals indeed. That is a recurring theme in this book.

Many of the remote locations I visited had only recently been opened up, and some areas are still very difficult to reach. But the rewards are fantastic, and you can usually experience them without crowds of other people. Before I started out, I would not have believed that it was still possible to travel up tributaries of the Amazon where no white woman had been before. Here is a continent so vast, and, in places, so wild, that it is still possible to experience some of the excitement of early exploration——to imagine what it must have felt like for Darwin, Humboldt, or Wallace as they pushed into unknown territory.

But you do not have to mount an expedition to enjoy many of the most spectacular natural wonders of the continent. It is possible to travel in relative comfort into the depths of the Amazon to see flocks of brilliant macaws, to watch whales and dolphins on an organized tour off the wild shores of Patagonia, or to experience the mighty Iguazú waterfalls from the balcony of a luxury hotel. There is a spectrum of location and experience to suit everyone's taste and mobility.

The book features special places our producers and camera teams have visited. Many are not easy to get to. This is why the end section is devoted to a unique eco-tourism guide identifying some of the best locations it is possible to visit for a memorable wildlife experience. There are so many wonderful places in South America that, if you have the time, you will discover many other special ones on your own.

In all the countries we visited, we met and worked with dedicated people committed to studying and saving these wild habitats and their animals and plants. It simply would not have been possible to film or research this book without the help and co-operation of the field assistants, scientists, and staff of the national parks and reserves throughout South America. These people not only provided the expert guidance and scientific information upon which this book is based, but also took me personally on many remarkable journeys. To them all I am very grateful.

I had the wonderful and fortunate experience of traveling by dug-out canoe, horse, bus, jeep, light aircraft, inflatable dinghy, and on foot to some of the most incredible wild locations in South America. I was always surprised at how little was known about such a fascinating part of the world. I also experienced many awe-inspiring sights that will stay with me forever. It is the goal of this book to share with you some of those natural secrets, to reveal the astonishing variety of exotic locations and strange animals that make up this extraordinary continent of extremes. I hope that some of you will be sufficiently inspired to experience them yourselves.

Karen Bass
Series producer, *Andes to Amazon*

THE
lost world

There were once dinosaurs in South America. Big ones. If you find yourself in the vicinity of Carmen Funes Memorial Museum at Plaza Huincil, Patagonia, you can see one for yourself. On display are the fossilized bones of one of the largest, if not *the* largest, dinosaur that ever lived. It is called *Argentinosaurus huinculensis*, a suitably tongue-twisting name for a gigantic, long-necked brontosaur that must have roamed what is now the Neuquén province of Argentina about 70 million years ago. How, though, did this enormous creature, with the mother of all appetites, come to be in a region that can be described at best as scrubby desert and where brontosaurus food is remarkable by its absence? The answer, of course, is simple: millions of years ago South America was quite a different place from what it is today.

Autana *tepuí* in Venezuela. This table-top mountain, riddled with caves and galleries, juts out from the dense rainforest. At its peak grows *Stegolepis*, a monocotyledon plant whose closest relatives are found in the sandstone regions of Liberia and Sierra Leone in Africa.

Jaguar, the largest and most powerful predator in South America. Stockier than the African leopard, it can climb and swim, but more usually stalks prey on the ground.

Argentinosaurus reminds us that our Earth is constantly changing. Wandering continents, changes in sea level and periods of mountain building all had an impact on South America's prehistory. By looking at key episodes, we can begin to understand how the continent's wildlife and pattern of natural habitats came to be the way they are.

Some of South America's oldest rocks are those of the Guiana and Brazilian Shields. These rocks date back billions of years and contain fossils of Earth's earliest life. They resemble rock formations in Africa, for at one time, these two great continents were joined.

In Venezuela today, some of these ancient rocks can be seen as dramatic, flat-topped blocks, known as *tepuis*, that thrust 5,000 feet (1,500 meters) or more out of the surrounding jungle in the Gran Sabana region of the Guiana Highlands. They inspired Sir Arthur Conan Doyle's *The Lost World*, a novel that depicts a fictional land where dinosaurs still roamed. Shrouded in mist, it is easy to imagine flying reptiles soaring around their peaks. The nearest you can get to an ancient beast, however, is an amphibian rather than a reptile, a primitive black toad, *Oreophrynella quelchii*, that can neither hop nor swim, but camouflages itself well against the algae-encrusted rocks and is an accomplished survivor.

The toad would have been here when British adventurer Sir Walter Raleigh landed on Venezuelan shores in the sixteenth century. He brought home tales of these "crystal mountains" and described the largest of the *tepuis*, the 9,430-foot (2,875-meter) Mount Roraima, as "a high church tower." Raleigh probably did not climb Roraima, but today the visitor can hike along a steep and narrow path to the top with its mazelike rock formations of the Labyrinth and the stone columns of the Valley of the Crystals. In the early evening light, the mountain's sheer cliffs glow like gold.

Raleigh went on to tell how "a large river leaps down from above without touching the mountain's wall in descent, as it goes toward the air and reaches the bottom with a roar and clamor that would be produced by one thousand giant bells striking one another. I believe there does not exist a bigger and more marvelous waterfall in the world." Was he describing another notable *tepui*, Auyan-Tepuí, the Devil's Mountain and site of Angel Falls, the highest waterfall in the world? Today, the falls drop 3,211 feet (979 meters), barely making contact with the vertical cliff face.

For the start of our story, however, we join South America during the early Cretaceous period (144–65 million years ago), when, along with Africa, Australia, Antarctica, and India, it was part of the supercontinent Gondwana. Dinosaurs such as *Argentinosaurus* ruled the land, and their reptilian relatives dominated the sea and air. In Patagonia impressive fossil bones indicate the presence of predators such as *Gigantosaurus* that would have made *Tyrannosaurus rex* seem puny. At about this time, South America began to split from Africa, producing some hydrological and botanical surprises.

The great basin we know as the Amazon probably drained not into the Atlantic, but toward the east into the Pacific and to the north into the Caribbean, through the Maracaibo Basin in northwestern Venezuela. The Amazon was clothed in cycads, ferns, and gymnosperms (naked seeds), but the time the continents parted coincided with South

▶
Angel Falls, the highest waterfall in the world. It runs off Auyan *tepuí* or "Dvil's Mountain" in Venezuela. The falls were named after US adventurer James Angel, who crashed his plane nearby in 1935.

America's first "invasion." Across all of Gondwana the flowering plants had been spreading, and little of the Amazon's ancient flora resisted the assault. Aside from ferns and tree ferns, the sole surviving gymnosperm today is the climbing vine *Gnetum.*

In the cooler southern regions of South America, the remnants of ancient flora survive. Giant conifers, such as the Patagonian cypress, grow for 3,000 years to a height of 165 feet (50 meters) and at the base have a trunk diameter of 30 feet (9 meters). There are also araucaria forests, including monkey puzzle trees, or Chile pines, that ooze resin from their trunks. During the Cretaceous period, they took a blow, as violent volcanic eruptions marked the splitting of Gondwana and coincided with the first phase of the building of the Andes. Ash covered the ancient woods, which can be seen today in Argentina as petrified forests. Southwest of Jaramillo, in Argentina, there is a beautiful semidesert where the landscape is formed from layer upon layer of differently colored rocks, and the ground is littered with fallen trunks of *araucaria* that could pass for recently living trees except that they are now made entirely of stone. They were preserved when they were covered by volcanic ash about 100–140 million years ago. There are other sites at Ormaechea and Szlapelis, near Sarmiento, where the trees were preserved when they sank into a swamp about 60 million years ago.

Family of marsupial mouse opossums. These little creatures live in most habitats throughout South America except high Andean *páramo* and *puna* regions, Chilean deserts and Patagonia.

By the end of the Cretaceous, about 65 million years ago, the dinosaurs were extinct and marsupial (pouched) mammals had been spreading out of the North American region of the northern supercontinent called Laurasia (Gondwana and Laurasia had split from the earlier single continent of Pangaea) and across South America into what are now Antarctica and Australia. They diversified and filled ecological niches left vacant by the disappearance of the dinosaurs and other creatures. Some eventually grew into giants – there were even marsupial saber-toothed cats – but the earliest forms were small, furry, shy shrewlike creatures that resembled the marsupial mice found in Australia today and whose descendants can be found throughout South America. These rat or shrew possums – belonging to three genera, *Rhyncholestes, Caenolestes,* and *Lestoros* – are some of the most ancient living mammals on Earth.

Rat possums have a rapid metabolism and must eat constantly. Their long, pointed jaws are filled with sharp teeth that can grab worms, insects, and crickets that are almost as big as they are. Rat possums have poor eyesight and will scamper about in the leaf litter, bumping into things as they go, following regular, well-marked runways with more than one individual using the same route. Like many small mammals, they have long whiskers on their

snouts to help them find their way. *Rhyncholestes* also have an excellent sense of smell. They are found today in the temperate rainforests of Chile, while *Caenolestes* live in the cloudforests and *páramo* of northern Peru and Venezuela, and *Lestoros* in southern Peru and Bolivia inhabit moss-covered slopes away from cold winds and rain.

Another descendant from an ancient family is the *monito del monte*, meaning "monkey of the mountain," which inhabits the southern beech forests of Chile and Argentina. Known locally as a *colocolo*, it looks and behaves like a little bush baby, and is so small that it can be cupped in the palm of the hand. Its ancestors appeared during the Eocene epoch (about 55–38 million years ago), but its only surviving relatives today live in Australia. In fact, if current evolutionary interpretations are correct, this group of animals probably evolved in Australia and dispersed back into South America. These creatures can be found in the forests on the slopes of the Osorno volcano, where they live among the humid bamboo thickets and monkey puzzle trees, but their range covers an area from the coast to the Andes foothills and from Concepción in Chile south to the island of Chiloé. The chances of seeing one are remote, however, for the little creature comes out at dusk and disappears into the night.

Much of the *colocolo*'s behavior has yet to be studied, but there are a few things known about it. It takes over birds' nests but also weaves its own nests between the stems of bamboo, much like a European harvest mouse. It has very big eyes, an obvious adaptation not only to its nocturnal lifestyle but also to the dark, dank places it inhabits, just like its ancient forebears. During foraging excursions, it will eat insects, although it has a preference for fruit, particularly a local version of the elderberry.

During the late Eocene, a type of short-tailed, rough-haired rodent also appeared in South America, and it gave rise eventually to capybaras, guinea pigs, mara, agoutis, paca, and porcupines. Accompanying the early marsupials as they spread across the continent were the ancestors of today's anteaters, armadillos, and sloths – the edentates, meaning "without teeth." This description is really only accurate for the anteaters – the xenarthrans – for both sloths and armadillos have well-developed teeth. Teeth or no teeth, though, these animals found that conditions in South America enabled them to diversify in a big way.

By this time, South America was, in effect, an enormous island. The edentates evolved unchecked, for they shared the continent with nothing more challenging than early marsupials and other small primitive mammals. Like the dinosaurs before them, they grew to enormous sizes. Three families of giant ground sloths evolved, and by the Pliocene epoch (about 5–2.3 million years ago), some species such as *Megatherium* grew to the size of modern elephants. They could rise on their hind legs and stand 20 feet (6 meters) tall. Their front paws were equipped with exceptionally long claws, probably for defense since, like modern sloths, their diet consisted mainly of leaves and they would not have needed this weaponry to handle their food.

Contemporary with the giant sloths were monstrous armadillo-like creatures. The largest species, *Glyptodon*, was 16 feet (5 meters) long and supported a rigid shell 10 feet

The Andes.
A geologically
young mountain
chain, many of its
volcanoes are
either active or
lie quiescent,
smoke venting
gently from their
craters until the
day arrives for
them to erupt
violently once
again.

MACHU PICCHU

Machu Picchu, the legendary lost city of the Incas, sits on a 150-square-mile (400-square-kilometer) igneous intrusion, known as the Vilcabamba batholith, which formed in the Permian period, about 250 million years ago, and was later exposed during periods of mountain building and erosion. Rock formations include a vein of serpentine 33 feet (10 meters) thick from which objects are carved for the tourist trade. The softer rocks have been eroded away, leaving spectacular steep-sided valleys and gorges, such as the Urubamba Gorge, upriver from Machu Picchu itself. Here the warm microclimate has enabled some species to live at altitudes above their normal range. The Urubamba River drops 3,300 feet (1,000 meters) during its 29-mile (47-kilometer) course through the sanctuary, creating many spectacular whitewater rapids and waterfalls.

While the city itself is the main reason for most people to visit, you have only to look around and you might see some of the natural gems that live alongside this historic site. Lizards and small harelike viscachas sun themselves on the ruins, while llamas can always be seen grazing on the terraces.

The area is famous for its orchids, with more than 300 exquisite species already identified and more being discovered all the time. There are orchids 16 feet (5 meters) high, such as *Sobralia dichotoma*, with a flower 3 inches (8 centimeters) long, as well as one of the smallest orchids in the world, *Stelis*, whose flowers measure barely ⅖ inch (2 millimeters) across. Some species bloom year-round, although the best time to see the great variety is in the rainy season between October and March, and the best place to see them is at 6,000–10,000 feet (1,800–3,000 meters), in the cloudforests.

At these altitudes, warm air from the Amazon meets the cold air of the mountains, shrouding the trees in mists. Their branches are festooned with lichens, bromeliads, and orchids, and their boughs are surrounded by bamboo and giant ferns. Here the spectacled bear and the Andean deer, or huemul, are rare visitors, but noisy flocks of plum-crowned parrots often pass through.

Flocks of tanagers and many species of hummingbirds may be seen flitting between the trees and flowers, and if you are lucky you might spot the lek where the male cock-of-the-rock displays on the banks of the Urubamba. Lekking reaches a peak between September and December.

Lower down, hiking on paths is unlikely to bring you close to wildlife, for there is too much disturbance, but there are many creatures hiding in the foliage. The light green plumage of the emerald toucanet enables it to blend in with its background despite its large black bill. These birds are often seen in pairs raiding fruiting trees. In the white waters of the river there are torrent ducks, and along the railroad track next to the river you might spot the spectacular lyre-tailed nightjar hawking for insects in the evening.

While most of the area around the ruins is covered in forest, a hike along the Inca Trail, which rises above 10,000 feet (3,000 meters) will reveal vestigial tracts of *Polylepis* woodland high up on the steeper slopes nearby, looking just like the enchanted forests depicted in fairy tales. Here you may spot the stripe-headed antpitta, since it is less shy than other birds.

At even higher altitudes, on the treeless mountain grassland or *puna*, you can see the black-chested buzzard eagle and the magnificent Andean condor. Aplomado falcons snatch green-yellow finches and other small birds, while the mountain caracara fills the niche normally occupied by crows elsewhere in the world and scavenges on corpses.

▶

Machu Picchu from the south. When it was rediscovered in 1911 by US explorer Hiram Bingham, the site was almost invisible, entirely covered by vegetation. .

(3-meters) long on its back. Its relative *Deodicurus* sported a massive tail with an armored tip like the mace of a medieval knight. These creatures needed their defenses, because, by this time, the marsupials had evolved to fill all the available ecological niches, including those occupied by the top predators. The edentates may have been large, but they fell prey to the more ferocious pouched mammals, the borhyaenids, including the hyena, wolflike mammals, and the marsupial saber-toothed cats.

The fossilized remains of all these creatures can be found at various sites around the continent, the most famous being the Cueva del Milodón on the road between Porto Natales in Chile and the Torres del Paine National Park. These were discovered by an American archaeologist, Junius Bird, in 1938. The largest cavern is open to the public, although the smaller caves are still being excavated. Outside the entrance to the main cave is a life-size stone statue of a *Megatherium*, showing just how big it really was.

It was during the Oligocene that the first primates arrived. They came to South America from Africa about 37 million years ago and began to diversify into the New World monkeys we see today, including the marmosets and tamarins, miniature clawed primates found only in South America.

The next major geological event in the history of South America occurred about 15 million years ago, during the Miocene, and had a devastating effect. At that time, an extensive belt of volcanic eruptions running the length of the continent marked the next phase in the building of the Andes, a violent and dramatic process that continues to this day.

As the mountains rose up, they upset the climate of the entire continent. Weather systems that flowed from east to west near the Equator and west to east at higher latitudes were disrupted. As a consequence, substantial rainfall fueled not only the tropical rainforests of the Amazon to the east of the Andes on either side of the Equator, but also the temperate rainforests or southern beech forests of southern Chile to the west.

This also meant that rainshadows were created by the Andes, on the western side from central Chile to southeast Ecuador, and on the eastern side from central Chile to Tierra del Fuego. The Atacama Desert, the driest hot desert in the world today, was formed on the western side of the Andes. Rivers running off the newly forming mountains evaporated within a few miles. Plants, such as low-growing cacti, that were adapted to the arid conditions survived; others disappeared. On the southeastern side, woodland gave way to savannah and then to scrub, forming the Pampas and Patagonia steppe. All the plants and animals had to adapt to the changes in order to survive, but there was one group that came to the top of the pile, and, like the dinosaurs before them, they erred toward gigantism. These were not mammals but birds. During the Miocene they grew to immense sizes and dominated the southern half of the continent.

The largest bird ever to have flown was a teratorn, one of the giant condorlike vultures that lived in Argentina during this period. Its fossilized bones were found in 1980, and it was given the scientific name *Argentavis magnificens*. Magnificent it must have been, for it had a wingspan of 25 feet (7.5 meters). It was a predator, catching prey with a nar-

row, hooked beak and swallowing it whole. The fossilized skeletons of small armadillos and maralike rodents have been found in the same rocks and they may well have been part of *Argentavis*'s diet.

The most frightening Miocene birds must have been the aptly named terror birds, which out-competed the marsupial saber-tooths to become the top predators. Standing 10 feet (3 meters) tall, with enormous bodies, powerful legs, and eaglelike beaks, they tore at the flesh of polar-bear–sized ground sloths and trapped now-extinct animals that resembled camels, hippos, rhinos, and horses by grabbing them with their clawed feet. They were the avian equivalents of *Tyrannosaurus*. Their surviving descendants are the seriemas, found today in Argentina, Paraguay, and Brazil. These, too, are fleet-footed predators, well capable of running down a lizard at speeds up to 25 miles (40 kilometers) an hour.

While avian mayhem was rife in the south, there were significant changes in the north. Until the late Miocene (about 10–8 million years ago), western Amazonia became a mixture of marine and freshwater wetlands, with the western reaches of the Amazon River draining to the north. Raised ground, where the present day Lower Negro and Zingu Rivers enter the main Amazon river channel, prevented it from draining to the east. It was the largest area of lake and swamp habitat the planet has ever seen, and it played host to a curious mix of marine and freshwater animals. The legacy today is an unexpected collection of what were once marine fishes in the Orinoco and Amazon river basins. There are stingrays, puffer fish, herrings, anchovies, gobies, and flatfish. Their nearest marine relatives are in the Caribbean Sea.

There are also dolphins. The tucuxi and the Guiana dolphin are closely related to ocean-going dolphins, such as the humpbacks of the Pacific and Atlantic. The tucuxi confine themselves to the main deep-water river channels of the Amazon, where groups of 6–20 animals swim and roll in tight formation as they hunt for catfish and crustaceans. They can often be seen from boats plying the Amazon. The Guiana dolphin is found in the other major river system, the Orinoco, and in coastal waters south from Panama along South America's northeastern coast. It is distinguished from the tucuxi by its darker color.

Eventually, the Amazon River broke through to the Atlantic, gouging its way down a valley between the Brazilian and Guiana Highlands. The area gradually drained and became the river and forest ecosystem we see today. Meanwhile, the other great river system, the Orinoco, flowed northward, forming a large delta of 70 or more channels as it entered the Caribbean Sea. Here, mangroves and wooded inlets have become a haven for birdlife, and the main river itself, together with the Meta River, was occupied by the ancient, long-snouted Orinoco crocodile, an animal reputed to have grown to 16 feet (5 meters) long but which nowadays averages only 10 feet (3 meters).

In the central Andes, debris eroded from young mountains formed the high, desert-like plain known as the *altiplano*. It stretches today from Cuzco in southern Peru through Bolivia into northern Chile and Argentina. A similar moorland known as the *páramo* covers the northern Andes from northern Peru through Ecuador and Colombia to Venezuela.

Laguna Colorado, at 15,750 feet (4,800 meters) in the Bolivian Andes. For part of the year The lake is home to the world's largest population of the rare James's flamingo. Its waters are sometimes colored red.

IGUAZÚ/IGUAÇÚ FALLS

Straddling the Brazil–Argentina border, the Iguazú Falls (Iguaçú in Portuguese) are nothing short of spectacular. They are about 2.5 miles (4 kilometers) wide – four times as wide as Niagara – with 275 cascades separated by islands and rocky outcrops. At the height of the rainy season, in January and February, rainbows dance in spray thrown 300 feet (90 meters) into the air as 58,000 tons of water per second tumble from the Paraná Plateau and crash in a thunderous roar into the horseshoe shaped canyon – "an ocean pouring into an abyss," as Swiss botanist Robert Chodat once described it.

Despite the number of visitors, the area is rich in wildlife. Thousands of dusky swifts nest behind the wall of water. On sunny mornings, flocks of 3,000 or more can be seen catching insects in front of the most spectacular waterfall, the Devil's Throat. In the distance you can hear troops of howler monkeys calling from the surrounding forest, and from August to September, your attention can switch between the stunning variety of orchids, the infinite variety of butterflies, and the flocks of colorful macaws. You might even spot a jaguar on the road.

On the Argentinian side, two circuits of paths, walkways, and footbridges take you to the islands and walkways directly above the falls. You pass cacti, strangler figs, slender trees protected by *Azteca* ants, palm trees containing the hanging nests of a local songbird, the red-rumped cacique, and wide-crowned trees festooned with lichens, ferns, and orchids. On the islands of the upper river you might see the rare broad-nosed caiman. Park rangers lead night walks on the upper circuit, while dawn and dusk are the times to explore the nearby Macuco Trail, a walk 2.5 miles (4-kilometers) through the Iguazú National Park to the Arrechea Fall.

A ferry runs between the mainland and Isla San Martín, where you get a panoramic view of the San Martín Fall. Small rubber boats will take you right into the horseshoe of the Devil's Throat. The most exciting views, however, are from a helicopter ride (arranged on the Brazilian side) over the falls and up the canyon.

▲

The falls seen from the Brazilian side. They were designated a World Heritage Site in 1984, and the surrounding subtropical forest is a protected haven for a wealth of wildlife, including 448 bird species and 250 species of butterflies.

On the *altiplano*, freshwater and saline lakes became the feeding and breeding grounds of creatures usually associated with warmer climates. Fossil footprints indicate that flamingoes have been visiting Chile's *altiplano* for at least seven million years. To exploit the new sources of food the lakes provided, these birds found themselves having to survive in extreme conditions – warm by day, but exceedingly cold at night. Their presence can be explained, perhaps, by the fact that during the Tertiary period when the lakes formed, the *altiplano* was not as high as it is now. Even today the region is snow-free for most of the year, and because it is so close to the Equator there are 12 hours of sunlight every day.

At various times during the Pliocene, North and South America joined up in the area of the Isthmus of Panama and then separated again. The proximity of the two continents meant that creatures from either north or south could take advantage of the opportunities in the new land. Coatis, intelligent and inquisitive, were among the first to do so. Foraging on the forest floor, they use a refined sense of smell to detect food, such as insects and grubs, and sharp claws to dig it up. They can rip apart decaying logs in order to get at the grubs inside, and will roll a large tarantula on the ground until all its irritating hairs are rubbed off. At dusk all the family, including the youngsters, help to build nests in trees, where they spend the night.

Together with racoons and mouselike rodents, coatis first reached South America from the north mainly by island-hopping, but eventually a land bridge was established and all kinds of creatures headed south, while others went north. The immigrants from the north included peccaries, horses, dogs, foxes, big and small cats, bears, tapirs, camel-like animals, deer, rabbits, squirrels, shrews, and a whole lot more. There were no wild goats, sheep, or oxen anywhere in the Americas at this time, and so their places were taken by the mountain living cameloids, the vicuñas, and guanacos, and the huemul deer.

By the time of the Pleistocene (1.7 million – 10,000 years ago), the invaders were doing well. Guanacos and vicuñas spread throughout the Andes; peccaries and tapirs adopted the rainforests, plains, and swamps; and foxes found niches almost everywhere. The jaguar began to stalk the rainforests, preying on tapirs, deer, and peccaries, and the puma spread to the southernmost tip of the continent.

Meanwhile, South America's geological superlatives continued to be created. In the Peruvian Andes, the Colca Canyon became the world's deepest gorge, and 86 circular craters gave us the Valley of the Volcanoes. In the south, an enormous icecap covered Patagonia during the Ice Age. Only the highest mountain peaks protruded through the thick frozen blanket. Today, its remnants form the largest ice field outside the Arctic and Antarctic, from which glaciers plunge westward toward the sea and eastward into lakes.

In the southern half of the continent, the advancing and retreating ice cover had a devastating impact on the vegetation. Many plants were lost. The survivors again were the large conifers, which have been represented continuously on the continent since the Jurassic. There was also the southern beech, one of the oldest living broad leaved trees, which covers much of the forested area of Patagonia today.

The Ice Ages also had a profound effect on the Amazon River. As water was locked up in the icecaps and the sea level dropped 100 feet (30 meters) or more, the rivers became torrents and eroded deeper and wider channels. Today you can see the result, particularly from the air. The lower reaches of rivers are more like long lakes. In two places – the lower Río Negro and mid-Río Amazonas – there are underwater canyons more than 330 feet (100 meters) deep. In the Amazon this might be explained by the rush of water from the Andes, but the source of the deep-water areas in the Río Negro, which runs off the eroded Guianan Plateau, is still a complete mystery.

Since the Pliocene, when the Amazon reached the Atlantic, the river has been transporting huge quantities of pulverized rock from the Andes and the Brazilian and Guiana Highlands. Giant sand-and-silt dunes over 33 feet (10 meters) high lie below the moving waters and are rolled gently along the Amazon river system until they reach the estuary, which is 125.miles (200 kilometers) wide. In the Atlantic, about 60 miles (100 kilometers) offshore, they deposit their silt onto the sea bed, where a dumpsite 15,750 feet (4,800 meters) thick, covering an area the size of mainland Britain, is spilling over the continental shelf and into the sea.

In the Andes, meltwater from the great freeze accumulated on the mountain

Valley of the Moon, near the old road out of San Pedro de Atacama to Calamba in Chile. Its striking sandstone rock formations sit in a vast desert landscape and glow eerily at sunset. At night, a full moon gives the rocks a frosted appearance.

plateau, forming great bodies of water such as the ancient Lake Ballivián. It has gone now, reduced to a series of lakes that includes Titicaca on the Peru–Bolivia border, the highest navigable lake in the world and the largest lake in South America. As Titicaca formed at 12,500 feet (3,810 meters) above sea level, it acquired its own fauna, including a flightless grebe and its own species of frog. This frog is confined to sediments in the shallows, where it spends its entire life underwater, safe from the glare of the sun but starved of oxygen. It copes with the help of a rumpled skin, resembling an ill-fitting suit, that increases its surface area and therefore its ability to absorb any available oxygen.

The water in many saline lakes evaporated, leaving inhospitable caustic saltpans, such as Bolivia's vast Salar de Uyini and Chile's baking hot Salar de Atacama, two of the largest salt flats in the world.

By the time the ice had retreated and the continent settled down once again, there was yet another invasion. This time it was by people. No one is sure when they arrived or from where they came – North America, Africa, or the Pacific islands have all been proposed – but the favored view today is that they originated in Siberia, and moved down the Pacific coast of North America on foot or by boat. One of the earliest human settlements in South America has been found at Toca do Boqueirão da Pedra Furada in Brazil. It is one of 200 or more sandstone rock shelters in the area. The main cave is about 230 feet (70 meters) long and contains exceptional rock art. Painted in red and yellow ocher, charcoal, and other pigments, the pictures are of abstract symbols, trees, sticklike cartoon people, and animals, including jaguars, deer, pigs, lizards, armadillos, flightless rheas, and freshwater crabs. There are stone tools, a circular stone hearth, and food storage pits – charcoal in the hearth has been dated at between 33,000 and 17,000 years old.

People rapidly colonized the continent. One site in a peat bog at Monte Verde in Chile is thought to be about 13,000 years old, and excavations there have yielded stone and wooden tools, charcoal, and the bones of llamas and mastodons. Ancient people also engraved the white boulders of Toro Muerto (left on the ground after volcanic activity) with pictures of local wildlife, geometric shapes, and men wearing what look like space helmets.

Artists and artisans these early humans may have been, but their rapid invasion brought trouble for the continent's wildlife. In the blink of an evolutionary eye, they successfully wiped out the megafauna. Some scientists believe that the crash was due to overhunting, although it has been suggested that invading humans introduced diseases, via themselves or their dogs, which caused these large animals to die out. *Megatherium* bones found with human remains in the Mylodon Caves in Patagonia confirm that the two coexisted about 9000 years ago. But *Megatherium* and its relatives succumbed, humankind survived, and we have decided the fate of all parts of the continent ever since.

Another cave with human artefacts is the Cueva de las Manos, meaning "Cave of the Hands." It lies out of Cochrane, on the road from Chile to Argentina. In four adjacent caves can be found not only rock art depictions of guanacos and other animals in charcoal, lime, ochre, hematite, and blood, but also the outlines of 829 human hands, 96 percent of

them left hands, indicating perhaps that the people were mainly right-handed and they painted with their right hands. The cave is in a gorge of the Pinturas River and was thought to have been occupied about 9,300 years ago.

Whenever they arrived and from whatever direction they came, people eventually settled and began to change the landscape. Long before the Incas built their extraordinary cities in the Andes, the slopes were terraced and cultivated, and ancient people settled all over South America. There were even extensive pre-Columbian "civilizations" in the Amazon, where terraced agriculture was practiced, rather than the "slash and burn" systems adopted today. Some of these ancient people left us mysteries to puzzle, such as the extraordinary lines on the Nazca Plains in Peru, which show animals and people in giant cartoonlike pictures hundreds of feet across, that can be appreciated only from the air.

There were mountain people and coastal people. In the mountains, they cultivated potatoes. Llamas and alpacas became the beasts of burden and also supplied meat and wool. On the coast, people fished from reed boats just as they do today. Using a relay of runners, they even supplied the Incas in the mountains with fresh fish every day. This idyll, however, was short lived. The next and most recent invasion took place over 500 years ago. This time the colonists arrived from Europe, mainly from Spain and Portugal. At first

◀

Llamas with their Bolivian herders. The llama is thought to be a domesticated version of the wild guanaco. There are two breeds: the chaku and ccara.

they came as conquerors, but soon they were followed by explorers and naturalists, who were to make some amazing discoveries.

In 1799, for example, Alexander von Humboldt chanced upon a cave system 6.5 miles (10.5 kilometers) long in the Caripe Mountains of Venezuela that was later to be named in his honor. What made these caves special to Humboldt was the presence of an extraordinary creature, the pigeon-sized oilbird, or *guácharo*. It is still there today, protected by the area's national park status, and visitors can experience the same chilling encounter that Humboldt must have had all those years ago. Led by lantern down a path beside a subterranean stream, you come to the first cavern, Humboldt's Gallery, and are greeted by the deafening screams of the 10,000–15,000 birds that live here. The cave is over 115 feet (35 meters) high and the birds nest or roost on ledges near the top. The flapping of their wings and their high-pitched screams echo around grotesquely shaped stalactites and stalagmites. Their accumulated debris is piled high on the floor.

The birds leave the cave at night to forage in the surrounding forest for fruits, especially palm nuts. They eat the pulp and regurgitate the seeds. Piles of decaying seeds and guano cover the cave floor, creating an entire cave ecosystem in which crickets, spiders, centipedes, crabs, and rats thrive, but where forests of spindly palm-nut seedlings sprout and die in the dark..

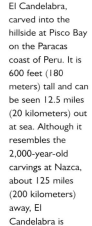

El Candelabra, carved into the hillside at Pisco Bay on the Paracas coast of Peru. It is 600 feet (180 meters) tall and can be seen 12.5 miles (20 kilometers) out at sea. Although it resembles the 2,000-year-old carvings at Nazca, about 125 miles (200 kilometers) away, El Candelabra is thought to be much younger.

The most spectacular time is dusk, when up to 250 birds a minute pour out of the cave mouth, which is 80 feet (25 meters) in diameter. They find their way in the dark using a primitive echolocation system and feed on the wing, hovering like hummingbirds as they pluck palm nuts from the trees. The seeds in the caves are mainly regurgitated by nestlings. The adults drop seeds as they go. Each night they spread palm-nut seeds over vast areas of the forest, a colony of 10,000 birds dispersing 21 tons of seeds a month.

There were once many caves containing oilbirds; now the caves are few. When the Europeans settled in the New World, they opened it up to massive exploitation. In South America, cattle and sheep farms took over the plains and plateaus; plantations replaced native trees; the rich adorned themselves with the skins of spotted cats and the wool from vicuña; hardwoods were hacked down to make toilet seats, and vast tracts of land plowed up for soy and sunflower oil.

The habitat most badly hit was the Atlantic mountain forest of Brazil, the most endangered tropical rainforest in the world. It once covered an area of over 40,000 square miles (one million square kilometers), but only 7 percent of that remains. The remnants still harbor an extraordinary variety of wildlife, which some authorities consider the greatest diversity of plants and animals in the world.

One species, the golden lion tamarin, was nearly lost forever. There are thought to be no more than 800 surviving in the wild, and half of those are in the Poços das Antas Biological Reserve to the north of Rio de Janeiro. Since 1971, the Golden Lion Tamarin Project, supported by a host of wildlife charities and scientific institutions, has tried to re-establish rainforest areas and reintroduce captive-bred tamarins to the wild. It has had some degree of success, increasing the wild population by 25 percent, and you can now go and see for yourself an animal that was brought back from the brink.

So, bringing our story up to date, we find that the South America of today covers about one eighth of the Earth's land surface. Triangular in shape, the continent is surrounded by sea – the Caribbean Sea to the north, the Atlantic Ocean to the east and the Pacific Ocean to the west. The Drake Passage separates the southern tip of the triangle from the Antarctic Peninsula, and in the northwest it is linked to North America by the Isthmus of Panama. It has the world's longest continuous mountain chain, its greatest river system and its driest hot desert. The continent's highest point is the peak of Aconcagua in Argentina. At 22,835 feet (6962 meters), it is the highest mountain in the western hemisphere. The lowest point is also in Argentina, at Laguna del Carbón, and is, in fact, the lowest point in all of the Americas. It lies in a large depression known as the Gran Bajo de San

Julián, not far from the road between Puerto Santa Cruz and Puerto San Julián. About 30 miles (48 kilometers) south of Puerto San Julián, and a further 11 miles (18 kilometers) along a track you reach a dry salt lake. At 344 feet (105 meters) below sea level, this place is 62 feet (19 meters) deeper than Badwater in Death Valley, California, the previous holder of the title.

Between the rarefied heights of Aconcagua and the oppressive depths of Laguna del Carbón, there are a great variety of habitats, and even wilderness areas still to be discovered and explored. The European invaders did not reach everywhere. Parts of the Amazon rainforest are still unknown to Westerners; the Chilean fjord coast and the southern beech forests are empty and unexplored. Mountains, deserts, forests, and sea remain barriers to development. It is sobering to remember that the Spanish conquistadors completely missed Machu Picchu, the lost city of the Incas set high on a ridge in the Peruvian mountains. It was not rediscovered until 1911.

South America clearly has many surprises in store for us yet. The pages that follow offer a flavor of the wildness that is South America – a journey through this land of extremes to meet the extraordinary diversity of plants and animals that live there.

▶
Pristine Atlantic rainforest in Brazil. The bromeliad *Vriesea wawranea* grows on tree trunks. Located close to the heavily populated industrial belt of Brazil, much of the rest of the forest has been destroyed.

◀
Golden lion tamarin. This monkey lives in heavily populated parts of the Atlantic rainforest of Brazil. A captive-breeding and release programme is trying to save the species from extinction, but fewer than 400 survive in the wild. A further 500 are to be found in captivity.

the andes

Our journey across the roof of the western world begins with the highest elevations at the lowest latitudes—places close to the Equator where the temperature drops way below zero, winds blow to hurricane force and the air is so thin it is difficult to breathe. It ends at sea level in the high latitudes, where glaciers plunge into the sea and the prevailing conditions are those more usually associated with the Antarctic. In between are stark moorlands, misty cloudforests, hot and cold deserts and dense tropical and temperate woodlands. The Andes is a place of extremes.

▶ Lago Gray, set in an elongated gorge against the background of the Paine Massif, Chile. Green and blue icebergs break away from the huge Glacier Gray, and the wind whips ice-cold droplets of water away from the glacier's snout. Lakeside beaches look as if they were paved with a surface of egg-sized rocks.

◀ Mountain viscacha. This long-legged, rabbit-like relative of the chinchilla has thick, soft fur, grayish or brown above and white or gray below. Males are twice the size of females.

Everything about the Andes is spectacular. It is the world's youngest and longest-running mountain chain, extending some 4500 miles (7245 kilometers) from the Caribbean coast of Colombia to South America's southernmost tip in Patagonia, and it is still being built. This is one of the most seismically active places on the planet, with the highest active volcanoes in the world—Tupungato (21,484 feet/6550 meters) in Chile and Cotopaxi (19,342 feet/5897 meters) in Ecuador.

A gentle reminder that the Andes are still being shaped by the colossal forces at the molten center of the Earth occurred in 1986, when Tupungato, just 50 miles (80 kilometers) east of Santiago, was awakened from its dormancy and blew its top. Many Andean volcanoes are actively smoking and many others have the potential to burst into life at any moment. In December 1999, for example, Tungurahua and Gua Pichincha, both in Ecuador, erupted in a flurry of activity. Tungurahua, whose name means "throat of fire," threw out molten lava and produced an ash cloud that rose nearly 7 miles (11 kilometers) into the air. Gua Pichincha, only 7 miles (11 kilometers) from the capital Quito, produced an extremely high cloud that enveloped the city, closing the main airport and causing city-dwellers to buy gas masks and stock up on canned food. Two scientists were killed in a previous eruption on the mountain in 1993.

◄

Ecuador's Cotopaxi volcano. At 19,342 feet (5897 meters), it has a perfectly shaped cone. Its eruptions destroyed the nearby town of Latacunga not once but several times, in 1742, 1768 and 1877. Herds of feral horses are often seen on its lower slopes.

In the cold and rarefied air of the mountain peaks and volcanic calderas, there are few living things. Lichens or algae may find a sheltered hollow or ledge, but surprisingly at least one hardy flowering plant is found up to 15,750 feet (4800 meters) on the scree slopes. It is the *qallu-qallu*, a low growing plant with a rosette of tongue-shaped, leathery leaves, able to survive in this desolate place because it contains an antifreeze that protects it from chilling nighttime temperatures.

Sandwiched between the snowy peaks and fiery craters is the next zone down—the high, dry plains, known as the *puna* or *altiplano*, where the soil between wind polished boulders is rocky, thin, and flecked with splinters of black obsidian. It supports no more than patches of grasses and evergreen shrubs that are molded by the wind into low, dome-shaped tussocks.

This is a harsh and barren place. Most snow, sleet, hail, and sometimes rain, falls in January and February. The rest of the year is dry and sunny, yet temperatures might vary from -4°F (-20°C) at night to 68°F (20°C) during the day. If a cloud should pass across the sun, the air temperature plummets by 27°F (15°C) in five to ten minutes. While mornings can be still and calm, westerly winds blow up every afternoon and evening, and so the cold feels very, very cold.

It is difficult to imagine that anything could live or would want to live on the highest parts, but there are unexpected sanctuaries. El Tatio in Chile at 13,800 feet (4200 meters) is the highest geyser field in the world. Due to its altitude, water boils at just 187°F (86°C), rather than the usual 212°F (100°C) at sea level, and the air is filled with great columns of steam. The ground is littered with chimneys and cones of crystallized silica and other salts, and the only water is that which comes boiling out of the ground. It is a frightening place, but there is a surprising profusion of life here, plants and animals adapted to live at the edge of what is possible.

The shallow runnels containing run-off from the geyser field are stained red and green with colonies of heat-resistant bacteria and algae, some of which wave in the current with long, ultra-fine filaments. Just a few yards from a boiling geyser, the air cools the water to the temperature of a comfortable bath, and in it, amazingly, lives a dark colored frog (*Telmatobius spinulosa*). Its tadpoles hide among the filamentous weeds in shallow water. The adult frog feeds both in and out of the water on aquatic larvae, tiny leeches, flies and the large spiders that scuttle between springs. It does, however, have a rather sinister habit—it eats the neighbors. This species is exceptionally cannibalistic, and frogs can be seen wandering about with the webbed feet of other frogs, only marginally smaller than themselves, sticking out of their mouths.

Nearby, not far from the Ollague volcano on the border between Bolivia and Chile, is another geyser field, but one that offers a quite different experience. Sol de Mañana, meaning "sun of the morning" because when the sun first rises its rays are filtered through the clouds of steam, is off the beaten track, but for the volcano enthusiast it is an extraordinary place. There are cracks in the ground where huge quantities of steam escape. It sounds

like a pressure cooker and feels like the bowels of the Earth. Everything vibrates, and the smell of sulphur hangs in the air, but the interest here is not in geysers but in the pools of boiling pastel-colored muds. Some are just a couple of yards across, others many yards, and each has bubbling mud—yellow, red and gray—like bowls of very thick, multi-colored porridge cooking.

The streams that drain away from the geysers, together with the run-off from melting ice and snow or from the infrequent rain, sleet or snow storms, flow down the sides of the mountains. Some are channeled into great depressions, the salt lakes or salars. These can be blue, green, pink, cloudy white, or multicolored, the color coming from the bacteria and diatoms that live in them. Most of the lakes are shallow, and at these high altitudes their waters evaporate very rapidly, concentrating the salts and forming high salt deserts, such as Salar Uyuni and Salar de Atacama, two of the largest saltpans in the world. Surely, you would think, no living thing could withstand these harsh conditions? Not true: brine shrimp endure the dry periods as drought-resistant eggs, and when water eventually comes, the emerging shrimps can survive in saturated salt solutions by excreting ions from their gills and producing concentrated urine from their maxillary glands. Up here on the "roof of the world," they are the salt lake's equivalent of the ocean's krill, and other creatures depend on them for food.

The salt lakes and their diatoms are a magnet for the flamingo, one of the few birds to take advantage of a caustic landscape that is 10 times as salty as the sea. It lives here in the biting cold and violent winds, making full use of its long limbs to wade into the brine and feed by hanging its head down between its legs. In this position, the bill is used upside-down, and the bird filters diatoms and shrimps from the water by passing it from one side of its bill to the other using its tongue as a pump. A mesh of lamellae, similar in function to the baleen in whales, filters out the food.

The *altiplano* is the only place in the world where you can watch three species of flamingo: the Andean, the Chilean, and the James's, the rarest flamingo in the world. They inhabit a crescent-shaped area about 120,000 square miles (315,000 square kilometers) in area, extending from southern Peru through Bolivia to northern Chile and northwestern Argentina. James's flamingo skims the surface for small items, such as algae, diatoms, and nematodes, while the Chilean has a deeper bill, which it sweeps from side to side to vacuum up brine shrimps, aquatic fly larvae and the small molluscs living on the lake bottom. The three species differ in that the lamellae in their mouths are spaced at different intervals, so they can feed side by side but eat different types of food and avoid competition.

At the end of September, during the South American spring, the birds arrive in the thousands to breed, and the first thing they do is dance—or at least march. Up to a thousand individuals strut shoulder to shoulder, heads turning this way and that, in a well-regimented display. Mates are found, couples separate from the main group, and partnerships are cemented. Nest building starts at the beginning of October. The nest itself is a raised, round platform of mud with a depression in the top that keeps eggs and chicks

▶
The Tatio geysers, a geothermal field at 14,170 feet (4320 meters) surrounded by high mountain peaks. They shoot plumes of steam up to 30 feet (9 meters) into the air and are surrounded by multicoloured mineral salts.

off a lake floor liable to flooding. Eggs hatch in December, and young birds take their first flight in April. At about this time, the endless table of white is stained with patches of black and gray. Closer inspection reveals that they are not rocky outcrops but large crèches of young flamingoes that have yet to acquire their rose-tinted plumage.

The nests are located in the middle of these vast deserts of salt and lakes of brine, some more than 4000 square miles (10,000 square kilometers) in area and as close to hell as anyone can imagine. Underfoot, a caked layer of painfully bright, caustic mud overlays a deep, smelly, gray ooze, and the air temperature here can soar to 120°F (50°C) during the day but plunge to freezing at night. No predator in its right mind—and there are Andean foxes, or *culpeos*, Andean mountain cats and Geoffroy's cats in the rocky areas nearby—would risk crossing these vast salt plains, where there is no place to hide or find shade and no water to quench a thirst, and so it is a relatively safe place for flamingoes. Even people are prevented from visiting these areas when the birds are breeding. The birds are skittish and will abandon nests at the slightest disturbance, and so the authorities take no chances.

On the surface of Bolivia's Salar Uyuni, the dark blemishes on the landscape really are outcrops—islands of volcanic rocks stranded in a sea of salt. Uyuni was once a lake, and parts of it still flood to a depth of 6 feet (2 meters) in the wet season, from December

◀

James's flamingoes on an *altiplano* lake. This small species of flamingo has a deep-keeled bill to filter out small food particles, such as algae and diatoms. Its bill excludes larger particles, so it can feed without competition alongside other species that eat larger food items. Flamingoes can be found at altitudes of up to 13,000 feet (4000 meters).

through to February. But, in the dry, the water evaporates to leave one of the largest salt flats in the world. The salt is only a thin crust, no more than 2 feet (60 centimeters) thick, and it overlays water or waterlogged ground like thin ice on a winter lake. Many visitors foolish enough to attempt to drive on it unaccompanied by a local guide have died. In the middle of this salt desert there is no fresh water and the distances to safety are just too great—if you leave your car and try to walk, you are likely to be dead within a day.

The rocky islands, however, are extraordinary oases in this nightmarish place and support an abundance of life. There are forests of candelabra cacti and small, stunted trees. Some of the larger islands even have their own characteristic communities of animals. On the island of Inkawasi, often referred to as Piscado in guidebooks, there are several species of small birds, a solitary *puna* hawk and mountain viscachas, among others. Resembling rabbits with long, fluffy tails for balance and cushion soled feet for grip, viscachas are amazingly agile, chinchillalike rodents found in groups of 80 or more throughout the Andes, from Peru to Patagonia. They have incredibly fine fur that keeps them warm at night, but it is useless if wet, and so they sun themselves in the early morning. For most of the year the viscachas eat the sparse vegetation, but each year on Inkawasi, they have a special treat: after the cactuses have bloomed, they feast on their fallen flowers.

The cactus flowers also attract black-hooded sierra finches and giant hummingbirds. The finches, very obvious with their black heads and yellow bodies, feed on the flowers, while the hummingbirds go for the nectar. One species of hummingbird, the Andean hillstar, ignores the cactus flowers and spends more of its time extracting the nectar from a small crimson flower that grows on the island. Both hummingbirds and finches, together with small ovenbirds, nest here, the hillstars nesting in caves and the sierra finches and giant hummingbirds wherever they can find a suitable site. The ovenbird builds its nest from cactus spines and bits of twigs in the elbow of a cactus branch.

The viscachas provide an ample supply of meat not only for the hawk, but also for Andean mountain cats. According to local people, some cats do travel from island to island across the salt. This is quite extraordinary, for the distance between islands can be 12 miles (20 kilometers) or more.

Where salars have been flooded, flamingoes are joined by a whole host of other waterbirds that have found ways in which to survive here, albeit temporarily. Puna plovers, Andean avocets and Wilson's phalaropes can be seen busying themselves in the shallows. They dip their long bills into the water, probably feeding on the brine shrimps.

The salt here is not simply a thin, flat crust but more like a ploughed field, with small caverns and crevices, crystalline formations and plenty of places for lizards to escape the cold of the night and the heat of midday. Iguanid lizards emerge from their hiding places in the middle of the salt flats at about 10 a.m., warming up quickly and then darting about chasing flies, which are so numerous in the "comfort zone," a layer of air just a few inches thick above the salt lake and the crystalline salts at its edge, that the humming of their wings can be heard quite clearly. If it becomes too hot—and salt surface temperatures can be as high

as 140°F (60°C)—the iguanids vanish for a while and return later in the day when the temperature drops. They keep cool by running through the tiny rivulets of fresh water.

As always in nature, where there is a potential resource, there is something ready to exploit it. So where there are lizards, there are lizard catchers. Sharing this inhospitable home is a small mouse with a penchant for lizards. The mouse is no more than 6 inches (15 centimeters) long, yet once it sinks its teeth into a 1-foot-long (24-centimeter) lizard, it does not let go, and the two tumble among the runnels of salt until the lizard is dead. This is no mean feat, for the lizards themselves are formidable beasts. They display constantly to each other, standing on tiptoe and arching their backs, and they will fight fiercely for the right to occupy the best feeding sites. Yet despite the difference in size and the potential for a disastrous outcome, the mice feed primarily on lizards.

A view over this extraordinary salty ecosystem can be found at the top of the 13,000-foot-high (4000-meter) Sillaguay mountain. A road runs to within 1000 feet (300 meters) of the summit, and it is here because many mountains and volcanoes in northern Chile and Bolivia have sulphur mines at the top. Local miners, working at 16,000–20,000 feet (5000–6000 meters), extract sulphur by hand; the mineral is then transported by small trucks to chemical plants, where it is turned into sulphuric acid for the copper industry.

From the top of the mountain, the vista includes other saltpans and lakes, some saline, others fresh, and these also attract birds. The freshwater lakes are almost all of volcanic origin, lava flows having blocked off meltwater streams. The shores freeze at night but melt in the morning. In the shallow waters of certain lakes at high altitudes, the *puna* toad is found. It is remarkable in having the smallest red blood cells of any known animal.

On Lake Chungar, surrounded by stunning snow-capped volcanoes in Chile's Lauca National Park, contender for the title of highest national park in the world, nests a noisy population of giant coots. They are constantly active during the breeding season, pulling up plants for food and refurbishment of their floating nests. Parts rot and sink periodically and must be repaired. The birds build two rafts—one for the nest and another for the male bird to survey his territory and launch an attack on any intruder.

Further south, at Laguna de Lejía, giant coots are replaced by horned coots, which can be seen nesting on small piles of vegetation diligently collected from the surrounding sparse moorland. Andean gulls and the strong smelling *culpeos* or Andean foxes raid coots' nests and also scavenge anything they can find on the lake shores.

Champion survivor in this region, however, must be the vicuña, a small and seemingly delicate animal in a huge landscape. It can be seen at the salt lakes nibbling at algae and sipping from any patches of fresh water that might have accumulated. Despite its fragile appearance, the vicuña is tough, the ultimate *altiplano* grazer—in effect, South America's high-altitude camel. It lives at altitudes between 12,000 and 15,750 feet (3700 and 4800 meters), where it has a daily routine alternating between an 45-acre (18-hectare) territory on the alpine grasslands during the day and a higher and safer 7½-acre (3-hectare) sleeping territory among the rocks at night.

The vicuña walks on the front ends of its hooves, and the pads of its toes are moveable to help it clamber over rocky terrain and scree slopes. In contrast to the upright posture of other camellike animals, the vicuña has a craning gait, pushing its head and neck forwards as it moves. It is superbly adapted to the strong winds, extremes of temperature and thin air. Its pelt is of the warmest and softest wool, which nearly caused its downfall: many vicuñas were killed for their wool until common sense prevailed.

Vicuñas live in small herds. There are bachelor herds of males and family herds, in which a single vigilant male defends his territory and harem of females and youngsters against any other male intruders. Grazing is scarce and territories large, and so fights sometimes break out between well-matched males.

Vicuña territories might well encompass a small freshwater lake or pond fed by meltwaters from higher ground. There are also freshwater streams running through marshy valleys called *bofedales*. These are oases in the high-plains deserts, but they are still buffeted by winds and exposed to the extremes of temperature. Rivers that flow freely during the day can be solid ice at night. It is said that the plants and animals living here experience all four seasons in a single day.

Most of these animals hide from the cold at night, and some survive simply by shutting down temporarily. The tiny Andean hillstar is the world's highest living hummingbird, so small that it cannot possibly maintain its body temperature through the icy *altiplano* night. Instead it goes into torpor, a state similar to hibernation, during which all its body processes slow down to a fraction of their normal pace. Each night it gets as close to death as it can, preserving just enough life to revive it in the morning. It roosts in places where it is bathed each day by the rising sun, which warms it back to life.

In a landscape devoid of trees, most birds tend to nest or roost in burrows or in crevices among the rocks. An entire flock of diuca finch might huddle beneath a rocky overhang, while ground tyrants use their beaks and feet to dig burrows as much as 3 feet (1 meter) long. The local woodpecker, the Andean flicker, also nests underground, often taking over tunnels made by other burrowing animals.

Reptiles living among the rocks have their own ways of surviving the cold. The Andean smooth-throated iguana hides in burrows or among the roots of low bushes at night. Thanks to its efficient heat gathering and retaining system, its body temperature can be 40°F (+4°C) when the air temperature is as low as +5°F (−15°C). In the morning, it flattens its body and angles it to the sun, exposing the maximum amount of dark skin. The colder it is, the blacker it gets. This way, it can absorb more solar radiation and warm up quickly. Even when the air temperature has only reached freezing point, this little creature will have warmed up at nearly 2°F (1°C) per minute until, in no time, its body temperature has reached 86°F (30°C).

When the sun rises, everything begins to melt and the entire ecosystem goes into reverse. There is a massive temperature increase from dawn to midday, winter to summer, in just a few hours. In the early morning, mountain viscachas may be seen sunning them-

selves. Each animal has its favorite spot, and fights break out if another intrudes. Wild guinea pigs or cavies are less adventurous. They wait in their burrow entrances watching for danger before venturing out and then skitter across the open ground for all they are worth. This is the time danger lurks for the unwary, for prowling among the rocks is the Andean cat, and when the rocks are warm and thermals form, the *puna* hawk is on the wing.

By day, the olivaceous thornbill makes an appearance. Rarely flying, it hops from flower to flower like a mouse. The Andean flicker, meanwhile, hammers at anything resembling a tree, including *llaretta* moss, a green cushion consisting of thousands of rosettes of tiny leaves. As each plant grows at a rate of no more than $\frac{3}{50}$ inch (1.5 millimeters) a year, a great cushion of rosettes 3 feet (1 meter) high and covering 320 square feet (30 square meters) could be many thousands of years old.

Unexpectedly, there is one species of small tree here. The *queñoa* or *Polylepis* grows on rocky hillsides but not on the open plateaux. Its trunk is gnarled, its bark like layers of cellophane and its leaves covered with small hairs, all adaptations to the wind and cold. It grows at higher elevations than any other tree in the world.

Come the evening, the viscachas graze on the cushion bogs, and it is time for another character to make its appearance: a small mouse with big round ears—the leaf-eared mouse. The two species feed together, the larger viscacha ever alert to the presence of cats, foxes and birds of prey. At least one viscacha keeps watch at any one time, emitting a high warbling whistle of alarm if danger threatens.

As night falls, the viscacha's closest relative, the chinchilla, emerges from its colonial burrow. A thick, silky fur protects it from the cold, and the cushioned soles of its feet enable it to clamber over smooth rocks. It never drinks and never bathes. The water in its plant food is sufficient for its needs, and dust baths in fine sand protect its coat from parasites.

As with the vicuña, the chinchilla's fine pelt once led to its being hunted relentlessly to provide Western society with elegant fur coats, and brought it near to extinction. It is protected now in the few places where it has survived. The viscacha failed to impress the fur industry; it sheds its hair as if molting continually.

With darkness, the freezing *altiplano* night returns. Some of the flamingoes, Andean avocets and *puna* teal keep warm by roosting close to the hot waters from geysers, but they must not stand too far from the vents. Even in summer on the Ascotan salt flats in Chile, the birds are sometimes frozen into the lake. At dawn, up to 2000 birds may be huddled together unable to move, all clucking like chickens. By 9 a.m., the sun begins to melt the ice, and they can extricate themselves. They skate off across the ice, their long, spindly legs going every which way.

But what happens when the real winter comes and the morning sun fails to heat up the landscape? The cold season can be sudden and devastating, appearing overnight with a chilling, ceaseless wind. Some, like the vicuña, just sit it out, protected by their warm fleece. Viscacha and mice hide in their burrows during the worst of the weather. But any flamingo that makes the mistake of spending the night too far from a hot vent may find that, without

Vicuña, a grazer in the *puna* grassland habitats of the Andes. It lives between 12,000 feet (3700 meters) and 15,700 feet (4800 meters) and, unlike the guanaco, does not migrate between higher and lower altitudes.

MAQUIPUCANA RESERVE

Just two hours' drive from Quito in Ecuador is the privately owned Maquipucana Reserve, a recognized model for ecotourism. The 18-square-mile (4700-hectare) reserve consists mainly of undisturbed cloudforest, with tree ferns, bromeliads, orchids, and *Heliconia*.

Visitors stay at the Thomas H Davis Ecotourist Center, where the impressive Umachaca Lodge is built of local materials and stands by a clean, free flowing river. Torrent ducks may be seen in front of the lodge, club-winged manakins have a lek nearby, and tree boas have been spotted in the area. The lodge is at 3300 feet (1000 meters), but the true cloudforest is a long walk away up to 9200 feet (2800 meters).

A short, self-guided nature trail and longer treks, including the "Two Rivers Walk" to waterfalls, may reveal hummingbirds, toucans, Andean cock-of-the-rocks, toucan barbets, and perhaps the long-wattled umbrella bird. Coatis are seen frequently; mountain tapirs, ocelots, and pumas only rarely. The spectacled bear was recently reintroduced.

▼

Male Andean cock-of-the-rock. He impresses the drabber female birds at a display site known as a lek. Several subspecies are found in western Venezuela, western Colombia, Ecuador, Peru and northern Bolivia.

the warmth of the morning sun, its frozen legs remain frozen. The chances are it will not survive. At Bolivia's Laguna Colorado, so-called because of the blood-red tinge to the water, the world's largest population of James's flamingoes may be caught by unseasonable freezing, with birds trapped permanently in the ice. Young birds fall over or are blown over by the strong winds; their heads become stuck in the soft ice, and when it freezes at night, they are trapped and unable get out. Local people come to retrieve the bodies, as flamingo fat is said to be good for rheumatism.

Most birds, however, migrate. Flamingoes head for lakes and saltpans at lower altitudes. James's flamingos leave the Salar de Tara in Chile and displace Andean flamingoes at the Salar de Atacama. The Andeans, in turn, move on to Lago Pozuelos in northern Argentina. On their legs they carry the eggs of brine shrimps, which then populate other lakes. Salt lakes in Brazil, Peru, and Chile are linked in this way. Come the following spring, the birds all fly back again.

In the northern Andes of Peru, Ecuador, Colombia, and Venezuela, the zone adjacent to the highland zone is known as the *páramo*. It has a greater diversity of plant life than the *altiplano*, and is wetter. It consists mainly of moorland, with small streams trickling through a boggy landscape of tortora grass, blueberries, high-altitude lupines such as the *taulli* with its purple and yellow flowers, anqush, a medicinal plant brewed into a tea to treat respiratory ailments, and the delicate *urca rosa*, a small blue mountain rose. There is even a tree.

In the mountainous areas of Colombia the wax palm looks completely out of place. At 200 feet (60 meters) high, it is one of the world's tallest trees, yet it grows in the mountains, towering over the alpine scrub some distance above the normal tree line.

Another giant is the 6-foot-high (2-meter) "tall gray friar," an enormous daisy with its stem clothed in soft dead leaves and a large rosette of green crowns at the top. Its living leaves have silky hairs, and the two flower stems that protrude from each crown bear flowers formed from dozens of pale yellow florets. It is unusual among plants in that, the higher it is found, the taller it grows.

An even more bizarre plant, probably the oddest flowering plant in the entire Andes, is also found in the *páramo*—the *puya*. Small species are found throughout the Andes, but the real giants occur mainly in Peru and Colombia. The *puya* is a strange form of bromeliad, and the giant species grows very slowly for between 30 and 100 years and then sends a flower spike covered in 8000 florets about 30 feet (9 meters) up into the air, like a floral telegraph pole. Then it dies.

While it is growing, small birds sometimes impale themselves on its spiny leaves and die, but it is in this hazardous place that the sierra finch and spinetails make their nests. The gigantic flower is visited also by the Andean hillstar, which comes to feed on *puya* nectar. This feisty little bird has big feet with which to hang on to the flower's conveniently situated "landing pads" for, unlike other hummingbirds on slopes lower down the mountain, it cannot hover for too long at this altitude and so must land. While it feeds, however, it is not

alone. Like airline passengers waiting to embark on their flight, a line of tiny mites runs up the hummingbird's beak and hides among the feathers on its head. The hummingbird unknowingly carries the mites to the next flower, where they all disembark to make way for another shipment.

In the summer, the flowers of the smaller species of *puya* also succumb to the rather brutal attentions of a visitor from the next zone down, the cloudforest. When it rains a lot, the *puya* are irresistible to the spectacled bear, a primitive species of bear recognized by the white markings around its eyes that resemble spectacles. The bear breaks down the flower spikes as they start to grow and eats not only the bottom parts, but also the white leaf bases, just as we would eat an artichoke. At this time, sugars that fuel the growth of the flower are concentrated at the base of the flower stalk, and bears like sugar.

As the name suggests, cloudforest trees have their canopies in the clouds. They are very dense and tangled, and the trees do not grow as straight or as tall as those in the rainforests at lower altitudes. Close to the Equator, these slopes are warmer and wetter than the slopes at a similar height further to the south. For much of the year the trees are green and host to ferns, orchids and bromeliads. And the good things in life, as far as a spectacled bear is concerned, are the bromeliads that grow in the canopy. So these bears have learned how to climb trees, and

▶
Spectacled bear, the most primitive of living bears. Here one tears apart a smaller species of puya to get at the sugars that have built up in the base of the flower stalk.

◀
Giant puya, a bromeliad and relative of the pineapple. It grows on the cool, dry, stony slopes of the Andes and has stiff, spiny-edged leaves that form a dense rosette. The tall flower spike is attractive to hummingbirds.

Guanaco. This relative of the vicuña is found in the Andean foothills of Peru, Chile, and Argentina. Some populations remain in one place, whereas others migrate annually, spending the winter months on the lower slopes and summers in the mountains. They are both browsers and grazers, with some occupying desert grasslands and scrublands.

their prize is either pineapplelike bromeliads—which they also eat like artichokes—or the succulent, fat-rich avocadolike fruits of the *ishpingo* tree. About 50 percent of the bears' diet is bromeliads, but they will also eat a wide variety of cloudforest fruits and other vegetation. They sometimes break the branches of the fruiting trees in which they are feeding and pull them together to make a platform that enables them to reach the smaller branches that won't support them, and this construction doubles as a day bed.

The perpetual shroud of mists and fogs means that epiphytes—plants such as bromeliads that grow on plants—can take water directly from the air. With so much moisture, they grow just as well as plants that germinate on the ground, and in these conditions hummingbirds have a distinct advantage over insects when it comes to carrying their pollen. Nectar is the incentive provided by the plant, and red is the color that attracts these feathered couriers, rather than the blues and purples that are seductive to insects. So the cloudforests of the Andes have the greatest diversity of hummingbirds anywhere on Earth. Competition among hummingbirds for what plants have to offer has led to extreme specialization, a kind of lock-and-key ecology. It also provides each species of plant with its own personalized service. The sword-billed hummingbird has a conspicuously long bill to allow it access to the nectar of the passionflower, while the booted racket-tail, with its unique hooked bill, achieves an especially tight fit when sipping the nectar from the *Coryanthes* orchid.

◄

Andean condor. This magnificent black-and-white bird, the largest flying bird in the world, soars on warm updrafts of air along mountain ridges. It spends much of its day gliding along mountain slopes in search of the carrion on which it feeds.

The hummingbirds are living jewels in the cloudforest gloom, but even they are eclipsed by an exuberant character known as cock-of-the-rock. Male birds, challengers for the role of top bird, romp strenuously at displaying areas known as leks, each competing to be the loudest and brightest performer to impress the females, which are rather drab in comparison. When the females have selected the performer of their dreams and mated, they retreat into the forest, their mottled brown plumage providing excellent camouflage as they merge with the greens and browns of the leaves, bark and bromeliads. They alone will bring up their young, the flamboyant males paying no heed to the future of their off-spring.

The male poison dart frog, on the other hand, is a very attentive father. This tiny creature takes full advantage of what bromeliads have to offer—ponds trapped in their crowns of leaves. The female lays eggs under damp leaves and the two parents guard them until the tadpoles hatch out. The male then places each tadpole on his back, carries them one by one up a tree and dumps them in a bromeliad pond.

The damp cloudforest is a paradise for frogs. One species in the genus *Eleutherodactylus* has forgone the aquatic tadpole stage completely. It deposits a dozen yolk-rich eggs in a burrow, and the young develop inside the jellylike covering. Froglets emerge having been nowhere near a pond.

While these three zones—the *puna* or *altiplano*, *páramo* and cloudforest—with their distinctive plants and animals can be identified in the northern and central parts of the Andes, the southern section is quite different. The southern Andes are dominated by the 8500-square-mile (22,000-square-kilometer) Patagonia ice sheet. This massive stretch of ice can be divided conveniently into northern and southern halves, and both have spectacular mountain landscapes.

On the edge of the northern ice field is the Chalten-Torré Massif, with the magnificent 11,168-foot (3405-meter) Fitzroy Mountain. In summer, the newly established village of El Chalten, near Lago del Desierto in Argentina, is a focus for tourists to the region. In winter the area is bleak and covered with snow.

The landscape in the southern ice field is overlooked by the dramatic rock towers and horns of Torres del Paine. The three distinctive high peaks of pink-gray granite are the Horns of Paine. They were thrown aloft by earth movements and carved by glaciers. The tallest reaches 9350 feet (2850 meters) above sea level, while the adjacent Paine Grande, with its four summits, is the highest mountain in this area at 10,000 feet (3050 meters) and a mecca for the world's rock climbers. Azure lakes, frozen in winter but ice free in summer, lie at their base. This is the domain of the Andean condor.

This magnificent bird—the acknowledged symbol of the Andes and found throughout the mountain chain—has a length of 5 feet (1.5 meters), wingspan of 10 feet (3 meters) and a weight of 26.5 pounds (12 kilograms), making it the largest bird that can fly. Its great black shape with broad straight wings is an unmistakable sight. Its wing-tip primary feathers,

longer than a human forearm, stream out as if feeling for lift, and it soars along mountain ridges, riding on the updrafts and thermals.

Condors make their nests on ledges on the highest crags, the female laying one egg every two years. Both parents share incubation duties for about 56 days, and both go in search of food. Once fledged, young birds, recognized by their brown rather than black plumage, accompany their parents for several years. Not until they are eight years old will they wear the full breeding plumage of black feathers with a white ring around the neck and splashes of white on the upper surface of the wings.

Condors find food by sight. They look for carrion on the ground and watch each other and any rapidly descending caracaras or turkey vultures whose movements give away the location of a carcass. Turkey vultures appear to pick up the smell of decaying meat on the wind, and the condor takes full advantage of this ability by following it to the source of food. They land upwind of a corpse and waddle towards it suspiciously, with wings folded. There is a pecking order at a carcass, the hierarchy established by the birds snapping at each other with their beaks. The beaks themselves are short and hooked, ideal for ripping flesh. When replete, the birds are often so stuffed that they are unable to take off and will clamber up the mountain in order to take advantage of an updraft that will get them airborne. In the air, they become the graceful icons of the Andes once again.

Another icon inhabiting these mountains is the huemul, or Andean deer, which shares the Chilean coat of arms with the condor. It lives mainly in the mountain forests, but ventures on to the scrubby areas above the tree line. Nimble and fleet-footed, even on the steepest slopes, it has filled the niche left open by the absence of mountain goats and wild sheep.

The mountain lakes are fed by streams that are frozen in winter but change overnight into raging torrents—the turbulent habitat of the torrent duck. As soon as lakes clear of ice, migrant birds fly in from the north to breed in the frenetic four months of summer. The haunting call of the great grebe announces it as one of the first to arrive, along with upland geese, black-necked swans, ruddy ducks, and noisy flocks of buff-necked ibis.

Male upland geese are highly territorial and will battle it out with any intruders. They have a special spur on the leading edge of each wing with which they almost "punch" their opponents into submission. The females are well camouflaged as they sit motionless on their eggs. They dare not move, for the black-chested buzzard eagle hunts overhead, ready to swoop down on any careless parent. Yet even more at risk are the buff-necked ibis. A buzzard eagle will hang in the strong wind waiting for the opportunity to swoop on the sitting birds. Chimango caracaras, birds the size of a crow but with the armory of an eagle, follow the buzzard eagles everywhere, the commotion caused by the larger birds providing these scavengers with ample food in the form of exposed eggs—after all, caracaras have chicks to raise too.

In the south, the vicuña is replaced by a stocky relative, the guanaco. It survives the 60 miles (100 kilometers) per hour winds and snow blizzards of winter, not by simply sitting out the storms like the vicuña, but by descending to more sheltered pastures where

TORRES DEL PAINE NATIONAL PARK

These magnificent mountains of the Paine Massif, including the granite obelisks known as the Paine Towers and the glaciers and azure lakes around their base, have been the destination of many travelers. In the nineteenth century, Lady Florence Dixie wrote of the towers after a 250-mile (400-kilometer) trek on horseback from Punta Arenas: "Their white glaciers with the white clouds resting on them, were all mirrored to marvelous perfection in the motionless lake, whose crystal waters were of the most extraordinary brilliant blue I have ever beheld." Today, it is a "must-see" site for travelers.

The Parque Nacional Torres del Paine was founded in 1959, and in 1978 UNESCO gave it World Heritage status. If there is one place to go in Patagonia, this is it. The best weather is from November through to April, although the park is becoming increasingly popular, and some visitors may find January and February too crowded. It has been described as a "wonderland" in the snow, between May and mid-September, and the persistent winds die down at that time, too.

Several hikes start from the park's administrative center, including the 8 to 10-day Torres del Paine Circuit across constantly changing terrain such as forests, streams, mountain passes, and grasslands. Animals to see *en route* include guanaco, rheas, and the shy Chilean deer. There are 105 species of birds in the park, including flamingoes, condors, black-necked swans, and eagles. If you are very lucky, you might spot a puma. Botanists will not be disappointed with the 200 species of plants, including *lenga* and *coigue* forests in protected valleys.

A shorter trail, the Lago Gray hike, starts at the administrative center with a ramble over grassland. It then follows the milky Río Gray to the clear, blue Lago Pehoé. From here, well marked trails take you to Glacier Gray and its blue glacier caves.

Mushroom gatherers will have a field day, with edible puffballs and other treats, although it is important to make a positive identification. There are edible greens and herbs in the moist meadows.

▼

Puma in Patagonia. This twilight hunter is an able stalker of prey from small rodents to full-size deer and guanacos. Found in forests, steppe and on rocky mountain slopes, it is surviving in the southern Andes despite being shot on sight by sheep farmers.

The mountains of
El Parque Nacional
Torres del Paine.
They are
composed of
Cretaceous
sedimentary rocks
penetrated by
granite. The highest
mountain in the
park is Grande
Paine, with four
principal summits,
the tallest of which
is 10,000 feet
(3050 meters).

conditions are less severe. In spring, the male guanacos have territorial battles. They push and shove to defend harems of females from all corners. All around, wild flowers transform stark mountains into alpine paradises, and the song of the long-tailed meadowlark rises over open areas.

As spring takes a firm hold on the southern Andes, chicks hatch out. At Twin Lakes, upland goose goslings head for the water just hours after emerging from their eggs. Grebe chicks do the same, but they rarely get their feet wet. The youngsters hitch a ride on their parents' backs and swim only when they move from one parent to the other. Adult grebes feed their offspring not only fish but also feathers, thought to be a kind of roughage to help them digest their mainly fishy diet.

On land, all the guanacos in a group give birth at the same time, a strategy designed to reduce losses to predators. A predator—even one with its own offspring—is not able to eat all the youngsters, and so inevitably some survive. It is the moment for which the harem masters have been waiting. The females come on heat just days after giving birth, but a male with a large herd will have his work cut out defending his females against the many young pretenders.

It is also the time when female pumas are out hunting. A puma mother with cubs to feed will work day and night to bring down enough guanacos to satisfy her growing family. As spring slips into summer, foxes, caracaras, and condors scavenge the leftovers.

Throughout the year, the sun is weak and the winters harsh, and on the lower slopes, running down to the coast, another rainforest grows below the tree line. This is the temperate rainforest of Patagonia. Lashed by constant rain all year round, the trees grow tall and dense. There are fewer species—high and low deciduous beeches, evergreen beeches, and monkey puzzle trees—than in the more northerly cloudforests, and their branches are festooned not with bromeliads but with mosses, ferns and beardlike lichens.

In northern Patagonia, the trees grow up to the 6500-foot (2000-meter) mark, whereas in more southerly areas where the temperatures are lower, they barely reach 2000 feet (600 meters). At higher elevations they are low and twisted, while at lower heights, the fertile soils and warmer temperatures enable them to grow tall. In places, the forests are bisected not by streams and rivers, but by glaciers. They slide down from the Patagonian ice sheet, and as explorer H.W. Hilman once remarked, it is "the only place in the world where one can see a hummingbird on a glacier."

Here, startlingly bright red fuchsias grow close to streams and are visited by the green-backed firecrown. In fact, many of the shrubs here have red flowers, or yellow-orange petals with spotted red nectar guides to attract hummingbirds. It is too wet and cold for there to be many bees, and blue or violet flowers, which usually attract insects, are noticeably absent.

The trees are home to austral parakeets, which travel through the forest in small, noisy flocks looking for food. Dead trees are the province of the highly territorial giant Magellanic woodpecker, the largest of the woodpeckers. The male can be 14 inches (35

centimeters) long, and is instantly identifiable by its bright red head. The female is black all over, except for a fleck of red above the nostrils.

In the forest's understory, the tiny Des Mur's wire-tail flits among thickets of bamboo, while on the forest floor, the black-throated *huet-huet*, with a black body, red cap and breast and exceedingly large feet, hides in the darkest recesses, only its unrelenting yap giving away its presence. The sharp call of the *fio-fio* and the cackle of the highly territorial *chucao tapaculo*, the recognized sound signature of the southern beech forest, let slip that they are here, too.

Stalking them among the bamboo might be the *guiña* or *kodkod*, a spotted cat with a dark band across its throat and large feet. It is smaller than a domestic cat but far more successful at catching small birds and mouse-sized rodents.

On more open areas with sandy soils, from October through to February, the yellow flowers of Wood's lady's slipper appear, while one of the more conspicuous plants in the cold, damp, and darker parts is Chilean rhubarb or *naica*, a plant often seen growing around suburban garden ponds in Europe and North America. In the southern forests, its gigantic, rhubarblike leaves hide the smallest deer in the world, the *pudú*. Standing no more than 15 inches (38 centimeters) at the shoulder and weighing 17.5 pounds (8 kilograms), the *pudú* is recognized not only by its small size and red-brown coat, but also by its pair of short, single-pronged antlers.

Each *pudú* occupies a home range of 40–65 acres (16–26 hectares) in which it travels along familiar trails and stops off at traditional resting places. It is active both day and night, periods of foraging interspersed with two- to five-hour rest periods. Curiously, *pudú* are less active on calm, sunny days, preferring to be out and about on windy days. Little else is known of this tiny deer and its slightly larger northern relative, since they are very shy animals and hide in the deep forest.

Moving southwards, the forests become thinner and lower until the Andes tail off into Tierra del Fuego and the Southern Ocean. In these southern latitudes, azure-blue glaciers carve icebergs into the Pacific to the west and drop into the Argentine lakes to the east, but in the northern and central parts of the range, the Andes is the starting point for another extraordinary South America phenomenon—the Amazon Basin.

The source of the Amazon is high in the Peruvian Andes. The actual spot is open to debate: some say the river starts at Lake Lauricocha, while others put the source in the Carhuastanta Crevice. Still others claim it begins in an underground glacier, known as Apacheta Crevice, over 16,000 feet (5000 meters) up on the volcano Chachani, near Arequipa.

Whatever the source, the water from these places plunges down the eastern slopes of the central Andes. By the time it reaches the port of Iquitos in Peru, the river is already 4.5–5.5 miles (7-9 kilometers) wide, and it still has another 2306 miles (3720 kilometers) to go before it reaches the Atlantic Ocean, making it the longest navigable river in the world.

the amazon
FLOODED FOREST

The Amazon's flooded forest is a curious Alice-in-Wonderland world, where for six months of the year the trees become islands, fish distribute their seeds, and dolphins swim in the treetops. While annual rainfall in most parts of the world is measured in inches, the Amazon has many feet of rain falling each year, about half of it due to water recycled by evapotranspiration from the soil and an ocean of trees, and the rest borne on trade winds that bring moisture from the Atlantic Ocean. The moisture is trapped within a basin that is bordered by the Andes to the west, the Brazilian and Guiana Highlands to south and north, and by the Atlantic to the east. It rains throughout the basin, although much of the rain falls in the foothills and on the higher slopes of the Andes. The air is forced upward by the mountains, after which it cools, and moisture precipitates out as heavy rainfall in the western Amazon or as snow on the highest Andean peaks.

▶

Anavilhanas Archipelago on the River Negro, from the air. Anavilhanas is the world's largest freshwater archipelago, covering a 55-mile (90-kilometer) reach of black-water river. Up to 400 islands are visible in the dry season, but half are submerged when the forest floods between November and April.

◀

Butterfly in the Amazon. The nostrils of a black caiman provide the butterfly with a drink. It is seeking salts, particularly sodium, which it also takes from the corner of caimans' and turtles' eyes.

The result of all this rainfall is an enormous flood that is caused partly by the annual wet season in the sub-Andean region of the upper Amazon and partly by backflow from the main stem of the Amazon itself. The main floods occur at different times in different parts of the Amazon, those in the northern and southern areas being separated by several months. The Amazon and Negro floods peak in June, for example, while the Madeira peaks in March. Rivers burst their banks and overflow into the adjacent floodplain forest. Water penetrates for a distance of 6–12 miles (10–20 kilometers) on either side of the main river channels—though it reaches 50 miles (75 kilometers) in some places—and floods the forest to a depth of 16–50 feet (5–16 meters), the most extreme floods occurring in the western part of the Amazon. Of the 2–2.25 million square miles (5–6 million square kilometers) of forest, at least 60,000 square miles (150,000 square kilometers) are flooded every year. It is a habitat where both plants and animals have had to adapt to extraordinary seasonal inundation, and there is no better place to see them than at Mamirauá (which means 'manatee' in the local Indian language), a reserve about halfway down the main channel of the Amazon River; there the flood season is between April and August. It is a protected area of floodplain at the confluence of the Japurá and the Solimões (Amazon), a two-hour motorized canoe journey from the nearest airport town at Tefé.

For sheer spectacle, it is the dry season rather than the wet that will bring you closest to Mamirauá's plants and animals. When the water is high, the animals are spread thinly throughout the flooded forest, but when the flood recedes, wildlife is concentrated in the rivers, streams, and isolated pools and in the long, ribbon shaped floodplain lakes.

The floodplain lakes are important habitats in the basin. They are sections of river that have been cut off from the main channel when it changed its course. While rivers in temperate regions change their direction infrequently, the waters of the Amazon change course constantly giving rise to these lakes. At low water the floodplain lakes are filled to overflowing with both fish and fish eaters, the close proximity of predators and prey making for uneasy neighbors. The action is apparent at dawn.

As an early morning mist drifts across Lake Mamirauá, a scattering of crusty heads betrays a dense population of caiman, both the black and the spectacled species. At 6 a.m. large flocks of egrets fly in and join them, each bird making its distinctive crowing call. The sound of splashing comes from the water and then a loud clap, like two pieces of wood being smacked together. A caiman's jaws snap shut on a big fish, and around it there is an explosion of fish and birds as they flee in all directions, the egrets crying out in alarm.

Suddenly a caiman leaps out of the water in a shallow pounce, turns on its side and with mouth open crashes back down. Its head reappears, jaws clamped tight to a fish. Then, with a flip of the caiman's head, the fish disappears down its throat. The concentration of fish and reptiles is so great that sometimes all a caiman has to do is plunge into the water and hit anything that happens to be there. Local fishermen have a nice trick in which they throw a harpoon randomly into the water and, with surprising frequency, hit a fish. The uninitiated visitor might be impressed with their demonstration of supernatural feats of

vision and marksmanship. The truth is that there are so many fish, it is hard to miss! The fish, in their turn, are at their lowest ebb in their annual cycle; many succumb to predators or become stranded in pools as they dry out. Some quite literally starve.

Black caiman can be enormous animals, a mature specimen reaching up to 20 feet (6 meters) in length, and some individuals have adopted a fascinating fish catching strategy. They move sideways, undulating their tails as they go, and gradually drive shoals of fish into the shallows. Once there, they turn sharply and thrust their mouths into the seething mass. In an effort to escape, small fish take off in all directions, but still provide easy pickings. Around the caiman, the water boils with the frantic movements of predators and prey, but by four o'clock in the afternoon activity stops. The caiman relax at the surface in shallow water with just their menacing heads exposed, but they attract to themselves unwelcome guests—biting flies. The flies, known locally as *mutuca* flies, are tabanid horseflies. They have a painful bite, as many a visitor to the lake will confirm, but for the caiman they are a constant irritation. Even its tough, armorlike hide does not protect it—the flies attack the softer tissues around the eyes and nostrils, and the only escape is in the water. As the caiman submerges, the flies circle around and wait for it to resurface, and as soon as its head emerges they swoop in and attack again.

▶ Black caiman. Although it is mainly active at night, the sound of splashing in daylight hours during the low-water season reveals that the caiman is taking prey that has been concentrated in gradually shrinking bodies of water.

At about ten o'clock each morning, neotropical cormorants fly in from their enormous roosts, where the smell of ammonia can be detected from over a half a mile (1 kilometer) away. They arrive in such large numbers that they literally black out the sky for 10 minutes or more. At Lake Mamirauá alone there are thought to be more than 15,000 visiting birds. They put down on the water where they appear to hunt cooperatively, forming great rafts which swim around in ever decreasing circles, herding fish into tight balls in order to pick them off one by one.

Some of the scattered pools at low water are avoided by frogs. Where courting frogs would be expected to occupy prime sites in residual water elsewhere in the world, in the Amazon's pools there are fewer. The reason is a particularly voracious fish, the goggle-eyed *traíra*, that is able to survive in just a few inches of water. It is an air breather, taking air into a specially modified swim bladder. It hides under the leaf litter and attacks just about anything it can swallow. So, these pools are off limits to frogs.

The larger, more permanent pools sometimes contain the magnificent Queen Victoria waterlily. Anchored to the bottom, it develops the biggest floating leaves imaginable, up to 6 feet (2 meters) across. The white flowers are also immense, about the size of a small football, and they are visited by insects, especially scarab beetles, which are attracted

◀

Queen Victoria waterlily. The large, showy flowers of this magnificent waterlily are attractive to insect pollinators.

to the butterscotch scent produced as the flower heats up to about 20°F (11°C) above the ambient air temperature. The beetles enter the flowers where they intend to spend the night, but when morning comes, they find that they are trapped. They chew at the starch filled spongy tissues of the carpels inside the flower, releasing the stamens. The stamens dust the beetles liberally with pollen; the flowers eventually open releasing the captive beetles. Off they fly and, attracted by the smell of butterscotch, they land on another first-night flower inadvertently pollinating it.

Fish are attracted to the *munguba* trees that overhang the pools. This is one of the few trees to release its seeds at low water. Its bright red pods crack open and release clouds of parachutelike seeds that are dispersed by the wind. The seeds resemble black pepper-corns surrounded by a tuft of white cotton. They float in the wind like the seeds of the kapok tree, the biggest tree in the floodplain.

The seeds first attract the attention of the little star parakeet, or *Periquito-estrelinha*. These birds fly in, jam their beaks into the open pods, and rip out the black seeds inside. In their eagerness to reach the food, cotton and seeds are hurled in all directions, and some float down toward the water. Such is the competition that South American 'river trout' or *matrinchão* leap out and grab the seeds before they reach the surface. If a seed is caught on an overhanging branch a fish will leap clear of the water in order to snatch it before any other creaturescan.

In the deeper lakes and rivers during low water, a sudden bout of heavy rain can have dramatic and unexpected consequences for the fish living there—a mass fish kill. At first light, there might be just a trickle of dead and dying bodies. They float belly up, their pale white undersides plain to see in the dark brown water. Cormorants and egrets line the riverbank. They ignore the dead, but pluck out fish gasping at the surface. As the sun rises, the trickle turns to a flood, and rafts of dead fish cover the surface from one bank to the other. Upstream the carnage can be seen for several kilometers. Black vultures crowd around the piles of decaying corpses deposited on the shore. The air is thick with the buzzing of flies, the smell overpowering.

This is not an industrial accident or agricultural run-off. It is an extraordinary natural phenomenon, and it takes place somewhere in the quiet backwaters of the Amazon in September and October, when rain falls and warmer bottom water, stripped of its oxygen by the decaying process of vegetation on the riverbed, rises to the surface. The process is so rapid that the fish are unable to adapt quickly enough and hundreds of thousands suffo-cate. Rainfall that should bring life brings death instead.

The sudden removal of fish from a stretch of water could cause serious short-term food shortages for the creatures that depend on them. The nutrient-rich floodplain lakes play host to the Amazon's giant river otters, or *ariranha*, although they are now extinct in the Mamiraúá Reserve. These unusually large otters are about 4 feet (1.2 meters) long and are characterized by mottled white markings on the throat, each with its own distinctive pattern. They spend more time in the water than other species of river otter. Their large,

paddlelike feet make them awkward walkers. They live in small family groups of up to eight or nine individuals; this includes the main breeding pair and a couple of litters that have stayed at home.

Although mating can take place at any time, new litters tend to arrive when the water is low and food is concentrated. They play, sunbathe, groom, and hunt, and whatever their activity, they make a huge amount of noise, chattering incessantly with irritating and whining calls. Swimming may not come naturally. A mother might appear to be drowning a cub, but actually she is teaching the reluctant youngster how to swim. She grabs the cub by the scruff of the neck, dumps it firmly in the water, and repeats this until it is able to swim by itself.

'Home' is a territory that is cleared of vegetation and marked with dung, urine, and scents from special anal glands. The otters flatten particular areas to serve as feeding or sunbathing platforms. They are active by day, diving to the mid-waters to catch fish, especially piranhas, *traíras,* and small catfish, sometimes at the rate of one every 10 to 15 minutes. Their whiskers are sensitive to fish movements, and they hunt cooperatively, blowing a bubble-net to corral shoals of fish, which they catch in their powerful jaws, but hold in their forepaws to eat.

Piranhas, one of the fish caught by otters, have a sinister reputation and are said to make light work of anything that falls into their midst. A shoal of red-bellied piranhas, or *piranha-caju*, is said to be able to strip a capybara of its flesh in less than two minutes. Of the 20 or so known species, only a few are recognized as killers. They have jaws filled with triangular, razor-sharp teeth designed to slice off bite-sized pieces of flesh. Blood in the water is said to whip a shoal—anything from a few to a few hundred fish—into a demonic feeding frenzy, and although the smell of blood or body fluids makes them more likely to bite, it is the sight of their prey that actually triggers an attack. Piranhas attack mostly small fish, including members of their own species.

Alongside the main river channels and lakes, there is another low-water habitat, the forest stream or *igarapé*. It is home to an extraordinary array of small fish—in fact, for the aquarium enthusiast, the streams of the Amazon Basin will seem very familiar. It is here that the small, brightly colored fish, seen so often in living rooms throughout the world, live naturally. In some areas of the Amazon, such as the middle Rio Negro, the aquarium trade is an important source of income to local people, and in these streams, scientists are discovering new species of fish at an astonishing rate. More than 1500 have been described so far from the Amazon Basin—10 times as many species of fish as are known in the whole of Europe—and the suggestion is that there could be just as many yet to be discovered.

There is one fish that actually looks like a leaf. The leaf fish, or *peixe-folha*, lurks on the stream bed, its body disguised as a decaying leaf, right down to the veins and its mottled moldy-brown color. It has huge extendable jaws and grabs anything that passes by, a habit it shares with the matamata terrapin, another creature that is camouflaged in the leaf litter on the riverbed. It strikes at unsuspecting fish with deadly speed and accuracy.

◀
Giant river otter. Having caught a piranha with its mouth, it holds the fish in its front paws to tear off bite-sized chunks. If the fishing is good, it can catch and consume a fish every hour.

Having an effective escape mechanism from these and other aquatic predators is a prudent survival tactic, and the deep-bodied hatchet fish, or *peixe-borboleta*, is a well rehearsed escape artist. It uses its expanded pectoral fins and the overdeveloped pectoral muscles that make up 25 percent of its body weight to leap clear of the water and fly a short distance, fleeing from the predatory fish that chase it.

Leaping is a very important survival strategy in this region. Fish seem to fly out of the water constantly—some to escape, others to feed. One species, the splashing tetra, even jumps to breed. The male and female jump simultaneously about 8 inches (20 centimeters) out of the water. She deposits her eggs on a leaf, where he fertilizes them. In these parts, it is safer to be out of the water, and so the male fish splashes water over the eggs to keep them moist until they are ready to hatch; then the fry drop back down into the stream.

These fish are not distributed evenly throughout the Amazon, for conditions can vary in different rivers. The eminent nineteenth-century naturalist Alfred Russell Wallace, a contemporary of Charles Darwin, spent several years around Manaus in the central Amazon of Brazil and identified three main types of Amazonian rivers—black waters, white waters, and clear waters. He also recognized that each water type had its own flora and fauna. Cardinal tetras, or *piaba cardinal*, so commonly seen in domestic aquariums, are

Piranha. Its jaws filled with razor-sharp, triangular teeth. This is a meat-eating species; others use their powerful jaws and sharp teeth to eat fruit and nuts.

found only in "black-water" streams and rivers of the Rio Negro drainage system. These originate not in mountains, but in lowland forests to the north of the Amazon River. They drain from infertile, sandy soils covered by stunted vegetation. Their waters are acidic and stained dark brown from the tannins and acids that leach from forest leaves.

The most impressive black-water river is the Rio Negro, the largest tributary of the Amazon and, at 500 miles (800 kilometers) long, one of the world's longest rivers. The forest that is flooded by this and other black water rivers, such as the Rios Tefé and Jutai, is known as the *igapó*. Along the riverbanks, the trees are much lower and the forest canopy less densely populated than elsewhere in the Amazon. Animals here range over larger areas in search of food, so populations are dispersed. The highest waters are in June, when stands of flooded palm trees host breeding black and yellow macaws and red-bellied macaws. The young feed on a purée of regurgitated fruit.

Many of the fish in black water streams—about 130 recognized species—feed to a greater or lesser degree on the decomposing leaves and vegetable material on the river-bed. Tiny shrimp with powerful claws start to tear the decaying leaves apart, and the detritus feeders follow in their wake. Classic among them is the *jaraqui*, with a suckerlike mouth and very fine, bristle-like projections on its lips. The fish works like a vacuum cleaner, the bristles dislodging algae and detritus from tree trunks, branches, and leaves and the mouth sucking up the debris. Angel fish, discus fish, and the pretty black and yellow banded head-standers are also algal grazers.

In the Tarumã-mirim, one of the black water tributaries of the Rio Negro near Manaus, lives a very unusual creature, *Phreatobius walkeri*, only recently recognized by the scientific community as a trichomycterid catfish. About 1.5–2 inches (4–5 centimeters) long, it resembles a small red worm. When wet, it can live in a film of water in litter about 2 feet (60 centimeters) above the level of the black water stream, but for the most part, it is found in submerged leaf litter. Its bright red color is due to high concentrations of haemoglobin (oxygen carrying blood pigments) in the blood, an adaptation to low oxygen levels. It is able to survive at the water level of the stream by moving around in the moist gaps between mats of leaf litter.

The white water rivers, such as the Ucayali, Huallaga, and Marañon, drain from the Andes and are loaded with silts and sediments. From April to August they are swollen with rain and snow melt, and the forest they flood is known as the *várzea*. These rivers are not white at all, but great ribbons of coffee colored water that weave their way through the deep green of the forest. Rivers such as the Madeira and the Amazon itself (known as the Solimões in Brazil and Marañon in Peru in its upper reaches) have neutral pH (that is, they are neither acid nor alkaline) and are rich in nutrients.

The third water type, the clear waters typical of the Xingu and Tapajós, originates in the Guyana Shield to the north and the Brazilian Shield to the south of the Amazon Basin. There is less erosion and so the rivers carry a lighter load of sediments. Some, including the Tapajós, have a visibility of more than 33 feet (10 meters), compared to 6 feet (2 meters)

maximum in black-water rivers and 6 inches (15 centimeters) in white water rivers—more like an aquarium than a river. The Xingu, however, carries silt, and visibility is no more than 3 feet (1 meter). Here, plankton blooms attract shoals of the *mapará* catfish. Each night they move from deeper waters towards the surface and the shore to feed.

Black water and white water meet near Manaus, where the Rio Negro and Rio Salimóes join. At first the waters do not mix, and so one side of the river is coffee colored and the other dark chocolate. From the air, the forest looks like a vast and featureless expanse of broccoli. Bush pilots find their way about by watching between the trees for the winding rivers. Each river has its own distinguishing color, like road signs in the forest.

The Amazon Basin presents us with a flood of superlatives. The river system carries about a fifth of the world's running fresh water at an average speed of 3 miles (5 kilometers) per hour from the mountains to the sea. It delivers over 6 million cubic feet (175,000 cubic meters) of water into the Atlantic every second—five times that poured in by the Congo and 12 times that of the Mississippi. The influence of the tides can be felt as far as Obidos, 450 miles (700 kilometers) from the mouth. More than 1100 tributaries drain an area of 2.25 million square miles (6 million square kilometers). The distance from Iquitos in Peru, where ocean going ships can tie up alongside native canoes, to the sea is 2300 miles (3700 kilometers), yet the drop to sea level is just 300 feet (91 meters). Throughout the basin, the temperature of the water in the main river channels rarely fluctuates more than a degree either side of 84°F (29°C).

The Amazon Basin is so big, it has its own weather systems. In one place it can be the wet season while in another it is the dry, depending on which side of the Equator you are standing. Generally, though, September through to December is considered to be the dry season, when the rivers are at their lowest. Low-water conditions are short-lived, however. In some places, the rivers and streams follow their established courses for just one or two months of the year, but when the rains come, this region is transformed into an aquatic habitat unlike anywhere else on Earth.

At the end of December and or early January, the rainy season arrives, and the waters begin to rise. Rivers overflow, causing lakes to drown, overwhelming streams, carving deep gorges from riverbanks, and pulling down trees. Some animals sense the coming transformation—detecting a change in barometric pressure or humidity, rainfall, or increased ground wetness for the landlubbers, and a change of conductivity, pH, or water temperature by fish. Whatever the sign, the animals move out or up. Any creatures that cannot swim, fly, or jump between trees must climb into the uppermost branches of the canopy, leave the flooding forest altogether, or drown. Predators are ready to intercept the dispossessed. Wading birds such as ibis and jacanas peck at small invertebrates on the ground. Lizards, tarantulas, ants, and praying mantis wait on tree trunks and the lower branches, ready to hijack the upwardly mobile spiders and insects, many of them beetles. The exodus is immense.

The white subspecies of the white and red uakari. It lives in a small patch of the upper Brazilian Amazon and is restricted to *várzea* forest, avoiding the margins of large rivers.

Leafcutter ants build their colonies in subterranean nests under the forest floor, and one species is an inhabitant of forests flooded by white water rivers. As the rains begin, the entire colony moves into the canopy, where the ants create a new home in a hollow bough. They take strands of fungus from their abandoned fungus gardens underground and carry these to the new site to start afresh. The fungus grows on leaves that the ants collect and chop up, but if their tree fails to have sufficient leaves for cultivation, they must turn to neighboring trees. To achieve this, they have been seen to 'walk' on relatively still water to reach adjacent trunks, orienting to the dark shape of the tree trunk on the horizon.

Some animals leave their escape to the last moment and are caught by sudden surges in water level. Sloths and snakes are good swimmers; most ants are not. Nevertheless, a colony of fire ants escapes the deluge by linking together and forming a raft. It floats downstream, at the mercy of the river and its inhabitants. Small fish dart in and pluck away ants from the periphery of the living ball, but the colony eventually makes landfall—a fortunately placed branch. In a surprisingly orderly manner, the ants unhitch and clamber onto their new home. The residents—lizards, spiders, and grasshoppers—are in panic because the ants smother and kill every living thing in their path. Some of the inhabitants bale out—but it is from the frying pan into the fire.

◄

Botos, considered to be primitive dolphins. They retain features such as the long, slender beak with many pointed teeth, flexible neck and broad flippers seen on fossil dolphins over 10 million years old.

The needlefish or *peixe-agulha* grabs any small invertebrate that happen to slip in. It catches small fish, too. Lurking and then approaching its target slowly, it suddenly thrusts forward with its jaws. *Aruaná* are like coiled springs, their powerfully muscular bodies allowing them to leap 3–6 feet (1–2 meters) out of the water to snatch insects and spiders from overhanging branches.

The water does not rise consistently at first, but in stages, each step called a *repiquete*. This is followed by a consistent rise right up to high water. Tiger beetles caught by the rising water can cope temporarily, either by breathing air trapped under their wing covers or by reversing into the holes in decaying wood made by beetle larvae. They can trap air at the end of the tunnel and, by using these bubbles, can remain submerged for a couple of hours. They emerge at night to go hunting on any logs, trees, or vegetation above water.

The rising water triggers another natural event, one that influences the lives of almost every animal in the flooded forest. Many of the trees begin to bear fruit, and it is bonanza time for red and white uakaris, New World monkeys easily recognized by their bald, vivid red heads against white fur. Uakaris live permanently in the floodplain forests of the delta-like area around Mamirauá, where the Rio Japurá joins the Amazon. You hear them before you see them—they make chattering sounds, much like chimpanzees, and crash through the forest. They travel in large, loose groups, with 50 or more individuals spread out over a foraging range of about 2.5 square miles (6.5 square kilometers). Because they can jump between trees, they travel through the topmost branches of the flooded forest. Thanks to the fruit, seeds, and flowers the forest provides, the uakaris almost never go down to the ground but thrive in the canopy. Their sharp teeth and strong jaws enable them to eat hard, unripened fruit, so they do well in the forest the whole year.

The red and white uakari is also known as the *macaco inglés*, or "English monkey." The locals maintain that the male's bright red face is like that of a gin-swilling European who has been out in the sun too long. But because its face is so human-like, the uakari is less likely to be killed for stewing. In reality, the uakari's red face may be a sexual signal, a sign of good health. A pale face is thought to indicate that a monkey is suffering from malaria.

At the edge of the flooded forest, some monkeys are driven out by the rising water, but other, more gymnastic species move in from the adjacent *terra firme* forests. Squirrel monkeys or *macaco de cheiro* are common, although another species, the blackish squirrel monkey, is more usually seen in the Mamirauá Reserve. These squirrel monkeys forage in trees that are coming into fruit, while red howler monkeys eat the leaves. Brown capuchin monkeys go on feeding raids, taking birds' eggs and chicks as well as tough-husked seeds, fruits, and flowers. Sparrow-sized pygmy marmosets—the world's smallest monkies—not only search for insects that have been driven up by the flood waters, but they also use their sharp teeth to make incisions in tree bark in order to suck the sap. Jaguars sometimes follow monkey troops through the branches, but the uakaris play safe: they spend the night on the very thinnest branches that will support their weight so as not to be surprised while they sleep.

One bird of the flooded forest that is wary of the marauding monkeys, particularly the intelligent capuchins, is the hoatzin. This strange-looking bird swims before it can fly and flies like a bloated chicken. Hoatzins prefer to nest over water. When the rivers are rising, foraging flocks break up into breeding groups—the breeding pair and a number of helpers from previous broods—which squabble for the prime sites, particularly on islands where predators are less common. Each group defends a strip of waterfront territory about 165 feet (50 meters) long.

The problem is that a hoatzin nest attracts predators, with its distinctive odor that can be detected some distance away. The bird feeds on leaves collected in the early morning. It snips them off with its sharp, scissorlike beak, and this food passes passed down into a gut like that of a ruminant. Unlike a cow, which has an enlarged hind gut where bacteria break down the tough plant cell walls, the hoatzin has a modified foregut, much like a kangaroo. Its greatly enlarged crop contains bacteria, and on its slow passage through the gut—the slowest of any known bird—the food is broken down, poisons detoxified, and nutrients, minerals, and vitamins absorbed. The consequence of this arrangement is that aromatic oils in the leaves give hoatzins a very distinctive smell. Local people call them 'stink birds' and avoid them, but for the brown capuchin monkey, the smell signals food.

◀

Hoatzin. It is not a great flyer, and though it can flap for 500 feet (150 meters) at a time, landings tend to be clumsy because the bird's unusually large crop causes it to topple forwards. After feeding, it perches with its breast resting against a branch, for which it has a special patch of skin.

The hoatzin chick, however, has an effective escape mechanism—it cannot fly but it can swim, and so when an inquisitive capuchin comes to call, it leaps over the side of the nest and into the water. There, it swims around underwater until the danger has passed. The chick has another trick. Each wing has a claw on its leading edge and another at the tip, giving it the appearance of some ancient birdlike dinosaur. Using a combination of claws and beak, the chick can haul itself up through the branches and back to the nest. When it is ready to fledge, the claws are lost, and the bird can flap away from danger rather than swim.

The adult hoatzin is quite striking, with naked electric blue skin around its bright red eyes and a crest of stiff feathers sprouting from the top of its head. Equally startling is the dark blue, crow-sized umbrella bird. The male impresses females not only by displaying a long wattle lined with iridescent blue feathers that dangles from its breast, but also by throwing forward over its face a crest of hairy feathers that resembles a 1960s rock 'n' roll haircut. Its booming calls are heard at dawn, and throughout the day it forages in the branches for the fleshy fruits available during the flooding season.

Birds and monkeys are not the only animals to take advantage of the fruiting bonanza. In the flooded forest, many trees have their seeds dispersed by fruit-eating fish. Silver dollars, or *pacu*, the *matrinchá,* and a variety of catfish eat the smaller, tasty fruits whole, the seeds passing straight through the gut unharmed and deposited in the fish droppings some distance from the parent tree. Trees can rely on more than 200 species of fish to distribute their seeds, some even germinating underwater.

It is a time of plenty for some and new life for others, but the flooded forest is not always the easiest place to live. The quantity of decaying leaves in the water means that oxygen levels are low, and this factor determines not only where fish live, but also whether they stay or move out of the flooded forest. Those that can make the necessary adaptations are the survivors. In the Amazon, fish tend to be more specialized to cope with low-oxygen conditions and so can change physiology, behavior, and body form in response to factors in the flood cycle, such as the lack of oxygen. Many have high levels of red cells in their blood and unusually shaped hemoglobin molecules to which the oxygen attaches when the blood carries it around the body. Others take in additional oxygen in various ways, but all head for the surface and either gulp air or skim the top few millimeters which, being next to the air above, contains a little more oxygen than the water below. Such is the desperate need for air that predators and prey rub shoulders at the surface.

The gigantic pikelike *pirarucu* is one of the largest known freshwater fish in the world and a voracious predator. Only the *piraiba* catfish, which frequents the main river channels, is bigger and heavier. The *pirarucu*, though, has teeth not only in its jaws but also on its tongue, which it can use like a second lower jaw. The 10-foot-long (3-meter) fish rises to the surface every 10–15 minutes to breathe, taking the air into a swim bladder that functions like a lung. From there, oxygen is absorbed by blood vessels in the swim bladder wall and carried round the body. At night, when oxygen levels are particularly low, many fish are forced to become less active—easy prey for the air-gulping *pirarucu*.

Some catfish also have to breathe air, and they absorb oxygen through the wall of their stomachs. Other species, such as the *tamoatá*, take in oxygen through their intestines.

The *tambaqui*—a large fish that grows to 3 feet (1 meter) long and weighs up to 66 pounds (30 kilograms)—spawns in the river channels at the start of the annual flood and follows the rising waters into the forest. It changes the shape of its lips within a few hours to accommodate low oxygen levels, developing a fluid filled, shovellike swelling at the tip of its lower jaw. When the fish swims along the surface, the swelling channels the oxygen-rich surface film into its mouth without taking in any of the deoxygenated water below.

By June, forests up to 50 miles (75 kilometers) on either side of the main Amazon River channel are flooded with water that can be up to 50 feet (16 meters) deep. There is no dry land anywhere. River people (the *ribeirinhos*), even those dwellings on hillocks, are forced to leave their houses and move either to a floating house or to a house on stilts next door. Chickens and cattle live on separate floating rafts, the cattle usually accompanied by a domestic cat that supposedly keeps the vampire bats away. Transport is by boat— nobody walks on dry land for three months.

There are even 'floating meadows'. As the water rises, patches of vegetation, such

as grass, bamboo, and reeds, either grow to keep pace with the rising water levels or float submerged at the surface. These rafts can be enormous—0.66 miles (a kilometer) long and about three hundred feet (100 meters) wide—and massively crowded with grasshoppers, other bugs, and spiders. Jacanas and other water birds forage for insects and other invertebrates on top, while fish and dragonfly larvae below grab any living thing that falls in.

Many fish species hide and breed underneath the meadows. Most occupy the raft's periphery, but swamp eels squirm a way through the tangle of roots and leaves. They have gills both for drawing oxygen from the water in the manner of most fish and for breathing air when oxygen levels are low. The eel surfaces, inflates its mouth and throat, then closes its mouth to trap the air.

Tambaqui, a large fruit- and seed-eating fish. Nasal flaps help it detect the biochemical changes taking place in trees that are about to fruit. It is attracted to the seeds and fruits as they plop into the water, smashing them with its nut-cracking jaws and seed-crushing teeth.

Strange trumpeting calls emanating from the floating meadows invariably belong to another of the Amazon's unusual birds—the horned screamer. Described as "a cross between a chicken and a vulture," it forsakes the flooded forest during the dry season but moves on to the floating meadows when the waters begin to rise. A plant eater, it has a fondness for the young leaves of water hyacinths.

With over a hundred species of fish and countless other creatures hiding below the meadows and lawns, including the juveniles of larger fish, this is a productive hunting ground for knife fish. They are known as "weakly electric fish," surrounding themselves with a pulsing electric field—usually less than one volt—night and day for their entire lives. They are so common that the electrical activity beneath the meadows is considerable.

Electroreception via receptors on the skin enables knife fish to detect voltage changes in the self-generated external field. Objects in their path or other fish distort the field, and the detectors pick up changes in its geometry. Electric knife fish can also detect the fields emanating from neighboring knife fish. This field is effective for just a few inches around the fish, beyond which they fail to detect objects, although using their lateral line system, they (like all other fish) can detect changes in water pressure well beyond this range. The electric field is so well developed that they can use it to locate food and find their way about at night in the turbid Amazonian waters. Under the floating meadows and among the swamp meadows, the smaller fish locate and eat aquatic insect larvae, whereas the larger species target other fish.

The weakly electric fish are often targeted themselves, particularly by the Amazon's "strong electric fish"—the electric eel, or poraquê. Despite its name, it is not an eel at all, but a gymnotiform like the weakly electric fish. It grows to a maximum length of 9 feet (2.75 meters) and is quite capable of stunning or even killing a person with a discharge in the order of several hundred volts, delivered not just once, but in short, sharp volleys of several hundred electric pulses. As an adaptation to poor oxygen levels, the eel must come to the surface to gulp air, which it absorbs through the folded lining of the mouth. Virtually blind, it is known to use low-voltage pulses—from about one pulse per minute to several per second—in the same way as the weakly electric fish to find its way around. It is seen hunting in small groups. Whether the eels cooperate or whether a fish hunting alone attracts others to the scene is unclear, but there is some evidence to suggest that, when an eel blasts its prey with a high-repetition pulse rate, all the other eels in the neighborhood race in to see what the fuss is about.

High water, however, is not the best time for predators. While fruit- and nut-eaters are enjoying an abundance of foods, most carnivores are having a difficulttime. Some switch diets. A predatory fish, known locally as bico-de-pato, which eats mainly fish during low water, takes to catching prawns and snatching fish scales when the floods come. Some predatory fish eat very little, relying on fat reserves to see them through the lean times.

At high water, there is more water in which to hide. Therefore, fish—in particular, young fry—are less likely to be caught, making it a good time for them to breed. The male

MAMIRAUÁ

There are not many places in the Amazon where you can experience living in an actual flooded forest, but the Mamirauá Sustainable Development Reserve is one. Until recently, the reserve has been the well-kept secret of researchers and wildlife film-makers, but now small groups of visitors are being welcomed. In fact, the steady trickle of enthusiasts is contributing to the development of the reserve, which was formed in 1990 to protect the *várzea* at the confluence of the Solimões and Japurá Rivers. It is part of the Ecological Corridor of Amazon rain-forest, which together with the Jaú National Park and the Amanã Reserve, covers an area the size of Denmark. Such is the extent of the flooded forest that if you visit during the wet season, your feet never touch dry land.

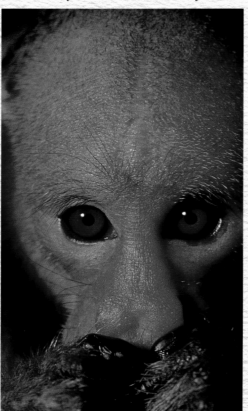

Transport is by boat, and visitors stay in a floating lodge that rises and falls with the waters as they incroach and retreat.

Wake-up call is often by a troop of red howler monkeys, and at high water the breakfast entertainment might include river dolphins in front of the deck. A rambling procession of squirrels, sloths, iguanas, many species of birds, and several species of monkeys may accompany an early morning canoe tour. One of the reserve's most spec-tacular monkeys is the white and red uakari, large troops of which can be encountered in the forest, often jumping gaps of 100 feet (30 meters) between trees.

Five species of kingfishers may be seen perched on branches overhanging the water, flocks of macaws and parrots pass overhead at dawn and dusk, and spectacular, metallic-blue morpho butterflies fly high in the forest clearings.

In the rivers, permanent islands have a covering of thick vegetation, and if you stare long enough at the leaves and branches, you might be in for a surprise: gradually you will become aware that sitting motionless in the trees are large, exquisitely camouflaged iguanas. Once you get your eyes focused, you can see them everywhere.

The reserve boasts 1000 black and spec-tacled caiman, along with 15,000 neotropical cormorants, and various species of herons. Altogether, there are about 400 species of birds and 45 species of mammals.

In the dry season, Lake Mamirauá boils with fish being chased by caiman and water birds. The constant noise from their flap-ping and the froglike calls of the *coro-coro* rat could keep you awake all night!

◄

White and red uakari. These monkeys move around the reserve in troops of 30 or more. Although their tail is too short to be of use for balance, they negotiate the branches with ease and leap across huge gaps between trees. Even in the low-water season, they rarely spend time on the ground.

aruaña ensures his offspring get a good start in life by hiding the fertilized eggs in his cavernous mouth, where the young subsequently hatch out. Each has a substantial yolk sac so it can remain in the mouth for two to three weeks. When the yolk is used up, the youngsters remain with their father for a further month to six weeks. Every so often he opens his mouth to let out the tiny fry for 10–15-second exercise periods, during which they feed quickly on algae, small aquatic larvae, and water fleas. If danger threatens, he opens his mouth and they all crowd back in.

Parental care is common in the Amazon, although some fish spawn in the better-oxygenated waters of the main river channels and return to the flooded forest to feed. The *tamoatá* overcome the low-oxygen problem by surrounding their eggs with a raft of air bubbles that serve a dual purpose—they also mimic the spawn of frogs and toads, which might deter some predators. *Loricaria* glue batches of a hundred or so eggs to their body, while the fry of discus fish graze the mucus on their parents' bodies. Cichlids, such as the *acar-boari*, can be seen herding their youngsters through the floating meadows. Some catfish excavate burrows in which they hide their young, and many other cichlids guard nests.

The wet season also triggers breeding among the *pirarucu*. The female deposits about 50,000 eggs in a hollow at the bottom of shallow water, but the male can fertilize no more than 500, and only a few of these will reach adulthood, despite the attention of the parents. The male fish escorts groups of hatchlings to the surface, their dark skin camouflaged against his head. It is thought that he produces mucus from glands on his head which the fry can feed on. They might stay close to their fathers for up to six months.

The *pirarucu* is caught for food. Much of it is salted and sun-dried for sale to local traders and markets, although a good proportion is sold fresh. It is the source of up to 45 percent of the local fishermen's income. They locate the fish by listening for the sound of it taking a breath at the surface, and harpoon its enormous body from a canoe. Frantic bailing is necessary for the fishermen to return home safely with their valuable catch.

Fishing, whether for food or the aquarium trade, is an important activity in the Amazon, and sometimes the fishermen do not fish alone. In the deeper parts of the river channels they are joined by schools of tucuxi (pronounced *too-koo-she*) dolphins that look as if they would be more at home in the sea than a river. In the flooded forest their fishing companions might be *botos* or Amazon river dolphins.

Some *botos* are pink, others gray, and their color depends partly on the clarity of the water. Muddy water contains pink dolphins; clear water has dark gray ones. Whatever its color, the *boto* swims in and out of the treetops, rising to the surface to breathe every 90 seconds. Like all dolphins, the *boto* finds its way through the submerged trees with the help of sonar, scanning the water ahead or locating potential prey, such as fish and crabs, by echolocation. Unlike its sea-going relatives, the *boto* has a flexible neck and a wide sound beam with which it can sweep its head from side to side and scan the Amazon's turbid waters. Its eyes are small and virtually useless in water, where you can barely see more than a few inches in front of your face.

One group of Amazon fish that is the subject of many stories, most of them pure myth, is the *candiru*. There are about 150 species of these catfish in the Amazon. The whale-*candiru* is a formidable flesh eater. It swims around in shoals taking circular chunks out of the flanks of larger fish and occasionally from dolphins and manatees. Local fishermen consider them to be as dangerous as piranhas. They are scavengers, too, and will quickly consume anything left in a fisherman's net, attacking first the soft underside and organs and then the muscles, reducing fish to skeletons in minutes. They sometimes attack people who happen to be in the water.

Another group of *candiru* are highly specialized feeders, some catching small crustaceans, some feeding on the body slime and scales of other fish, and others that burrow into sick fish and dead corpses, eating their flesh from the inside out. But the most famous is a smaller species of the *Vandellia* genus, 2 inches (5 centimeters) long, which has a particularly unpleasant habit. In the wild, it infests the gills of larger catfish and other river fish, extracting blood from the veins. It does this by following an odor trail of urea (expelled into the water from a fish's gills) back to its source. The gills of a large fish can be packed to overflowing with parasitic *candiru*.

For anybody swimming or urinating in the water, and particularly menstruating women, the *candiru* can have a nasty surprise. It is reputed to follow a urine or blood trail and enter the urethra or nose of humans, where it gets stuck. Preposterous stories abound in the press, claiming that when a man relieves himself from the riverbank, the fish can swim up a stream of urine and into his urethra. But to quote Amazon researcher Will Crampton, "This fish can no more swim up a stream of urine than I could swim up the Angel Falls."

By September, in the middle basin of the Amazon at least, the rains cease and the waters begin to fall. The endless procession of Amazonian wildlife—from roundworms and flatworms to fish and turtles—reverses and begins to make its way back to where the main river channels, streams, lakes, and oxbows emerge. Except for a few overlooked palm tree seeds, the forest's cupboard is almost bare. As the water level continues to drop, the *tambaqui* must move out of the forest. The nuts and fruits it has consumed during the wet season enable it to put on ample fat reserves—about 10 percent of its body weight—to take it through the dry season. But during this period, it does something odd—it supplements its reserves by switching to foods of animal origin. It has been known to take small fish, mayfly larvae, and cockroaches; yet when the freshwater plankton blooms, it becomes a filter feeder, extracting zooplankton from the water with its long, fine gill rakers.

One of the last trees to bear fruit is the piranha tree or *piranheira*, a relative of the rubber tree. As the floods subside, it loses its leaves and a new crop of fruit appears immediately. Many fish feed on the fruit, but the tree itself is covered with hordes of the caterpillars of a noctuid moth, eager to consume the new growth of leaves. Many of these caterpillars drop into the water and are gobbled up by the fish that gather below. The commotion attracts piranhas. They not only eat up any caterpillars that fall in but also attack the fish that try to feed on them. Eventually, the caterpillars pupate in cocoons suspended from

the branches, and the tree produces its second crop of leaves. The moths emerge at low water, just as the flowers appear, and pollinate the plant. The price the tree must pay for guaranteed pollination is its first crop of leaves.

On other trees, the hijackers that exploited the mass exodus from the forest floor as the water rose, anticipate the return leg of the migration. About a month before the forest dries out, spiders and centipedes move down the trunk and take up the prime positions that will enable them to intercept the beetles and ants returning to the ground.

As the forest floor begins to reappear, however, not all aquatic animals are eager to leave. Freshwater bivalve mussels bury themselves on dry land rather than risk the concentration of predators in the remaining stands of water. Their bodies slow down to save sufficient energy for survival until the waters return once again.

Up in the trees, balls of freshwater sponges festoon branches that were submerged at high water. As the flood recedes, they are left hanging, but they do not die. The organism—a simple collection of living cells joined by a matrix of channels and chambers—produces a drought-resistant reproductive body known as a gemmule. It consists of a protective sphere of silicon spicules encasing the reproductive cells, and it is sometimes retained, especially by older sponges, or released to disperse elsewhere. The gemmule keeps the sponge's cells safe until the water returns. The sponge itself can also resist the drought by shutting down its vital processes (metabolism) and protecting its living cells with a siliceous casing.

Where there are puddles of mineral-rich water or wet sand, millions of colorful butterflies flap down like living confetti. All males, they crowd together on the damp sand, each one drawing up minerals and salts through its tiny curly proboscis. The main salt they seek is sodium, essential for the working of nerves and muscles, but the male butterfly would have transferred much of his sodium to the female in a sperm package during mating. Now he replenishes his supplies from the wet sand.

By October, the waters of the River Xingu have reached their lowest point, and yet stretches of the river near its mouth are over 10 miles (15 kilometers) wide. It looks more like a sea than a river. Waves whipped up by the wind break on broad, white sandbanks or *praias* exposed by the falling water, and even as far as 625 miles (1000 kilometers) from the sea the river is noticeably tidal.

The organisms of the exposed sandbanks are protected by law—no tourists are allowed to come here. These sandbanks form a stage for a performance that must go unobserved except for the hidden lenses of the film-makers' cameras because the stars are so easily frightened and vulnerable.

During the dry season, 5000 giant river turtles, or *tartaruga,* arrive here to deposit their eggs in the sand, in the same manner their ancestors would have done 65 million years ago. With a carapace over 3 feet (1 meter) across, they are the largest of the thriving freshwater turtles of the world, and they cause the rippling sands to turn into something resembling a war zone.

▶ Butterflies, Tambopata riverbank in Peru. Huge swarms of butterflies suck up water permeated with minerals from the damp sand. Many are males replacing salts they have transferred to the females when mating.

On an early October morning, first one, then two, then myriad heads appear on the surface of the river. As the numbers grow, the females haul out onto the three or four sandbanks in mid-river, appearing between 7 and 10 a.m., and bask in the sun for six or seven hours a day. A line of motionless bodies stretches for 0.3 miles (500 meters) along the water's edge. The females arrive two weeks before egg-laying, the two weeks of sun-bathing thought to be an aid to egg development. As they bask, the sky may be filled with yellow butterflies. In a living blizzard, millions of them fly from west to east across the river throughout the day, and then every day for an entire week. Where they are going and why they go nobody knows, but they do it every year without fail.

Then, at six or seven o'clock one evening in middle to late October the first wave of female turtles begins to dig. It is unusually quiet, with no sound but the lapping of waves and the movement of sand. Using her back flippers, each turtle excavates first a body pit and then a flask-shaped hole in which she deposits 60–130 round, leathery-shelled eggs. The hole is covered, the sand is tapped down, and she returns to the river. Her offspring must develop, hatch out, and be gone before the river begins to rise once more.

But space is at a premium here. The turtles are forced to use the sandbanks in mid-river because they have been moved on by settlers who have built their riverside homes

▶

Giant river turtles. On an island in the River Xingu, many females bask in the sun while the eggs developing inside them reach the final stage before laying. Only the females haul out, the males remaining in the river.

on prime nesting sites along the shore. Turtle after turtle digs and lays, each of them digging up the eggs of the previous wave. The chaos continues well into the morning. Black vultures make light work of any eggs that are exposed, but those hidden below the sand are relatively safe—as long as the river does not flood early. In the dry season, the weather pattern follows a three- or four-day cycle—hot, hotter, then hot and stuffy with thunderstorms in the afternoon of the third day. When evening comes, the clouds disappear, stars cover the sky, and the sound of mosquitoes fills the air. In fact, at precisely 6:30 on the Rio Xingu, the mosquitoes rise from the ground and take to the air. Researchers, visitors and locals alike make sure they have finished the evening's chores by 6:25 and then race for cover.

By January, as the rivers rise once again, mosquito larvae have ample water to grow in, but the emerging adults are faced with less and less land on which to find their mammalian prey. Concentrations are so dense, local people stop talking. Every time anyone opens his mouth, it is filled with mosquitoes. They get in the eyes, the nose, the ears—the invasion is unbearable. In the nearby *terra firme* forest, the mosquitoes are replaced by a plague of equally irritating sweat bees—but that is the next part of our journey.

the amazon
TERRA FIRME

Sweat bees are the bane of anyone who ventures into the Amazon's forests. Perspiration attracts the tiny creatures, and as soon as you leave the forest floor and climb up into the canopy they arrive in great swarms. The 500-plus bees attracted by the moisture on your skin are an insufferable and unbearable plague. They get in your eyes, nose, and ears, in your armpits and down your pants, and if you look up, they go straight for the whites of your eyes. And if that is not enough, there are sweat wasps. The impact of their sting belies their small size, and they will sting for apparently no reason at all.

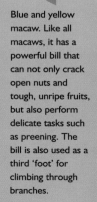

▶ Cannonball tree. The flowers develop on a tangle of woody stalks that push out from the bark on its trunk – an adaptation to a life in the understory, where the flowers attract insects, hummingbirds, and bats. The tree gets its name from its 8-inch (20-centimeter-diameter) cannonballlike fruits.

◀ Blue and yellow macaw. Like all macaws, it has a powerful bill that can not only crack open nuts and tough, unripe fruits, but also perform delicate tasks such as preening. The bill is also used as a third 'foot' for climbing through branches.

Sweat bees and wasps may be the most obvious inhabitants of the rainforest, but hidden away in the dense green jungle is an incredible wealth of wildlife, possibly the greatest diversity of plants and animals in the world. Along the Urucu river basin, near Tefé, for example, 14 species of primates are present within a single 250-acre (1-square-kilometer) plot. This rivals or even surpasses the West African sites often claimed to harbor the richest primate communities. The place is vast – it is possible to fly over unbroken rainforest for several hours by jet plane – yet every single ecological niche is filled to overflowing.

In one 1500-acre (6-square-kilometer) site near the Tiputini Biodiversity Station in Ecuador, scientists counted 3000 species of plants, 530 species of birds, 80 species of bats, and 11 species of primates. There are countless free-living amphibians, reptiles, fish, and invertebrates, each with its own internal and external parasites. Taking the insects alone, there are known to be 60,000 species per 2.5 acres (1 square hectare) of forest, and 80 ant species and 650 species of beetle have been identified on a single tree, including 28 different fig weevils in one fig tree alone. Throw in the algae, fungi, and micro-organisms and the bio-diversity count is mind boggling. Yet to the first-time visitor, it looks as if there is nothing here at all.

Animals hide themselves well in this *terra firme* forest, which is on higher ground than the flooded forest and far enough from the river to avoid its annual inundation. Without a seasonal deposit of silt, its soils are thinner and less fertile because most of the nutrients are tied up in the trees. Nevertheless, there is a wealth of wildlife living here, and the plants and animals are segregated vertically into at least four main levels – floor, understory, canopy, and emergents. The levels are not as distinct as the textbooks would have us believe. Parts of the forest are high, others lower, but each level has its own environmental conditions and is occupied by its own collection of plants and animals.

On the ground floor, everything appears to be in silhouette. It is dark here both night and day. Very little sunlight – no more than 2 percent of available light – filters down from above. Fungi, mosses, and a few herbs that tolerate deep shade live here. Saplings try to stretch to the canopy above, but in an undisturbed rainforest there are no impenetrable thickets. You can see great distances in the gloom and walk without hindrance.

The forest floor itself is a dense mat of roots. On ground level, fallen branches are imprisoned in a tangle of roots and hyphae from organisms desperate to find and extract minerals and nutrients. In the humid conditions, debris dropping to the forest floor is broken down rapidly by fungi and bacteria, and the nutrients released are quickly taken up by the trees. Where a leaf in a temperate forest might take a year to decompose, it takes just six weeks in the tropical rainforest.

Yet even here on the forest floor, there are animals hiding. Cockroaches, crickets, and small frogs scatter this way and that; flocks of trumpeter birds disturb the leaf litter and peck at anything that breaks cover. Tapirs forage for tubers and roots, pacas and agoutis feed on nuts and fruits falling down from above, and piglike peccaries snuffle about in the leaf litter for just about anything edible.

The agouti is one of the few animals that can break into a Brazil nut. It is a forgetful scatter hoarder, and hence it contributes substantially to seed distribution throughout the Amazon forests. Its caches, however, are often dug up by peccaries. The collared peccary or *javelina* roves the forest in herds of no more than 10 individuals and defends territories of 75–700 acres (30–280 hectares), which it scent marks with secretions from a rump gland. Peccaries also leave piles of dung in key sites, allowing clumps of forest to grow from undigested seeds. Although there is no 'leader', the group tends to follow whichever peccary is at the front of the line, usually one of the mature females. The white-lipped peccary or *huangana* travels over much greater distances and may be found in groups numbering 200 or more. One herd in Paraguay was reported to contain more than 1000 animals.

The largest of the forest herbivores is the tapir, which feeds mainly on leaves and fruit. Rarely seen by day, it is never far from the mud in which it wallows to keep cool and to protect its hide from parasitic flies. Its splay feet support a bulky body, but when moving through the forest it is surprisingly quiet, except when dashing blindly through the undergrowth if disturbed.

Under its feet, in the leaf litter, are giant earthworms such as *Rhinodrilus fafner*, which can be up to 6 feet (2 meters) long, and its only slightly less colossal cousin

► Brown agouti, a common yet secretive animal of the forest floor. It feeds mainly on fallen fruits and is ever alert to the sound of them dropping through the canopy. Its principal predators are ocelots and jaguars.

Glossoscolex giganteus, which grows to 4 feet (1.3 meters). But most animals here are small and less obvious. Termites, cockroaches, beetles, and millipedes use organic litter as a source of food, while there are centipedes, scorpions, and spiders ready to catch and feed on them. There are also ants. Millions of them.

Ants are present at all levels in the forest, including the bushes and trees of the understory, just above the forest floor. In the *terra firme* forest, they account for about 75 percent of all insect predation. Because of considerable competition, the ability to call up and recruit other members of the colony to help bring down prey and transport it away is important. Crazy ants, *hormigas locas,* are quick to find food and summon help, but they can be thwarted by the more aggressive *Azteca* ants, which use chemical sprays to take over a kill. Fire ants coat their food with chemicals which render it unpalatable to other species.

The ants themselves, however, are very palatable to the southern anteater or tamandua. Like many of the understory animals, it has special adaptations to living in trees – a prehensile tail, opposable digits and enlarged claws. It forages among the trees for arboreal termite and ant nests, which it tears apart with the large claws on its powerful forelimbs to get at the insects and their larvae inside. It avoids species that defend themselves with noxious sprays, although the *tamandua* itself releases an unpleasant odor from its anal gland that has earned it the nickname "stinker of the forest."

The understory is less dense than a first-time visitor might imagine. The image of an impenetrable hell is true only in certain parts of the forest, such as in clearings and at the forest edge, where the tangle of plants is especially dense. The rest is less crowded. Even so, only 2–5 percent of the available sunlight reaches this level, and so plants must have adaptations to enable them to cope. Some have dark green leaves that collect every last of photon of sunlight, others rotate their leaves and follow the sun. Dwarf palms and other understory trees and shrubs rarely grow more than 10–13 feet (3–4 meters) high, and below them are bushes and smaller ferns that are green all year round. Many, such as the Swiss-cheese plant, will be familiar to houseplant enthusiasts, for these plants, adapted to life with little direct sunlight or rainfall, adapt well to growing indoors.

There are frogs that have also adapted to these conditions and have developed ways to achieve independence from their normal aquatic lifestyle. The glass frog lays its eggs on leaves. These are guarded by the male, and if they are in danger of being dehydrated, he will moisten them with water from his bladder.

Water reaches the lower levels of the forest by running down trunks and dripping off leaves. The sound of dripping may go on many hours after a rainstorm, giving the impression that it is still raining. The constant wetting coupled with high humidity is a recipe for rot. To rid themselves of excess water, plants have water-repellent leaves and shapes that allow water to run off easily, including 'drip-tips' that aid draining. Some tropical trees, however, tap into the tiny nutrient-laden streams that run down the trunks of their neighbors – a kind of "nutrient scavenging." By putting out rapidly growing, upwardly mobile roots – known as apogeotropic roots – they race up the trunks at a rate of 2–2.5 inches (5–6

TIPUTINI

The Tiputini Biodiversity Station, owned and operated by the Universidad San Francisco de Quito in collaboration with Boston University, has been described as the best place in all of Ecuador to see wildlife. Those wanting to learn more about the rainforest can visit the station, which is about 200 miles (300 kilometers) southeast of Quito, in eastern Ecuador, and participate in one of their educational workshops.

The journey to Tiputini, the traditional home of the Waorani people, is an adventure in itself. A 45-minute flight or 10-hour bus journey from Quito to Coca is followed by a 2-hour boat journey on the Napo River to the village of Pompeya, a 1½-hour overland trip to the Tiputini River, and another 2-hour boat journey downstream to the station. There are well-marked trails through *terra firme* and *várzea* forests, and a 125-foot (38-meter) tower from which visitors can view the forest canopy.

Jaguars are spotted occasionally by the river, as are tapirs, giant otters, capybara, and caiman. There are 520 recognized species of birds present. Twelve species of monkey inhabit the canopy, half of them seen regularly close to the camp. Woolly monkeys, rarely seen anywhere else in the Amazon, are a particular attraction here.

▼

Brazilian tapir, the largest *terra firme* forest animal. A good swimmer, it spends time in the water feeding, cooling off, or divesting itself of parasites. Water is also a refuge when escaping its main predator, the jaguar.

centimeters) in 72 hours, some climbing right up to the canopy. One specimen of butter-nut tree was once found to support 15 climbing roots. A root from an adjacent *Swartzia* grew 44 feet (13.4 meters) up to the subcanopy, where it subdivided into small rootlets that infiltrated a large decomposing branch.

Vultures by day and opossums at night tend to lead as animal scavengers. They can reduce any large carcass – tapir or deer, for example – to a skeleton within days. There are also some unexpected insects that are quick to arrive – bees.

One type of stingless bee (*Trigona*) has five large, pointed teeth on each mandible with which it can cut into flesh. Once a carcass has been located, a bee will lay a pheromone trail and recruit further help. Members of the swarm descend and stand around in a circle, tearing at the skin. They make a small hole through which the rest can enter and methodically demol-ish the insides of the dead animal. As they chew, they spread an enzyme over the meat and partially digest it before taking it back to the nest, where they regurgitate it to others.

By arriving in a swarm, the bees dispell any competition, such as flies and ants. One species of *Crematogaster* ant is not attacked and, in turn, does not harass the bees. The bees, it seems, have sole occupancy during the day, while the ants take over at night. The most common carrion is amphibian or reptilian; 60–80 bees can reduce a dead frog to its

◀

Leaf cutter ants. Foraging ants snip off leaves and flowers and, following a scent trail, carry the pieces back to their nest. They do not eat the leaves but turn them into a mulch on which a nutritious fungus is cultivated. The ants feed on the fungus.

bare bones in 3 hours or a woolly opossum in 24 hours, but a thousand-strong swarm may tackle a dead monkey and strip it bare in a few days.

With little or no wind down here, most plants must rely on insects, hummingbirds, and bats for pollination. Some produce strong smelling flowers at night, so at dusk – between 5:30 and 6:30 every evening – the forest becomes remarkably fragrant as flowers pollinated by bats and moths begin to open up. Others adopt a flowering and fruiting strategy known as cauliflory. They produce their flowers and fruits, not on their crowns like most other plants, but on their trunks. The flowers are thus more conspicuous to understory insects and hummingbirds and easier to visit for climbing and clinging bats. The insects, in turn, are food for saddle-back tamarins and moustached tamarins, two insect eating primates commonly found in the understory.

Sharing the understory with them is another, much rarer monkey – Goeldi's monkey. Small, squirrellike, active, and agile, it lives in isolated family groups in the lower levels of the forest and is an opportunistic feeder. In the wet season, when food is abundant, the Goeldi's family will roam in a circle, collecting fruits and hunting insects and small mammals. In the dry season it must forage over a wider area. Goeldi's monkeys can bound across 13-foot (4-meter) gaps from tree to tree, adopting a 'cling and leap' method using their powerful hind legs. They retain a vertical posture and twist, even in mid-air, to land feet forward.

Groups are active for much of the day, foraging at all levels of their forest home, although they seem to be most comfortable below 16 feet (5 meters), and make for this part of the forest to hide when disturbed. Their trails are marked with urine and smears from glands on their chest, and their highways tend to be the lianas and vines that twist their way up from the forest floor through the understory to the canopy. Almost half of rainforest trees have climbing plants attached, including climbing palms, climbing ferns, and the climbing gymnosperm *Gnetum*. Some trees have several attached.

The vine-like lianas seem to bypass the understory and make for the daylight as fast as they can. They are among the fastest climbers. They start as free-standing plants, growing rapidly to about 3–6 feet (1–2 meters) tall, but the quick growth results in a spindly stem, so they must then rely on sturdier plants for support. Unlike a tree, which grows straight upwards, a liana's dependence on other vegetation might take it on a rather circuitous route to the light. Its growth, therefore, might be as long horizontally as it is vertically.

Lianas might constitute about 5–10 percent of all the above ground forest plants, but their leaves cover about 20–25 percent of the canopy. They can do this because relying on other plants for support enables them to have larger and more efficient water-carrying xylem vessels in their stems. Normally, a tree gains greater strength and rigidity when its xylem loses some of its water-carrying capacity as sapwood and becomes part of the internal support system – the heartwood. Lianas can afford to be 'bendy' and retain their xylem vessels for longer. In this way, they can function with a greater leaf area than an equivalent sized tree.

The weight of lianas may be one cause of falling trees, and their profusion of leaves

certainly puts some trees in the shade. But they also anchor trees together, at least temporarily. In this way, the tables are turned and some old trees could well rely on the lianas to keep them upright during their final days. On the other hand, if a liana laden tree falls, it probably takes its neighbors with it. It is also quite possible that trees have come and gone during the lifetime of a liana, so it is older than the trees supporting it. Lianas and vines can be some of the oldest plants in the rainforest, with specimens more than 500 years old.

Some trees, such as the umbrella or trumpet tree, are protected from a liana invasion. When young, they play host to a species of *Azteca* ants that cut away any stems that attempt to take over their tree. These ants also protect against plant eating insects, which they bite with strong mandibles, secreting caustic chemicals that they rub into the bite. The ants live in the hollow, compartmentalized stems of the trees and are fed via swollen leaf hairs and swellings on the petioles that secrete oils and glycogen, a high-energy carbohydrate. The ants also tend and 'milk' sap-sucking mealy bugs inside the plant's stem.

Most forest animals find lianas useful and depend on them for food, shelter, or as a means of traveling through the forest. Sloths seems to prefer trees with lianas to those that have none. They make climbing easier, providing more handholds for an animal that is so very careful and deliberate about where it places its hands and feet.

The sloth is an upside-down creature. It hangs from branches by its powerful limbs, and its fur grows down with a parting on its stomach. It has a two-layered coat: a fine underfur and a coarse outer coat with blue-green algae growing in the grooves of its corrugated hairs that give it a tinge of green, protective coloring against marauding predators. Its coat also plays host to a moth that has wings but rarely flies; instead, it scurries about in the sloth's fur. If a sloth should have to swim (and sloths are good swimmers) the moth will sit on the sloth's head, the only dry place it can find!

There are two types of sloth — ones with two claws on the front limbs (*Choloepus*) and ones with three (*Bradypus*). They

◄
Guarana liana fruits. This liana is pollinated by bees and its fruits are dispersed by birds. A caffeine-rich stimulant, claimed to be an aphrodisiac and valued highly by South American Indian tribes, is made from the liana. It was brought to Europe in 1775, and is today used as an ingredient of some commercially produced tonics and sports drinks.

eat leaves, which they digest in a stomach with many compartments, each containing cellu-lose-digesting bacteria. A meal might remain in the stomach for a week before being passed on to the relatively short intestines. About once a week, the sloth crawls down carefully to the base of the tree in which it is feeding and makes a depression into which it defecates, returning valuable nutrients to the tree. The sloth's moth companion also makes use of the dung, scuttling off the sloth to lay its eggs there. Once hatched, the larvae feed on the dung.

The tree and its lianas might also play host to courting manakins. These are small, colorful birds the size of chickadees. Females are less flamboyant than males, which are mostly colored black and white with splashes of red, orange, or blue depending on the species. Courtship is often quite a performance and is certainly a noisy and colorful affair.

The most dramatic is the 'catherine wheel' dance performed jointly by three male swallow-tailed manakins. When a female arrives, the first male approaches her, leaps into the air and then flies backwards in a flurry of twangs and whirrs to the back of the line. As he lands, the second bird follows suit, and so on until the three aspirants are performing in a seemingly endless chain. In the end, the males themselves seem to choose the winner, and only this dominant bird mates with the female.

Another extraordinary performance is given by the male wire-tailed manakin. He

► Brown-throated three-toed sloth. A baby is suckled by its mother for only a month, but it will stay with her for up to 9 months, perching on its mother's stomach and grabbing leaves to eat.

might also be joined by a support male, the two performing an exquisite *pas de deux* in order to entice a female closer. When she arrives on the display perch the lead male has a unique display. Some of his tail feathers are modified into downwardly curved, wirelike filaments, much like a splayed-out wire brush. The male backs up to the female, raises his curious tail, and wiggles it from side to side just under her chin. Experienced female birds will place themselves at the right height and in the right place to be tickled. This display appears to establish a temporary bond between the pair prior to mating and is one of the few known examples of tactile stimulation in birds. The male's behavior is all the more remarkable in that he performs this ritual throughout the year and displays at virtually anything that presents itself near his perch. Even an unsuspecting agouti, rustling in the bushes nearby, will trigger an impromptu performance!

The next level up in the *terra firme* forest – the canopy – is a dense umbrella of leaves that blocks out most sunlight and rain from the understory and forest floor. From below it looks like a solid green ceiling. Rising to about 150 feet (45 meters), it is the engine that drives the forest. While decomposition is the main process on the forest floor, in the canopy photosynthesis takes place in a big way. Among the leaves, there are also flowers and fruits in abundance, so the animals that live up here need never touch the ground throughout their lives, not even to find water.

Despite the heavy rainfall, conditions in the canopy resemble a desert, and the only standing water is trapped in the tree tops, in bromeliads. Like most tropical rainforest epiphytes – including orchids, ferns, mosses, and lichen – they are specially adapted to an arboreal life, occupying any available surface, such as branches and tree forks, and extracting water and nutrients from the atmosphere. Some species have taken things even further. Bromeliads such as *Aechmea brevicollis* and *A. mertensii* place their roots in arboreal ant nests, from which they extract their moisture and nutrients.

Bromeliads are high living members of the pineapple family. Each plant has a rosette of stiff, spiny leaves that can be up to 6 feet (2 meters) long in some of the larger species. The inner leaves or bracts are often bright red and the flowers white or reddish purple. Some grow on the ground, but many species are found attached to the branches of trees. The leaf axils of many arboreal bromeliads fill with water and are known as tank or 'aquarium' bromeliads. Small plants may have less than a few ounces of water, but large specimens may contain as much as 2 gallons (9 liters) of water, and in 250 acres (1 square kilometer) of forest there could be over 450,000 gallons (2 million liters) of water stored in bromeliads.

Special structures in the cuticle – the waxy surface of the leaf – enable the bromeliads to absorb water and minerals from their pools directly though their leaf surfaces. The pools are microhabitats in themselves. In areas where surface water is scarce, insects with aquatic larvae, such as mosquitoes, midges, and dragonflies, depend on them. In fact, they provide homes and food for a variety of forest residents, with as many as 470 species

▶

Macaws at a clay-lick alongside a river in Manu National Park, Peru. Each morning, hundreds of birds squabble at the clay-lick for the best perches on the clay seams. They can be seen during most of the year.

recorded living in them.

Larger and older bromeliads have blue-green algae growing in their pools. These fix atmospheric nitrogen that then becomes available to the plant. The algae are also food for an entire community of small creatures, and within a short time a bromeliad can play host to quite a food chain. In the 'aquarium', top predators are represented by water beetles, dragonfly larvae, and frogs, while in the drier, older leaf axils around the periphery of the plant, spiders, centipedes, scorpions, ants, praying mantis, snakes, and lizards lurk in the accumulation of organic debris that is the 'terrarium'. Vine snakes, for example, stake out bromeliads in order to catch tree frogs, and crane hawks, with their exceptionally long legs, specialize in snatching frogs and other small animals from bromeliad pools.

In these pools there can also be carnivorous bladderworts that capture small aquatic insects and their larvae in tiny bladder traps. There is even the suggestion that some bromeliad pools are like carnivorous pitcher plants, producing enzymes to digest insects that fall in. Most bromeliads, however, are safe havens.

Frogs use bromeliad pools as nurseries. Male poison-dart frogs wrestle for the right to occupy a pool, since pool owners attract the females. Tree frogs take possession too. One species carries its eggs on its back, but when they hatch, its tadpoles are released into

Male reticulated, or red-backed, poison dart frog carrying a pair of tadpoles on its back. This tiny frog hides in the axils of bromeliads, emerging to eat springtails, mites and small flies.

the pools. The young of another species complete their development on their mother's back, and enter the bromeliads as tiny frogs.

One poison-dart frog mother deposits a single tadpole in each of several bromeliads. She avoids pools already occupied by the offspring of the same species, because the resident tadpole sends her a signal – it shakes its tail. Having found homes for all her brood, she revisits each pool in turn, depositing an unfertilized egg which the tadpole consumes.

When they grow up, some species of frogs, such as *Aparasphenodon brunoi*, shelter in bromeliads during the day, but do so in a curious way. *Aparasphenodon* has a strange bony lid on the top of the head with which it can fit snugly into the plant's central tube. It withdraws its eyes into its mouth cavity and here it sits, well protected from predators and from drying out. The plant benefits, too, because the living plug helps it retain water.

The trees themselves tap into the nutrients trapped or stored by epiphytes by putting out adventitious roots. These are roots that grow from unusual positions, such as from a leaf or stem, and run into the thick mats of organic material beneath the epiphytes, giving them access to water and nutrients that would otherwise be denied to them. They also grow roots directly into the bromeliad pools. If the load of bromeliads and vines should become too much, some trees have the ability to 'self-prune'. They can shut down the branches overloaded with bromeliads and other hangers-on so that they wither and break, thus saving the rest of the tree from the same fate.

The tallest forest trees, such as the silk cotton or kapok tree, are what are known as the emergents – the topmost level in the forest. They grow to immense sizes, towering as much as 200 feet (60 meters) above the ground and reaching up beyond the canopy to bathe in maximum sunlight. Their massive trunks can be 16 feet (5 meters) in circumference, the base supported by roots that fan out in the thin soils rather than dig deep. Huge buttresses brace the tree against high winds. These broad leaved, hardwood evergreens are exposed to greater variations in temperature, wind, and rainfall than the trees in the canopy, so their leaves have a thick, waxy covering.

Up here, birds and butterflies are active by day, but at dusk the night shift takes over. Having spent the day huddled with the rest of its family group in a hollow tree some 100 feet (30 meters) above the ground, members of a group of goggle-eyed night or owl monkeys appear to follow a well-rehearsed daily routine: they wake, stretch, urinate, and defecate, and then an adult heads off across the lianas towards a feeding tree. The rest of the group follows, parents first, children second. Here, they feed on fruits and young leaves, and any insects or birds' eggs they might chance upon. This is the only known nocturnal monkey, although much of its foraging activity takes place at dusk or in bright moonlight.

The number one night hunter, however, is the jaguar. It is at home in dense forest, particularly areas close to water, and may patrol a territory of up to 200 square miles (500 square kilometers). Ground dwelling creatures such as tapirs, peccaries, and agoutis are on the jaguar's hit list, and it even goes fishing and digs up turtles' eggs. It is also an active predator in the trees. Despite a stockier body and shorter legs than its relative the leopard,

it climbs with surprising agility. In the trees, sloths are often the target. They tend to sleep on high, slender branches where jaguars cannot go, but when they move from tree to tree they are vulnerable. Monkeys and birds fall prey to jaguars too.

Of the smaller cats, another climber and swimmer is the ocelot or *chibi-guazu*. It rests by day and does most of its hunting by night on the forest floor, stalking young deer and peccaries, monkeys, opossums, bats, sloths, coatis, agoutis, and pacas, as well as snakes and other reptiles. Its elegant striped and spotted coat, once in great demand from fashion houses, renders its almost invisible in the forest. It also ambushes birds, which represent about 20 percent of its prey. Stalking does not usually work, however, for birds simply flap away. The cat must rush the target and pin it down with the front paws and claws.

Daylight hours are the province of the harpy eagle, considered by some ornithologists to be the most powerful eagle in the world. It has short wings and a long tail for optimum maneuverability in the forest as it glides among the tree-tops, with extraordinary precision, at 35–50 miles (60–80 kilometers) per hour. Its feet are the most powerful of any bird of prey. The tarsus is nearly 1 inch (2 centimeters) thick and ends with a foot spanning 10 inches (25 centimeters) and armed with menacing daggerlike claws 1.5 inches (4 centimeters) long that could pierce the body of a monkey and kill it instantly.

The harpy eagle ambushes from the air. It can spot movements through the foliage of the canopy and swoop down nearly vertically, braking at intervals by raising its tail and furling its wings. It can fly briefly upside down and snatch a young sloth hanging beneath a branch, but a third of the prey items brought back to a harpy's nest are monkeys.

The canopy and emergent trees are the kingdom of the monkeys, and the *terra firme* forests are far richer in the number of species than the neighboring flooded forests. One of the typical *terra firme* monkeys is the woolly monkey, known to the locals as *barrigudo*, meaning 'pot-belly', on account of its enormous appetite. It is a timid creature; if anything frightens it, a cry will clear the area, so it is rarely seen.

It lives in the highest parts of the canopy and is widespread throughout the forest. Its behavior is dependent on the season, for even here in the rainforest rain does not fall every day. In the dry season woolly monkeys are found in small family groups, but in the wet season they travel in parties of 30–60 animals, chirruping constantly to each other. While other monkeys cross from tree to tree in single file, woollies sweep across like a weather front. They are known to feed on the fruit of at least 220 species of trees and drink from bromeliad pools. They are often joined on their fruit foraging expeditions by toucans and are also followed by small forest hawks that pick up the insects the monkeys disturb.

Some monkeys, such as black-handed spider monkeys and Geoffroy's tamarins, benefit the forest trees by helping to disperse their seeds. The seeds go straight through the gut unharmed. Other creatures are more destructive. Some trees make their fruits highly visible and attractive to animals, but the function of the fruit is to offer a nutritious covering so that the seeds are left to germinate once the fruit has been consumed. Unfortunately, a few animals, including sakis and macaws, have discovered that young seeds can be richer in

▶

Juvenile harpy eagle. It will grow up to become to be one of the most powerful eagles in the world. A short-winged forest species, adapted to flying in and around the canopy, its daggerlike talons are capable of instantly killing a young monkey.

MANU

The Manu Biosphere Reserve is the largest tropical rainforest reserve in the world and perhaps the most species-rich protected area on Earth. About half the size of Switzerland, Manu is unique in having three major habitats: tundralike *puna*, clothed in pale yellow *ichu* grass, populated by viscachas, huemel deer, small cats and the Andean condor; mist-enshrouded cloudforest with trees festooned with lichens, bromeliads and orchids, brilliantly colored birds, such as hummingbirds and cock-of-the-rock, and spectacled bears; and lowland rainforest, home of howler monkeys, scarlet macaws, black caiman, and giant otters, where the sound of insects is overpowering and 43 different species of ants may occupy a single rainforest tree.

There are 13 species of monkeys, 3000 identified species of plants, over 1000 species of birds – 10 percent of the world's total – 120 species of amphibians and 99 reptile species including two of the Amazon's most venomous snakes, the lancehead and the bushmaster, which are so well camouflaged that they blend in with the leaf litter on the forest floor. This is also the best place in the Amazon to see giant otters and congregations of macaws.

Dry season is from May to September and the wet from October to April. Different species of trees flower all through the year, with patches of the same colored flowers appearing throughout the canopy at any one time.

Located in southeastern Peru at the furthest tip of the Amazon River system, Manu is just 160 kilometers (100 miles) from Machu Picchu, and yet most of the reserve is so remote, two ethnic groups living in the forest still remain to be contacted.

◀

Red and green macaws and scarlet macaws at a clay lick along the exposed bank of the Manu River. Macaws gather in such numbers only at clay licks, arriving in the early morning. If enough birds arrive, they will eventually drop down to the mining face.

▼

Red howler monkey. It eats leaves and spends much of the day lounging around while digesting them. At dawn and dusk, males from different troops call loudly to each other, making a sound similar to a distant lion's roar.

nutrients than the flesh, so they eat the seeds and discard the covering.

A troop of about 20 bearded sakis, resembling arboreal poodles, wake up at 5 or 6 a.m. in their sleeping tree, maybe a silk-cotton tree. They defecate their pellets, call to each other, and move off into the forest in search of the 50 or so different species of trees in which they will find food. A favorite is the breadnut tree, which the monkeys visit when the fruits are small and the seeds soft. Sakis have strong, sharp canines for breaking into fruits and nuts; they also have cheek teeth for crushing seeds. With this dentition, they destroy all the seeds they eat. Along with red and green macaws, which also crunch up the hard, protected nuts and fruits, they can be considered 'seed predators'. By the time a seed has passed through their digestive system, it has no chance of germinating.

The bearded saki is a good climber, leaping in the trees from higher to lower crowns, but the title of champion leaper must go its close relative, the white-faced saki, known as the 'flying jack'. It occupies the lower parts of the canopy and the understory, and can leap horizontally between trees. Males and females are quite different. Females have a dull brown color and blend in well with the greens and browns of the forest, whereas males have bright white faces. It is thought that their conspicuous colors may help draw predators away from the females and young. Many a field researcher has been led on a wild goose chase, only to find that the male responsible has lured them away from the troop and then vanished in an instant.

Some monkeys forage in mixed groups. Gray-cap squirrel monkeys associate with brown capuchins, and different kinds of tamarins form mixed species troops. These alliances appear to improve the group's chances of spotting a predator before it attacks, as well as increasing its ability to locate sources of food. Some insect eating birds follow the troop, grabbing any insects the monkeys may flush out.

Emperor tamarins take nectar without damaging the flowers, and because their faces are inevitably covered with pollen, they become unwitting pollinators. Mixed species troops of moustached tamarins and saddle-backed tamarins, on the other hand, destroy flowers. In one study site, a troop was seen to destroy 44,000 flowers from 10 *Symphonia* trees within their home range in six weeks.

Tamarins and squirrel monkeys, however, are not totally vegetarian. They will take prey, such as invertebrates, when it is available, and some species actively hunt. Squirrel monkeys spend about half their waking lives searching for insects, and marmosets take advantage of the insects flushed out by army ants. White-faced sakis are also partial to insects, especially wasps, but they are uncharacteristically possessive about them. If a saki finds its more usual food, it gives a 'good food call' to let the rest of the troop know, but if it should chance upon a wasps' nest it keeps very quiet. It will eat all the nest, whether it is active or vacated, ignoring the stings of the irate occupants.

Howler monkeys make themselves known every morning. Their extraordinary growling dawn chorus echoes through the still forest, one of the most evocative and haunting sounds of South America. The sound is made when air passes through a cavity in

Strangler fig, Peru. It uses another forest tree for support to reach the canopy. Over a period of perhaps 200 years, it slowly strangles the host tree, and eventually only the strangler fig remains.

a large bone in the monkey's throat, known as the hyoid. Males have larger hyoids than females, ensuring that their calls carry for well over 0.5 mile (1 kilometer) across the canopy and through the trees.

Howlers live in large social groups. Each troop shares its home range with other troops, and the morning call is a way for each one to indicate its position in the forest. The calls of one troop are answered by the distant calls of another, but if two troops are in close proximity there is complete uproar and fights can break out. The morning chorus limits conflict and also makes weaker troops aware of where the stronger troops are located so that they can avoid contact.

Unlike other monkeys, howlers rarely leap, preferring to climb slowly and methodically through the canopy, using their tail as a fifth limb and safety anchor. The patch of skin on the underside of the tail tip has the same sensitivity as the palm of the hand.

Howlers will eat ripe fruits, but their main food is leaves. They are the least active of all monkeys, traveling very short distances and spending 80 percent of the day resting – a consequence of their diet, perhaps. Why animals have taken to eating leaves at all may seem a mystery to those who study them. After all, leaf eaters are presented with a food not only difficult to digest and low in nutrients, but also laced with all manner of poisons –

◀

Black spider monkey. It hangs in a tree using its tail as a fifth limb. A bare patch of skin on the underside of the tail tip helps it to grasp branches.

alkaloids, tannins, and other deadly substances. Tropical forest trees are particularly toxic. At first a tree might focus more on growth and less on defence, but when it matures it switches tactics: the older the tree the more noxious it becomes.

Some, like the rubber tree, produce a sap which dries into a thick latex that would gum up any insect mouth parts. Others produce substances that block protein absorption or interfere with the nervous system. They can even produce chemicals that suppress the ability of insects to molt when growing, causing them to be crushed inside their armorlike exoskeletons.

Nevertheless, many tropical forest animals rely on leaves for food, and confronted with such an arsenal of chemical defence substances, they must find ways and means of reducing their exposure or detoxifying the poisons. Fruit eaters have the same problem, particularly those, such as parrots and macaws, that beat the rush and eat fruits before they have ripened. Some animals simply change food plants regularly so that no single poison accumulates in their bodies for too long. Others are able to neutralize plant poisons by eating clay – a natural kaolin mixture that lines the gut and takes up as much as 60 percent of the toxins in the food – but to get to it they must leave the trees and take their lives in their hands when they move down to the ground. Macaws and other parrots follow a strict routine. The smaller birds, such as the blue-headed parrot and mealy parrot, arrive in the trees around the clay-licks at dawn. The larger macaws follow later, between 8 and 10 a.m., and socialize for an hour or two. If no more than 20 birds turn up, or it rains, the group will abort its visit and disperse. If there is a quorum, the birds begin to drop down towards the clay.

Animals are wary of leaving the safety of the trees because the clay-licks draw not only the clay eaters, but also their predators. Attracted by the commotion, predators make a bee-line for the licks. At Peruvian sites, such as those in the Manu National Park, pumas stalk monkeys and peccaries, while elsewhere in the Amazon, jaguars are the greatest threat.

Spider monkeys, therefore, are understandably nervous at clay-licks. Like the macaws, they gather in the surrounding trees for an hour or more before climbing down, and the slightest noise can send them scampering back into the canopy again. When their reluctance to be at ground level is overcome, first one then two monkeys will hang by their prehensile tails over the lick. A long arm will come down from the branch and gingerly grab a handful of mud. Soon, the entire troop festoons the branches, and great helpings of clay are pushed into open mouths, the monkeys choking and retching on each handful in their eagerness to swallow as much as they can in the shortest time. Some drop down into the mire so that first their legs and arms and then, as they throw caution to the wind, their entire bodies are smothered, giving them the appearance of mud wrestlers. A baby's head is coated as its mother bends over to grab a handful of clay. All the members of the troop scrape at the same place on the lick, as if they were mining a particularly productive seam of minerals.

When the monkeys are gone, peccaries, deer, and a whole host of birds take their turn. Not all are concerned with detoxifying their food – some are more interested in the dietary supplements found in the clay, especially essential minerals such as sodium. Many bats and tapirs visiting clay-licks are females, some pregnant. Might the clay be important for development of the young? Like the spider monkeys, the tapirs mine their clay at the same spot, often placing their heads into a single hatchlike opening to get at the best seams. Although they arrive alone, a steady stream may visit a lick each night.

The tapirs are often bothered by vampire bats, as well as a moth that sucks the lachrymal secretions from the corner of their eyes. The bats in turn are troubled by boa constrictors and dwarf caimans, which catch them as they come down to the lick.

Everything comes down from the canopy and back to the forest floor eventually. What nutrients go up through the trees and lianas must come down, whether it be in the form of rotting timber, discarded fruits and seeds, or dung, and animals play an important role in the recycling and distribution process. Just as fish in the flooded forest have become reliable agents of dispersal, so too have monkeys and other canopy residents in the *terra firme* forests. Woolly monkeys are especially helpful. They travel great distances through the trees, carrying undigested seeds in the gut and depositing them far from the parent tree.

The forest floor below can be a nutrient desert. As soon as food drops from above, something, somewhere, is ready to get at it. Ground living birds such as curassows feed on the fruit pulp and seeds raining down from above. Any that is overlooked is quickly recycled by the forest itself. Tree roots grow so rapidly that they are able to tap temporary sources of nutrients, such as those leaching out of decomposing fruit. They even grow out of the ground and actually over the fruit. Insects and other invertebrates, plant roots, fungal hyphae, and microrganisms are all waiting. The competition is fierce.

Within two minutes of a glob of woolly monkey scat hitting the forest floor, dung beetles fly in. Males fight vigorously for possession. Some meet females at the dung sites, others bury the dung quickly and lead the females to it. The females lay their eggs in the dung, providing their offspring with ready-made accommodation, complete with food. They also contribute to seed dispersal as undigested seeds grow from the buried dung balls.

The dung beetles react so quickly because they must beat flies to the prize. Fly maggots grow quicker and feed faster, and so would starve out the beetle grubs. One species of dung beetle has solved the problem with the help of a tiny friend: it carries a mite that parasitizes fly larvae.

One of the most impressive animals of the forest floor is the army ant. Some species are column invaders, others swarm raiders, but whatever their strategy, they kill and collect every living animal in their path. The secret of their success is the ability of up to a million individuals to work as one – a gigantic superorganism. The ants themselves are almost blind, relying on a chemical sense and imperceptible sounds and vibrations to find food and to communicate. Each member of the community has its role to play, whether it be foraging, defending the colony, carrying food or larvae, or attending the single egg laying

▶
Emerald tree boa. An adept climber, it searches for prey using vision and heat sensors. It lunges at its target, grabs it in its mouth, and then coils its body around the victim, killing by asphyxiation.

queen.

Food consists mostly of hard-bodied creatures, such as other insects, spiders and scorpions, and with so many mouths to feed, including a fully packed nursery, the colony is invariably on the move to find new supplies. The workers spill out and scour the forest for food. After an hour or two, the first food is brought back to the nest, and towards the end of the day a raiding front may be 650 feet (200 meters) away. Such is the speed with which they communicate that, if prey is encountered, a hundred or more ants can be summoned to subdue it within a minute. The workers catch and pull apart the prey, while others grab its legs and spreadeagle the victim until it is dismembered and dissected. Raiding caches of choice pieces are set up at points along the column, and workers arrive to carry them back to camp when the hunting is finished for the day.

Army ants, like most armies, have their followers. An advancing column of raiders is accompanied by an entire menagerie of animals, including birds and butterflies, each one intent on taking advantage of the panic and mayhem created by the advancing ants. Antbirds are the most obvious. They do not eat the ants themselves, but pounce upon the insects that are flushed out ahead of the ant columns. There is competition for the best feeding sites at the head of the column, and so a hierarchy of antbirds is established. Large species, such

as the ocellated antbird, take the prime positions just ahead of the ants, where most insects are attempting to flee. Smaller ones, such as the spotted antbird, spread out on either side or position themselves behind the army.

These antbirds cannot survive without army ants, and yet they are vulnerable to their stings. It is said that if they are stung more than three times, they will die, so if ants should run up their legs they 'snap' them violently to throw off the invaders. Whatever they do, they are careful not to squash the ants, for then an alarm pheromone is released, and the ants will seek out the attacker.

At dawn, and in the same spot each day for generations, another cortege forms. This con-

Army ants. This column has captured a katydid (grasshopper) and is dismembering it. The pieces are taken back along scent-marked trails to the ants' bivouac. In a relatively short time, the colony of a million or more ants will eat everything in its neighborhood and then will have to move on.

sists of mixed species flocks of insectivores and omnivores that make their way through the dense foliage. Each species has its own feeding station. There are some in the top of the canopy, some in the lower tree levels, some in the bushes, and still others on the ground. They occasionally forage with the army ants, but usually go about their own business higher in the forest canopy.

These mixed species flocks are often led by antshrikes that call the assembly together and lead it off to search for food. They also stand guard while the flock forages, and in return are provided with a constant supply of food flushed out by the searching, probing, gleaning birds. Occasionally, a flock leader will take unfair advantage of its position when a juicy morsel is about to be eaten by another bird. It emits a false alarm call to startle or distract the target bird long enough for the leader to nab the prey. The rest of the flock is rarely fooled and can usually tell a fake alarm call from the real thing, so the ruse probably only works on specific targets.

The ant procession does not end there. Following the antbirds are ant butterflies. These brightly colored creatures feed on nitrogen-rich antbird droppings, locating the ant columns by the odors given off by the ants themselves. The vivid patterns on their wings are warning colors. The butterflies protect themselves against the birds by being toxic to eat. Their caterpillars acquire poisons from their plant food, often *Solanum* – the plant family which includes deadly nightshade – on which they feed and grow.

Most animals flee when the army ants approach. Some adopt simple predator-avoidance strategies to see them safely through an attack. Standing still seems to work because army ants are programed to attack a moving target. Spiders will drop from a branch and dangle by a thread until the ants have passed. Only the ants at the front of a swarm or column tend to attack. If an animal should chance upon a column carrying its plunder back to the colony's headquarters, it is unlikely to be set upon, except for any defensive behavior on the part of soldiers guarding the column.

Not all animals become victims. In fact, some animals actually live unharmed among the ants. Many ants play host to mites, and there are species of silverfish and ant-mimicking beetles, wasps, and millipedes that live in the ants' bivouac or join the marching columns. They disguise themselves by secreting the colony odor.

The ants themselves, however, are not indestructible, for the army is also accompanied by swarms of tiny flies. Some follow the ants in order to deposit their eggs on escaping insects, but others are interested in the ants themselves. Tiny phorid flies are parasitic on army ants. Leafcutter ants overcome the fly menace by having a caste of mini-ants that provide cover. They ride shotgun on the leaves being carried by the larger ants, and if a fly should try to attack, the worker's mini-companion chases it away.

In the Amazon, ants are just a part of the rich mix of wildlife that inhabits the rainforest, but to the south of the basin is a plateau region where ants and termites play a leading role in everyday life. That plateau is the *cerrado* of Brazil.

plains
TO PATAGONIA

South of the Amazon Basin lies a series of high plateaux where you can see forever. The ground is carpeted in grasses and shrubs, and there are small, gnarled trees with thick, corky bark. This vast area of grassland and scrub is known as *cerrado* or savannah, and it covers South America's high plains, the Planalto Central—about 1650–2600 feet (500–800 meters) above sea level—and surrounding areas.

Ten Brazilian states share the 800,000 square miles (2 million square kilometers) of *cerrado*, an area the size of western Europe, and it is rich in wildlife. Some estimates suggest that 5 percent of the world's species of animals live here, and there are over 10,000 recognized species of plants, including 420 different grasses and shrubs. There are valuable medicinal plants and more than 100 species that are considered to have economic value, such as *caviúna-do-cerrado*, which produces fine wood.

▶

The Pantanal. During the wet season, this vast area of Brazil is a mosaic of water and vegetation. From the air, it appears there is no dry land anywhere.

◀

Mara, a harelike rodent that behaves like an antelope. It can gallop at speeds up to 30 miles (45 kilometers) an hour and, when danger threatens in the form of a fox, it will even stot (leap into the air, to show that it knows it has been seen).

Rivers and streams are lined by narrow corridors of gallery forest with many species of trees, including *copaiba,* whose oil heals wounds, and the instantly recognizable buriti palms with their crowns of broad palm leaves. Stands of tall, dry forest tower over patches of swampy ground that flood in the wet but revert to grass in the dry season. In the more humid areas, low scrub trees, 6–10 feet (2–3 meters) tall, are festooned with lichen and epiphytic ferns. Clinging to trunks and branches are the unmistakable red clay nests of arboreal termites, and flying between trees are the brightly colored vermilion flycatcher or *verão*, and a woodcreeper or *arapaçu*, recognized by its red-brown plumage and long downwardly curved bill. A flash of red and black betrays the presence of the local helmeted manakin, which would seem more at home in the dense forests of the Amazon Basin.

In fact, animals in the *cerrado*'s woodland areas are a mixture of those from the Amazon and others from the Atlantic rainforests, particularly species with an affinity for water, such as tapirs, water possums, and muskrats. With no ground living monkeys present, like the baboons and vervet monkeys of East Africa, black howler monkeys have taken over the niche and, although they spend most of their time in the trees, they are seen foraging on the ground as they travel across the floor of the *cerrado* between the trees of the gallery forests.

Today, about half of the original *cerrado* remains. During the past 20–30 years great tracts have been cleared for cattle and then ploughed up on a huge scale for arable agriculture, particularly soy, corn, and sunflowers. Although the soils are poor, vast quantities of lime and fertilizers have made them productive, and when you drive on the endless straight roads you travel for hours through flat agricultural land like that of Kansas, with nothing to break up the unvarying view of endless monoculture.

The *cerrado* is the second largest habitat in Brazil and represents just over a tenth of the world's savannah, but it is far more endangered than the rainforest. It has been estimated that 40–50 percent has disappeared during the past 30 years, compared to 15 percent of the rainforest. The problem is that the *cerrado* appears flat and featureless, at least superficially. The science here is less glamorous than in the mysterious rainforest. Only a handful of dedicated scientists are taking a serious interest in its ecology. Conservation projects are beginning to appear, but only 2 percent of the remaining *cerrado* is protected as either a national park or a reserve. It is in these remnant areas that you can get a glimpse of what the *cerrado* was like decades ago, oases for wildlife and wildlife watchers alike.

Reached by paved highways out of São Paulo and Belo Horizonte is the Serra da Canastra National Park, where the Casca d'Anta waterfalls mark the sources of two of South America's great rivers, the Araguari and São Franciso. Here, the water plunges 650 feet (200 meters) down the Canastra escarpment. About 150 miles (250 kilometers) north of Brasília is the Parque Nacional da Chapada dos Veadeiros, which has spectacularly eroded rocky plateaux of buttes and mesas covered with scrub, great valleys of green grass, and swampy areas of palms. One of the most visited sites, located just outside the park, is Moon Valley, where the landscape resembles the surface of the moon. There is the Chapada dos

Guimarães, near Cuiabá, with its dramatic escarpments, caves and waterfalls, such as the 282-feet-high (86 meters) Véu da Noiva Falls. But the wildlife jewel in the *cerrado*'s crown is undoubtedly Emas National Park.

Emas is in the middle of Brazil, to the west of Rio de Janeiro. Here, the entire ecosystem is driven by fire and water, the patterns of grass, scrub, and trees determined by when the previous bush fire passed through and when it last rained. The seasons are marked, half a year each of wet and dry, but, fires aside, there is little change in the landscape from one half of the year to the other—the grass is simply green in the wet season and brown in the dry. In the wet season, from October to March, mornings are clear, but in the afternoon clouds build up; the atmosphere is hot and humid, and it rains almost daily. From April to September, the dry season brings blue skies with handfuls of white fluffy clouds. It is hot during the day, but the nights are cold, clear, and sharp.

Emas is one of the best places in South America to see the rare maned wolf, a solitary animal that you will probably smell before you see, for maned wolves must be among the smelliest animals alive. If one crosses your path when the air is still, you will still be able to detect it hours later.

The maned wolf is neither wolf nor fox, but is allocated a genus all its own, *Chrysocyon*. It has a red-brown coat and blackish mane, but is instantly recognizable by its unusually long legs—it resembles a fox on stilts. Unlike other dogs and foxes that have opted to push their way *through* long grass, this creature chooses to go *over* it. It does not run fast like other long-legged plains animals. Instead, it paces; that is, it moves both feet on one side forward at the same time and does not change its loping gait as it increases its speed.

By day, it curls up in the shade of a termite mound or tree, for it is active mainly at night. Its scent marks everything in its territory, urinating on many of the termite mounds it passes and rolling in every grassy tussock. It might travel alone for many miles each night, scent marking, foraging, and hunting.

During the dry season, the maned wolf mainly hunts small mouselike rodents, using its own special hunting technique. It walks and listens. It has a pair of large, mobile ears like radar dishes, and when it hears a rustle in the grass it stops, stands, and points them directly

▶
Maned wolf, named after the patch of black, erectile hairs on its shoulders. It stands about 34 inches (87 centimeters) at the shoulder and moves with a characteristic loping gait, even when chasing prey.

EMAS

Emas, the wildlife jewel in the *cerrado*'s crown, is 20 hours' drive west of Rio de Janeiro, and 5 hours' drive from the nearest town, Campo Grande, on the eastern edge of the Pantanal. The area is completely flat and criss-crossed by a network of dirt roads and fire breaks along which you travel in four-wheel drive vehicles.

It is pot luck whether you find it easy to view wildlife at Emas. If there have been no fires, the grass is 10 feet (3 meters) high on either side of the flat, straight road and you see the park's wildlife, maybe a tapir, giant anteater or rhea, for little more than 10 seconds when it crosses the road. So a good time to visit is at the end of the dry season, when fires are more likely to have burned down areas of grass, as they did across the entire park in 1999. After that conflagration, you could see for ever.

Then there is a lot to see, including giant anteaters, tamanduas, peccaries, capybara, armadillos, maned wolves (which you can also hear howling at night), as well as a multitude of birds including rheas, macaws, toucans and numerous birds of prey perching on the many termite mounds. If you are there at the beginning of the rainy season (September–October), go on a night safari, since at this time the termite larvae glow, resulting in an incredible bioluminescence show.

Parts of the park are open to visitors and others are not. Visitors are forbidden to cross the main river that runs through the middle of Emas, so you must enter and leave the park on the same side of the river. There are no official tour operators, but local guides in the towns of Chapadão-do-céu in Goiás state in the south and Mineiros in the north have been trained to escort tourists. The roads to the towns are good, but those in or approaching the park are dirt roads—dusty in the dry season, and quagmires in the wet—so four-wheel drive vehicles are essential.

There are very few people, not too many mosquitoes because of the elevation, but lots of flying termites and ants at the beginning of the rains.

◄

Luminous termite mound. At night during October and November, the mounds light up like office blocks, with pinpoints of light produced by luminous beetle larvae, whose glowing abdomens lure flying termites to their death.

at the ground. It then leaps, trying to pin down its target with its paws. It sometimes misses the first time, so it starts to stamp its feet on the ground, attempting to drive the mouse into the open where it pounces again . . . and again, until it drops down onto all fours, placing its front paws on either side of the prey. It will continue this performance until it catches a meal or the prey escapes.

In some parts, where disturbance from people is less, the maned wolf can be seen out and about during the day. You can spot it from a distance because it is sometimes followed by an aplomado falcon, which perches nearby and then swoops down to snatch insects such as grasshoppers that the wolf has disturbed. The same bird does not follow it everywhere, for the wolf travels through the territories of several birds. Each resident shadows the wolf diligently to the edge of its patch, and then its neighbor takes over.

Another alliance you might spot in Emas is that of the great rhea and the very rare pampas deer. The rhea is a flightless, ground living bird related to the ostrich and emu, and it shares with them a usefully long neck. The pampas deer is relatively small compared to, say, a red deer, but it has a first-class sense of smell. By sticking together, the rhea and the deer complement each other's senses. The rhea can raise its head above the long grass and spot danger—such as a jaguar or puma—approaching, while the deer can smell it.

If a maned wolf should chance upon a rhea, it avoids it, but it might well try to snack on any eggs. While the eggs are hard to crack, the wolf might get lucky and break one, spicing up its end-of-season diet of beetles. The adult rhea, however, is not on the maned wolf's menu: it's too big.

By the end of the dry season, when there has been no rain for five or six months, every living thing seems to be struggling to survive. The grasses turn brown, but some of the local plants are faking it. The impression that they are under stress is superficial, for 6 feet (2 meters) down there is water, and most plants tap into this reservoir and continue to transpire even in the dry season. They are not short of water and, as a consequence, bloom in September, *before* the rains arrive.

At this time, the atmosphere is electric. The first big thunderstorms do not bring rain, but the lightning brings fire. It touches down in the dry grass and triggers bush fires. The sky fills with smoke, and on some days the sun almost fails to appear. It is like living in a twilight zone, but with spectacular sunsets. The fires are low-intensity, quick to burn, and move rapidly across the plains. They burn the grasses but do no more than singe the trees. Some of the grasses actually stoke the fires. They are loaded with highly flammable oils that burn easily, and because they are the first grasses to recolonize scorched areas, it is to their advantage to fuel frequent fires. The entire area can burn unchecked for many days—these fires stop only when they reach a river or when it rains.

Any living thing that can hide in a hole is safe from the flames. Trees, too, often survive. The flames may scorch the thick, corky bark at the base of the trunk, but the crown is usually left unscathed. Underground, roots and rhizomes are untouched. Animals on the surface must make a run for it or be caught by the hawks, caracaras and seriemas that hunt along the fire line for the insects and rodents flushed out by the flames. For many plants, the passing fire is a time for rejuvenation, and some depend on it to release their seeds.

After the fire comes water. Following the first sprinkling of rain, many birds lay and incubate their eggs so that chicks hatch out when conditions improve. The rain regenerates the grasslands, and the fire blackened ground is quickly transformed into a green carpet of grass. Flowers are everywhere. Insects emerge, and the larger animals start to breed.

The Emas grasslands, however, are not dominated by large herbivores. Aside from a few pampas deer and tapirs, the antelope of the Serengeti and the buffalo of the American prairies are replaced here by ants and termites. They are the main grazers, and it is these tiny creatures, working together as superorganisms, that drive the entire ecosystem.

Termites and ants are not related: termites are actually colonial cockroaches while ants are more closely connected to wasps and bees. At Emas, there are 90 known species of termites, and as far as the eye can see, there are termite mounds. The mud walls of these mounds are as hard as concrete, and inside there are interconnecting passageways and galleries with walls of softer chewed wood. Occupying a central 'royal chamber' is the enormous, sausage shaped queen and her consort. Her rippling abdomen can be 6 inches (15 centimeters) long and 1.5 inches (4 centimeters) wide, and she is an egg-laying factory, producing 33,000 eggs a day—one every couple of seconds. Because of the queen's size, the royal couple are incarcerated in their chamber for their entire lives. A ring of soldier termites guards the queen, and workers busy about her, bringing her food, taking away eggs, and stroking and cleaning her abdomen.

The eggs are placed in small nursery chambers surrounding the royal apartments, where they are looked after by workers. Nearby are larger galleries with convoluted walls and ceilings where leaves and other vegetation are stored. Radiating from the mound are tunnels through which the workers head out to forage for leaves. With several million bodies, all busy, bustling and breathing, oxygen

Bush fire on the *cerrado*. Fire dominates the savannah, and some plants depend on it to survive. The fires are quick-burn, however, and the inferno is fuelled by plants that are packed with inflammable oils. The fires pass so quickly that the tops of some trees are left unscathed.

consumption and the production of carbon dioxide and heat are high, so the high-rise structure has automatic air-conditioning. The hot air rises into the upper parts of the mound and is channeled towards the outer buttresses, where stale air and fresh air from the outside are exchanged through the porous walls. The air cools and drops back to the cellar at the base of the nest. Here, it replaces the warm air that is rising, completing the circulation.

The mounds take quite a battering during the wet season. For an hour or two every afternoon, massive black clouds gather and the sky goes dark. Then the storm front passes through. Accompanied by startling displays of thunder and lightning, massive quantities of rain fall on the plains in extraordinary monsoonlike downpours. They can be seen approaching from several miles away. When the deluge arrives, the wind and rain thrash anything standing or exposed.

It is at this time of the year, on a particularly hot, muggy evening in October or November, after a heavy downpour, that the termite nests take center stage in an amazing natural performance. The colonies produce winged termites capable of reproduction, and they all emerge at the same time on the same night. They have well-developed eyes, but the males locate females by smell—that is, if they get that far, for as they emerge there is a tiny creature ready to intercept them.

The activity starts in late afternoon, when winged termites are seen crowding round the tops of the mounds. As darkness falls, however, you gradually become aware that the termite mounds are covered in myriad luminous specks, like the lights of a high-rise office block. Closer examination reveals that the tiny pinpoints of light are produced by the larvae of a beetle (*Pyrearinus termitilluminans*) with a luminous tip to its abdomen. Each termite mound has hundreds of larvae living in its outer skin.

The grub excavates its own narrow, 4-inch-long (10-centimeter) tunnel, and this leads to a larger inner chamber. It sits with its head in the tunnel, its legs anchored to the sides and its glowing abdomen protruding from the tunnel entrance. At the tip of the luminous abdomen is a pair of pincerlike claspers, ready to seize anything that comes along. Winged termites are attracted to the light, but they are grabbed the moment they land and dragged quickly into the inner chamber. The beetle larva catches, caches, and reappears to capture again in less than 30 seconds, for it must be ready to store as many termites in as short a time as possible in order to have sufficient food to complete its development during the rest of the year.

Beetle larvae are not the only tenants. With a scarcity of trees on these grasslands, the termite mound is the highest structure around, so parrots, parakeets, flickers, kestrels, and other birds that normally nest in tree hollows have taken to nesting in the top. Large *teju* or caiman lizards, armadillos, and burrowing owls dig underneath. Ants may take over parts of the nest that have been damaged, sealed off, and then abandoned by the termites.

On the nights the termites swarm, the ants swarm too. The winged ants head for the highest point in the area, a termite mound, tree, or bush, where they congregate for mating. Down below, worker ants gather at the entrances of their colonies and grab anything that lands near them. There is considerable congestion at the nest entrances as workers catch flying termites, snip off their wings and drag them struggling into the ants' nest. Thus, a termite might emerge from one part of the nest ready for procreation and end up being hauled back into another part as prey.

Any trees in the area might be hiding another species, the ambush ant. As its name suggests, it catches its prey by setting a trap for other insects. About 100–200 ants hide on the undersurface of a leaf and use their antennae to detect the slightest vibration from the top side. If a flying termite lands there, they all swarm out onto the top of the leaf, catch the prey, drag it back below where they dismember it, and then carry the parts back to the nest.

The most conspicuous ant in these parts, however, is the leafcutter. As soon as the first sprinkling of rain has triggered new growth, it is out on the plains cutting up the fresh, green blades of grass and transporting them back to the nest. If there is a flowering tree nearby, the ants ransack its branches. Along the ground, a file of ants, guarded at intervals by big-jawed soldiers, trails between the tree and the nest. By midnight the single file turns into several broad columns, each one 10 or more ants abreast. In the tree, they snip away tiny pieces of leaves and petals and either drop them down to be picked up by more ants below or carry them back to the nest themselves.

◀

Giant anteater. It protects its claws by walking on its knuckles, which gives it an ungainly, limping gait. Its long, narrow tongue has tiny backward-pointing spines covered with sticky saliva that helps it lick up termites and ants.

The colony, marked by an immense pile of loose soil on the surface, comprises a thousand or more underground chambers, some the size of footballs, others no bigger than a fist. In about 400 of them there are subterranean gardens, for these ants are agriculturists—they grow fungi resembling bread mold for food.

The amount of vegetation collected in a day is about the same as that consumed by a cow. It is brought down to the garden chambers where fungus cultivation follows a precise sequence of events, each step attended by a different worker caste. First, the foragers dump their loads onto the floor of the chamber, and slightly smaller ants snip the leaves up into pieces just $\frac{1}{25}$ inch (1 millimeter) across. Even smaller workers chew and knead the tiny snippets into moist pellets which they place on the garden. Finally, the very smallest caste scurries about, moving material and making best use of the space available.

Resembling a gray sponge, the fluffy frass garden of leaves, excrement, and other refuse produced by the insects and their larvae is riddled with channels and holes, providing ample surfaces over which the fungal hyphae can grow. The fungus digests the cellulose and proteins, making them available to the ants, which then harvest it. The garden is kept tidy by the tiny ants that are able to run through the narrow channels. They 'weed' the garden, plucking out spores and strands of alien fungi. They also pull out the chunks of the cultivated fungus, which, together with leaf sap, is the colony's food.

The efficient working of the colony and the ratio of different types of workers is regulated by chemicals, and should the balance of castes and the stability of the colony be threatened, one caste may be removed in favor of another. The large soldiers, for example, are expensive to make and maintain. When times are tough and food is scarce, they are the first to go. Some of the workers grab them by the legs and pin them down, while others cut them up and cart them back to the nest. The soldiers, which are far bigger than the workers taking them apart, could easily fight their captors, but they do not. They and their executioners are programed to work only for the good of the colony.

With such a large number of ant and termite colonies on the plains, it is not surprising to find one or two larger animals that exploit them as food. The biggest of these predators is the giant anteater, and those individuals living on the *cerrado* have a preference for termites rather than ants.

An anteater's day follows a well rehearsed routine. It spends the morning hidden underneath its tail, which it spreads like a giant hairy parasol over its entire body. It then becomes active about 1 or 2 p.m., with a peak at 6 p.m., and retires by 2 a.m.

About 20–30 percent of termite mounds on the *cerrado* are uninhabited, but with so many from which to choose, the anteater has more than enough food for it to "graze" at one mound for just a few minutes and then quickly move on to the next. It rarely stays long at one nest. Is it an efficient resource manager, taking just a few termites from each nest, or does it remain only as long as it can stand the chemical defence weapons of the termite soldiers? Nobody is sure, but whatever the reason it is often seen using the side of its claws to brush the termites off its long nose before moving on.

A more compact version is the collared anteater or southern tamandua. It is semi-arboreal in the scrubby, forest areas of the *cerrado* and eats mainly the ants and termites that build their nests in trees. It uses its keen sense of smell to detect its prey and then breaks into nests or deadwood, penetrating cracks and crevices with its long sticky tongue and licking out the ants and termites. Like the giant anteater, it also climbs down to the ground and digs into the larger termite mounds, but it avoids some of the more aggressive ants and termites, such as army ants and leafcutter ants.

Another termite eater is the giant armadillo. Unlike the giant anteater, it has teeth, albeit a set of primitive peglike molars. With a 3-foot-long (1-meter) body and 20-inch (50-centimeter) tail, it is the largest member of the armadillo family. Supported by its tail and hind legs, it sits upright and attacks the termite mound with its sturdy front claws, inflicting considerable damage. It then licks up its prey at leisure with its sticky tongue. The holes it leaves behind are very obvious, but the chances of spotting the perpetrator are remote—for, like most of its kind, the giant armadillo is active mainly at night.

Between cloudbursts, the termites emerge to repair damage to their mounds, not only from anteaters and armadillos but also from the heavy rain. The mounds get buffeted in the wind, and mud is washed away. The respite enables others to get about too.

Common long-nosed or nine-banded armadillo in the wet season. This is a widely distributed species, found from Texas to Argentina. Pantanal animals, however, must adapt to extreme changes in water level, and the armadillo is fortunately a good swimmer.

Blue and yellow macaws sit out downpours in stands of buriti palms. When the rain stops, the birds fly out in loose groups, parents and offspring foraging together. They can travel considerable distances in a day, searching for food. They even come down to the ground to drink at pools, where, it is said, they are sometimes caught by maned wolves.

By the time the wet season is well underway, the maned wolf switches its diet from meat to fruit. It eats the *fruta do lobo* or wolf's fruit from a tree called *lobeira* with which it has a special relationship. At this time of the year, wolf's fruit can form 90 percent of the maned wolf's diet and is highly prized, partly because of its medicinal properties. It reduces infestations of the giant kidney worm, which is common in maned wolves. In return, the maned wolf appears to help the tree by distributing its seeds.

The maned wolf marks its territory not only with urine, but also with dung, which it deposits on raised areas, such as the spoil heaps of leafcutter ants. The wolf fruit's seeds pass through the maned wolf's gut unharmed and are expelled with the dung. The leafcutters pick through the dung and take the seeds into their nests, where some germinate. The result, after a few years, is a small patch of trees among the ant nests, and some of them will be wolf fruit trees. The maned wolf comes each year to eat the fruit in its territory, and so the cycle continues.

During the rains, the *cerrado* drains quickly. Although some rivers flow directly into the Atlantic or north into the Amazon, many drain towards the west. In the wet season, a huge surge of water tumbles down spectacular waterfalls along the western escarpment and into a vast basin filled with wildlife, known as the Pantanal. The Pantanal is an extensive mosaic of savannah, forest, swamps and lagoons situated in the upper Paraguay River basin. Run-off from the *cerrado* feeds its great rivers, such as the São Lourenço, Cuiabá, and the Aquidauana. Their waters flow westward across the Pantanal until they hit the Serra do Amolar range of mountains and are diverted south in the great Rio Paraguay.

Most rivers in this area are muddy, but at places such as Touro Morto and Bonito, spring-fed waters are crystal clear. Touro Morto has dark ground and a green background, while Bonito has white sand and bluish water. As if in a fish tank, there are schools of red-bellied piranha and one or two of its fruit-and-nut-eating relatives, the *pacú,* which have flat, crushing teeth rather than the razor-sharp dentition of their infamous relatives.

Although the annual rainfall is less here than on the higher *cerrado*, during the wet season the Paraguay River and its tributaries burst their banks, turning the Pantanal into a gigantic wetland the size of England. As it fills with water, fish move out of the main river channels and into the flooding countryside. The local subspecies of caiman, the *jacaré,* takes full advantage of the spill. Where water gushes from breaches in riverbanks, the caiman form a line, their jaws partly open, and let the rushing water flow through their open mouths. If a fish swims in, they snap their jaws shut and swallow it. Any fish that escapes the living barrier heads into the flooded swamp to traditional breeding sites to spawn.

It is hot and humid here throughout the year, but not all parts of the Pantanal are equally affected by the seasons. While the eastern areas become parched during the dry

▶

Freshwater lagoon,
Pantanal. In the dry
season, the lagoons
become a focus for
wildlife, including
caiman, wading
birds, coatis and
anacondas.

PANTANAL

The Pantanal is basically a huge swamp. Access is either by river, via the port of Caceres on the Paraguay River, or by a single road, the Transpantaneira, a long red wound that winds in from the north for 60 miles (100 kilometers). The route includes 114 trestle bridges, all in a bad state of repair. You take planks from behind your vehicle and place them in front in order to proceed. The distance is relatively short but the journey might still take two days. Whatever the hardships, though, the drive is well worth it.

During the wet season, the wildlife is spread widely across the region, but in the dry season the pools along the road are a magnet. Zillions of birds, including jabiru storks, egrets, whistling herons, snail kites

and more make this a birdwatcher's paradise. There are also capybara, peccaries and caiman either in or visiting the pools, and if you are really lucky you might spot a jaguar and some of the smaller cats.

▲

Hyacinth macaws. They will gang up on intruders, such as hawks, that invade the *bocaiuva* trees in which they feed, making growling sounds and screaming until the unwelcome visitors leave.

Accommodation is mainly at working cattle ranches, called *fazendas*, which are well organized for eco-tourists. They have trucks, boats and horses to take visitors on wildlife-watching excursions and teams of guides. Some even have their own wildlife reserves. At the Fazenda Caiman, for example, the owner Roberto Klabin has created a nest-box program for the rare hyacinth macaws, and about 40 pairs are breeding there. At the Fazenda Barranco Alta there is a giant river otter protection program, and it is the best place in the Pantanal to spot a jaguar.

Like other parts of the natural world, however, this haven for wildlife is under threat, in this case from grand waterway and hydroelectric schemes, gold mining and uncontrolled tourism. The great abundance of fish attracts sports fishermen from all over the world, and already permit controls and closed seasons have had to be introduced to conserve stocks. Poachers sell rare jaguar furs and caiman skins to an illegal international trade in animal skins that reached its peak in the 1980s. In the Mato Grosso Pantanal National Park, which covers about 340,000 acres (135,000 hectares), poaching has been reduced somewhat by park rangers, but it is still rife.

There are also the ranchers and their cattle, but they have been here for more than two centuries—cattle and wildlife living successfully cheek by jowl. With their ranches inundated by water each year, they never overgraze the land. This simple natural phenomenon has enabled people and wildlife to live in harmony.

The main flood is from December to May, but as the water recedes the land can support only a four-wheel drive vehicle until July. From then until December you can drive over the Pantanal, although the rains come again in October.

season, the western strip is flooded for most of the year. Some areas receive more water than others and are more like rainforests, while really wet areas form permanent swamps.

The landscape is a patchwork of different types of vegetation, each scrap of land often dominated by a single species. Grasses grow in the places first to drain, while cat-tails are common in the marsh. Distinct palm tree woodlands form near rivers and on patches of water-logged ground. Other well watered areas are dominated by the gold tree or *paratudo*, or the balsam-of-Peru, which produces valuable wood and an aromatic resin. The strangely shaped strangler fig or *figuera mata-pau* can be seen to smother the relatively common *bacaiúva* palm, using its victim's tall, scaly trunk to support its own stem.

The floral symbol of the Pantanal is the 50-foot-high (15-meter) *piúva* tree, a hardwood with beautiful pink flowers called *ipê-roxo*. It bursts into flower for about three months in the dry season from June to August. The *cambará* flowers from July to September and contributes to the pageant with great swathes of yellow flowers. From August to September the *paratudo* bears yellow flowers and the *algodão-do-pantanal* has trumpet shaped ones. The *urumbeva* is a tree dwelling cactus with large white flowers.

There are lagoons (*baías*) with floating meadows, or *camalotes,* of water hyacinths and giant waterlilies. Fish spawn beneath them, fry hide in the tangle of roots and they

►
Pantanal or jacaré caiman. Its eyes sit high on its head and, at night, can be picked out with a spotlight, glowing orange-yellow. Each nocturnal animal has a different eye shine—the eyes of a marsh deer glow green-blue and those of a jaguar red-orange.

become a magnet for wildlife when the water is low. Here, you might catch a glimpse of a sunbittern, a refugee from the Amazon, and you can see wattled jacanas searching for insects, their yellow plumage more than evident when they hold out their wings momentarily. Troops of inquisitive coatis come to forage for anything edible—water snails, fish, snakes, and frogs—while overhead, snail kites are wet season visitors. They swoop down to feed on the molluscs and other aquatic invertebrates. In the dry season, they are replaced by savannah kites, which hijack rodents escaping from bush fires.

In the east, the height of the dry season sees vast areas of parched, cracked mud with nothing growing. As the soil is very permeable, even the large rivers have low water. Fence posts are topped with the abandoned clay-oven nests of the ovenbird. Scattered around the region, a handful of salt lakes dry out to form small saltpans or *barreiros*, where animals come to lick salt. Trees are close to death and wildlife is concentrated in freshwater pools beside the only road, the Transpantaneira Highway, which advances 60 miles (100 kilometers) into the Pantanal.

The road is built on an embankment above the swamp, so when the water is high it is like driving across a lake. At the height of the dry season, however, there is merely a series of pools on either side of the road. These form in the hollows where the soil was

▶
Coati, a relative of the racoon. The females and young live in groups. Males are solitary, though before this was realized, a lone male coati was once known as a coatimundi, meaning "lone coati," and thought to be a separate species.

◀
Jabiru storks, egrets, caiman and domestic horses sharing a waterhole in the Pantanal's dry season. Fish become concentrated in the pools, providing the fish-eating birds and caiman with a feeding bonanza.

▶

Two species of
trees burst into
flower, each with
its own distinctive
color. Trees of the
same species
throughout the
Pantanal tend to
blossom
synchronously, as
they do in other
parts of tropical
South America.
This helps ensure
successful
pollination.

scraped out to build the embankments. The resident wildlife has been quick to find the amenity, for as the water recedes many fish, such as eels and *traíra*, a 12-inch-long (30-centimeter) fish with large overlapping scales and brushlike tail, are trapped and wallow in the liquid mud. These creatures can tolerate the low oxygen levels and high temperatures in the pool, and they provide a glut of food for caiman and waterbirds alike.

The scene is a must for birdwatchers. Thousands of great egrets, snowy egrets, great blue herons, white-necked herons, wood storks, and jabirú storks or *tuiuiu* crowd around the pools. As many as a thousand or more jabirús might be seen fishing together. They strut about, jabbing their open bills into the water and snapping up distressed catfish.

The caiman with which they share their shrinking pools can be as much as 6–10 feet (2–3 meters) long. At night, they and their offspring may have traveled considerable distances overland, from pools that have dried up completely to places where open water still remains. A female caiman may have a brood of squawking youngsters following closely in her footsteps. She will have nested on land still exposed at the end of the wet season, sometime between December and May, building a mound of vegetation and depositing 20–40 round, white eggs inside. She will have had to guard it fiercely, for coatis, crab-eating foxes, and *teju* lizards are skillful nest robbers. Despite the diligence of their mother, fire

ants will have found their way into cracked shells and killed the embryos inside before they had a chance to hatch. After 60–90 days the surviving hatchlings are released by their mother and taken to the water, where they are vulnerable to predatory great black hawks. At the remaining waterholes in the dry season, they are plagued by horseflies which bite them on the softer skin around the eyes and nostrils.

The constant sound you hear, however, is not from flies or even birds. Aside from the isolated calls of macaws, the rattle of the piping guan, the startling yodel of the southern screamer, the occasional grunt of a caiman, or rumble of a rhea by day and the interminable frog chorus and distant rasping of a jaguar at night, the Pantanal is dominated by the lowing of cattle.

This is cattle country. Some 99 percent of the Pantanal is privately owned, much

Anaconda mating ball. At breeding time, a female anaconda produces a scent that attracts males, who wrap themselves in a coiling ball in their attempt to mate with her.

given over to huge *fazendas* or ranches. Each ranch covers hundreds of square miles and during the dry season the white, humped zebu cattle graze the withered grasses until nothing is left; then they are moved on, much like the wildebeest migration in East Africa. The cattle were brought here from India in the 1920s because they are able to survive local diseases, live in the intense heat, and then readjust to the wet season floods.

The zebu share the shrinking waterholes with peccaries, feral pigs, and groups of the largest rodent in the world, the capybara. These enormous animals, about 3 feet (1 meter) long, resemble giant guinea pigs and fill a similar ecological niche to that of the hippopotamus in Africa, feeding on land but using water as a refuge. Their ancestors were even bigger—one extinct capybara was the size of a North American grizzly bear!

Its living descendants are almost always found near water, and during the dry season they wallow in the mud to keep cool and avoid the flies. Their slightly webbed feet, together with the fact that their eyes, nose, and ears are positioned near the top of their head, enable them to be adequate swimmers; they can remain below the surface for five minutes or more. The males also have a large and very obvious scent gland on top of the snout which produces a sticky white secretion. Both sexes have glands near the anus, and each capybara produces its own distinctive odor, so individuals can recognize each other by smell.

Capybaras are grazers. They feed on grasses growing near water, and can make full use of the short, dry grass remaining at the end of the dry season. They are active day and night, bathing in the hot afternoons and eating in the early evening. They continue through the night, alternating feeding with short bouts of sleep. In the morning, they tend to rest.

By the end of the dry season, temporary groups of 100 or more capybaras may be seen congregating around any pools that are left. But as the rains begin to fall and the Pantanal starts to fill up, they split into smaller bands of about 10 individuals on average, though sometimes as many as 30 or 40. Each band is led by a dominant male, and includes females with youngsters and a sprinkling of young males. Males from other bands often try to infiltrate the group but are chased away by the resident males.

If danger should threaten a group, the first animal to spot it emits a barking alarm call, and the others immediately stop what they were doing and stand alert, as if waiting for instructions. Further barks send them rushing into the water, where the adults form a protective phalanx around the young.

Natural dangers for capybaras in the Pantanal include jaguars, caiman, and foxes, and young capybaras can be prey for vultures and feral dogs. During the transition between dry and wet seasons, when animals are on the move between vegetation and water, another threat comes from the largest snake in the region, the anaconda. Growing to 33 feet (10 meters) in length and weighing 440 pounds (200 kilograms) – even more if the early explorers are to be believed—these are formidable predators.

The Pantanal is a paradise for wildlife enthusiasts. It is, after all, the largest continental wetland on Earth, the Brazilian part alone covering 55,000 square miles (140,000 square kilometers) of the states of Mato Grosso and Mato Grosso do Sul, as well as extending into Bolivia and Paraguay. During the annual floods, the waters bring a fresh covering of silt, clay, and organic material to the land. The diversity and numbers of the wildlife it supports are staggering—650 species of birds, 80 mammals, 260 fish, and 50 reptiles, and these are only the ones known to science. There are estimated to be 10 million caiman here, the largest concentration of crocodilians in the world.

The place is also a stopover for birds on migration, and about 75 percent of the species found in the Panatanal spend only part of their year here. The three major flyways that pass through the Pantanal bring ospreys and yellowlegs from North America, wood storks and southern lapwings from Argentina, and even flycatchers from the eastern slopes of the Andes.

One of the resident birds is a species endemic to the Pantanal. The hyacinth macaw, the largest parrot in the world, is thought to number fewer than 3000 birds in the wild, and its very rarity makes it valuable merchandise in the international pet trade. The macaw's natural nesting and roosting sites are in palm trees. Parent birds remain together for life and share responsibilities for bringing up their chicks. Two eggs are laid but usually only one chick makes it to its first birthday. The larger sibling grabs all the food and the smaller bird dies of

◀

Capybara with young. Youngsters constantly emit a guttural purr, thought to be a contact call between mother and offspring. If an adult should give a loud "cough," the group scampers for the safety of the water.

dehydration and starvation. Toucans and coatis sometimes steal and eat unattended eggs.

On foraging excursions, macaws might travel up to 15 miles (25 kilometers) in a day and are often seen hanging from the fruit clusters of Pantanal palms. They also follow cattle, picking out palm nuts from cow-pats because the nuts are softened as they pass through the cows' guts. In the wet season, macaws and cattle can find themselves running out of space. As the Pantanal fills up, the *pantaneiros* or Pantanal cowboys round up their cattle and drive them towards higher ground. They head for large areas of dense jungle that rarely flood, known as *cordilheiras*, and small islands of green, called *capões,* meaning 'little forest in the open land'.

It is the time for nesting. The basketlike nests of black, crow-sized oropendolas hang like garlands below branches. The birds weave grasses, pliable twigs and leaf fibers into a 6-foot (2-meter-long) tight mesh tube with a bulbous end. Nearby, the large basketlike colonial nests of monk parakeets are home not to one but to maybe 10 separate families.

Top predator in the *cordilheiras* is the jaguar. Before poachers killed these magnificent cats for their spotted skins, they kept peccaries and capybaras in check. Now, they are rarely seen, although the carcass of a dead cow might lure one into the open in daylight. Though not usually known for scavenging, the jaguar will, like any self-respecting big cat, seize the opportunity if it should arise, and just such an occasion came to light when the BBC film crew were in the Pantanal.

The carcass of a zebu cow lay in a swampy hollow, attracting the attention of a gaggle of about 100 black vultures. Little did the crew know that lurking in the bushes were a female jaguar and her cubs, until suddenly the mother burst from cover and chased the vultures away. Showing her considerable strength, she then hauled the carcass out of the water and on to a rise near the bushes where her cubs were hiding. Here she rested. Meanwhile, the vultures were not to be outdone. As the jaguar guarded her prize, they gradually inched forward, seemingly for hours, until they reached a critical distance; the jaguar then leapt up and chased them away; and so this went on well into the evening.

Ocelots and other wild cats and foxes frequent the Pantanal, but the least-known hunter to be found here is the bush dog. With its rounded ears, squat legs, a short and powerful muzzle, a stocky body just 25 inches (65 centimeters) long and standing no more than 10 inches (25 centimeters) at the shoulder, it looks more like a badger than a dog. It is exceptionally elusive and little is known about its behavior in the wild, though it is thought to be mainly a cooperative hunter, with packs of 10 or more animals capable of bringing down prey, such as capybaras and rhea, that is much larger than themselves. They chase their victim into the water, where they show considerable agility, diving and swimming around until the prey is subdued. They then haul it onto the bank and feed.

A bush dog's home is a burrow hidden in thick scrub, and it is territorial. The male scent-marks with urine in the usual canine way, by cocking its leg, but the female backs up to a tree and performs a headstand before urinating. The bond between male and female partners is strong, both sexes looking after the needs of the young. Males take food back to

females nursing cubs, and the litter squabbles over food much less than other dogs and foxes.

As the water rises, predators and prey make strange bedfellows on the smaller islands. Caiman and capybaras lie within a few yards of one another, and the turkeylike, bare faced curassows walk between their prostrate bodies.

One familiar bird, the muscovy duck, seems very much at home here for the simple reason that this *is* its natural home. It was taken to Europe in the sixteenth century, but in the Pantanal it can be seen feeding in the wild. Its bill is lined with lamellae that form a filter with which it can sieve out small aquatic crustaceans and fish. The roseate spoonbill feeds on similar creatures, but uses a sideways sweep of its spoon shaped bill to skim the surface waters.

By April the rains tail off and the waters in the Pantanal gradually recede once more. The only drain is the Rio Paraguay. It carries water and silt downstream to the Paraguay depression where the alluvial soils are unusually thick. Geologists have drilled down for over 260 feet (80 meters) without hitting bedrock. Here conditions are similar to those in the Pantanal, except that the vegetation includes both grasslands and dry, thorny *quebracho* forests that provide tannin for the leather industry. Outside Brazil, the area is known as the Gran Chaco, and it is shared among Paraguay, Bolivia, and Argentina.

To the south is the Pampas, the vast treeless plain of central Argentina, which rises

◄

Pantanal caiman lining up shoulder to shoulder at a spillway. When the river floods, they lie with their mouths open into the current, like living fishing traps, waiting for fish to be swept in before slamming their jaws shut.

gently from the coast to the Andes mountains. In the east the fertile, humid grasslands have become the breadbasket of Argentina, while in the west the drier areas in the rainshadow of the Andes support cattle, horses, and sheep.

Pantanal caiman sometimes pass through these habitats, but they do not walk. They become marooned on floating rafts of water hyacinths and grass, and float downstream towards the sea, through Paraguay and into Argentina, reaching Buenos Aires or Montevideo before their transport breaks up and they must head for the shore. Apart from the tales of fearstruck residents of suburban Buenos Aires, there is no evidence that caiman have established themselves near the river mouth.

Further south again, the rainshadow created by the Andes has even greater impact. When the high mountains rose up in the southern part of South America, they cut off the lands to the east from the rain bearing winds of the Pacific. Today, just 6 inches (150 millimeters) fall each year and the ceaseless cold, dry winds suck out the moisture from the parched soil. This is the Patagonia steppe.

Islands of hard rock that have resisted erosion rise above the plateau where gullies and narrow canyons have been carved in the soft rocks. Reptiles, such as the *matuasto* lizard and Patagonian gecko, hide among the boulders, finding places sheltered from the wind and where the day's heat is preserved. Dry river courses litter the landscape, some marked by patches of the endemic creole willow. No more than half a dozen rivers make it all the way to the sea.

In valleys close to the Andes, where the soil is relatively fertile, there are small trees such as the *lenga* or "flag tree." Searching for seeds among their branches might be the carbonated sierra finch and seed snipes. On the rest of the steppe, just a few grasses and low shrubs grow on the sandy and rocky soils. Spiky, hedgehoglike tufts of slow-growing *coirones* can survive in freezing temperatures, and these grasses live for many years. Beneath them, other plants with tiny flowers can grow sheltered from the wind.

The shrubby *calafate*, with its reduced leaves, woody stems and protective thorns, is typical of the area. It produces purple berries, and it is said that anyone who eats them will return to Patagonia. In its branches can be seen one of the commonest and tamest birds in the region, the rufous-collared sparrow. Almost invisible among the dried out vegetation below is the elegant crested tinamou, which travels along the ground in groups of six or seven individuals in search of seeds and small insects. At breeding time, the usual sex roles are reversed, with the male taking charge of incubation and raising the chicks.

Depressions and hollows fill with water, forming wells or brackish lagoons. They are temporary summer homes for black-necked swans, a variety of plovers and coots, and Chilean flamingoes that feed here but nest further north. In the summer months, vegetation along the margins of lakes also provides food for flocks of ashy-headed geese.

The largest body of water in the region is the Lago Argentino. Its turquoise waters add color to the endless browns and grays of the steppe. It is invaded by the impressive Perito Moreno Glacier, which in 1988 advanced right across the middle of the lake, isolat-

ing the top part from the bottom. Water continued to drain into the upper part but, blocked by the glacier, failed to flow into the lower half, and the water level there dropped. Only when the tip of the glacier broke up and the floodgates opened did both parts of the lake reach equilibrium once again.

The smaller, shallower lakes and ponds dry out in high summer, from December through to March, but they attract large numbers of a rather unusual but charming animal peculiar to the Patagonian steppe. This is the mara, a long-legged, harelike creature that is actually a rodent and close relative of cavies and capybaras. Over a hundred at a time may be seen grazing the dry lakebeds. When the scrub on the surrounding steppe is dried to a frazzle, the lakebed provides the only suitable vegetation on which maras can feed.

Like many steppe animals that wish to avoid the wind and have protection from predators, the mara is a burrower, although it differs from the others in that adults dig burrows but do not live in them. Burrows are reserved for babies and are communal, with the offspring of up to 20 couples hiding inside. In effect, their parents have created a rodent day-care center, where the adults take it in turns to stand guard.

They may be seen in the open, for they are active by day—although, as they are the same height as thornbushes, as often as not only the pointed tips of their long ears are visible. If a visitor should approach too close, they will take off with a stiff-legged stotting gait reminiscent of the gazelles of Africa. Indeed, about 38 million years ago, when rodents invaded the continent and there were few hoofed mammals to fill the available ecological niches, it is likely that these long-legged rodents took over the place normally occupied by antelopes, and curiously, they behave just like them. They rely on speed and flight to dense cover to avoid predators and just like antelopes, have white-rump patches that are highly visible when fleeing. Danger can be in the form of an Andean fox that can be seen hunting during the day. Should a fox approach a den, the adults stot in an attempt to distract it.

Couples tend to arrive at the den in shifts, so there is always a pair on guard. At these times, the entire group of youngsters can be seen romping outside. Adult maras, however, are not very tolerant of each other. Another trait they share with antelopes is territoriality. Despite the communal den, each couple has its own piece of territory which holds sufficient food to support the two adults and their offspring. And, if a female is about to give birth, the cosy community life breaks down momentarily. Her partner will not tolerate the presence of other adults. The father-to-be runs towards the other couple, his head low and neck outstretched; as they turn away, he prances about in a zigzag fashion and waggles his rump at the departing male in a display of ownership. When the newborn pups have arrived and their mother has licked away the membranes, given them their first feed and led them down into the burrow, things return to normal.

Pupping occurs between August and December. Parents are monogamous, the female always taking the lead and the male following dutifully behind. Their territory might be a 500-acre (200-hectare) patch of rather sparse steppe, although they tend to graze in 90-acre (35-hectare) chunks for about six weeks at a time. The male defends his partner wherever she may go, grunting softly to maintain contact and standing guard as she feeds. A nursing mother needs more food than her partner. If they are the first couple back to the den after a day's foraging, however, his attempts to defend her come to nothing as 40 baby maras race out from the burrow entrance and attempt to feed from her. Mothers call their young with a high-pitched squeal and identify their own by sniffing their rumps. A wily interloper will keep its rump firmly against the ground to disguise its scent and steal a drink.

During the night, while the young are safely tucked away underground, the adults sleep in dense patches of scrub about 0.33 miles (500 meters) away. The first couple to arrive back at the den in the morning is mobbed in the usual way, not only by youngsters but also by burrowing owls, and sometimes the situation turns nasty. The problem seems to be that the adolescent maras emerge from their burrows and, being curious, go to investigate the smaller owl burrows. Seeing the hole, they do what any self-respecting young mara would do: they dig. The owls understandably take umbrage and try to drive off the hares, at which point the highly protective parents retaliate. The result is a full-scale war in which the owls dive-bomb the young maras and their parents chase the owls. Oblivious to the feud are another pair of burrowers, unique to Patagonia and relatively common. They are two species of armadillos—the greater hairy armadillo and the smaller *pichi*.

The hairy armadillo gets its name from the white and brown hairs that not only project from the scales of its body armor but also sprout from its limbs and belly. Its armor consists of a head shield, a small shield on the neck, and a large carapace with 18 bands that protects the rest of the body. When attacked—perhaps by a Geoffroy's cat or a pampas cat—it will either try to burrow into the ground or draw in its feet so that its armor is in contact with the ground.

The chances of seeing a hairy armadillo or the predators that try to catch it are few because they are active mainly at night, although an armadillo is occasionally seen during the day. It sometimes burrows under animal carcasses to get at the maggots, but more usually digs in the ground for grubs and insects. In winter, its diet switches more to tubers and roots. Places where it forages may be indicated by circular hollows in the ground, created when it digs. It pushes down with its head, then turns its body in a circle so that a conical hole is created.

The smaller *pichi* can be found as far south as the Straits of Magellan, where it survives the cold winters by hibernating. It too forages for insects and worms. In Argentina, the young of both species are born in January and February.

Another, unexpected burrower feeds on the Patagonia steppe but lives on the coast. Where the steppe falls into the Atlantic Ocean, there are steep 200-foot-high (60-meter) cliffs of reddish-brown sandstone. Near Viedma in Argentina these cliffs are home to thousands of Patagonian parrots. In the absence of trees, they behave like the maras, armadillos and burrowing owls and have resorted to burrowing into the soft rock to create nesting tunnels. When they forage for food, however, they must head inland, to the sheltered gorges, traveling many miles each day before returning to the cliffs, where huge flocks swirl round in the updrafts.

Below the parrots, the Atlantic coast is bordered by sandy and multicolored pebble beaches that provide haul-out sites for fur seals, southern elephant seals, southern sealions, and Magellanic penguins.

The traditional breeding sites of the penguins are on bare patches of steppe at the top of the Atlantic beaches. The largest is at Punta Tombo, about 80 miles (120 kilometers) south of Trelew, where a spit of land extends 2 miles (3.5 kilometers) into the sea. At the end of August, the adult males return first. They seek out the nests they occupied in previous years and undertake renovations while waiting for their lifelong partners to arrive. Choice nesting sites may be surrounded by shrubs, but new couples must dig afresh in more exposed areas, using beaks, feet and fins to excavate a burrow 20 inches (50 centimeters) deep.

By the end of Septem-ber, nests have eggs, and after 40 days, during which both parents take it in turn to be on incubation duty, the chicks hatch. They are covered with a gray, fluffy down and weigh just 3 ounces (80 grams). Gulls, skuas, and petrels cruise the colonies for wayward chicks, but if all goes well and the parents bring sufficient food, the fast growing fledglings will be taking their first dip in the sea by February. In March, they are able to fend for themselves. Meanwhile, the adults molt and prepare to move northwards towards the Brazilian coast where they will spend the winter at sea.

About 250 miles (400 kilometers) to the south of Punta Tombo—as the crow flies or the penguin swims—the estuary of the Deseado plays host to penguins, too. It is also the site of one of the largest colonies of red-legged cormorants in the world and is visited daily by small groups of the distinctive black and white Commerson's dolphins. About 20 dolphins enter the estuary, swimming usually in twos and threes and often upside down. It is thought that this is one way to scan the sea floor and search for food in shallow water. They are also adept at rounding up fish, making fishing easier for gulls and cormorants too.

Part of the large breeding colony of Magellanic penguins at Punto Tombo, on the Patagonian coast of Argentina. The birds mate for life and nest in burrows that they retain and refurbish each year.

Offshore, an enormous continental shelf extends out into the Atlantic, the outermost edge marked by the Falkland Islands or Islas Malvinas. The sea here is rich in nutrients, which is why the Patagonia coast is home to such large numbers of marine

birds and mammals. At Punta Tombo alone more than 800,000 penguins arrive each year, making it the largest penguin rookery outside the Antarctic. Another key site is about 100 miles (150 kilometers) to the north, at Península Valdés. Here, 7000 southern sea lions, 50,000 southern elephant seals, and 1500 right whales congregate to breed each summer.

The right whales—so named because they swim slowly and float when harpooned, so early whalers thought they were the "right" whales to catch—head for the peninsula's two horseshoe shaped lagoons, where they spend the southern winter. Recognized by their enormous size and the barnacle infested bonnet on their snout, they arrive each year to drop their calves and mate. Individuals are present from April to December, but the peak of activity is in September and October. With a two-to-three-year breeding cycle, only a small number of females are receptive at any one time, and so the males crowd around, sometimes as many as 20 of them jockeying for position next to the same female. Many are scarred from the head butts and pushing fights, but somewhere down in the blue, away from the prying eyes of humans, mating takes place and a new generation is conceived.

The babies—if a 16-foot-long (5-meter) newborn calf can be considered a "baby"—are born and nursed in the confines of the bay. Both mother and offspring are repeatedly harassed by gulls, which swoop down and peel skin and blubber from the whales as they come to the surface to breathe—attacks which can last from minutes to hours. But, gulls aside, the whales and their calves are relatively safe in the two bays at Península Valdés, for they are protected from their main predators, the killer whales or orcas that patrol the Patagonia coast.

Orcas are the top predators in this area, and in December, when the right whales and their growing calves head south into the Southern Ocean, they run the gauntlet of these voracious killers. Baby whales are the target. The orcas pursue mother and baby, each member of the pod playing its role in the chase. Some flank the larger whales as if herding them, others swim ahead, attempting to stop the whales from escaping, and a third group swims underneath to prevent the victims from diving. The hit squad will then try to separate mother and calf, and drown the youngster.

While some pods chase right whale calves, others specialize in beach raiding. At Punte Norte on the northeastern corner of Península Valdés, the orcas are especially cunning. Between March and May, when young sea lions crowd the beaches, the orcas behave in the most extraordinary way. They have learned how to ride the surf and surge right on to the beach, grab a careless youngster and return to the sea without running aground. Curiously, some adult sea lions will actually enter the water during an orca attack, instead of high-tailing it out of the danger zone. An adult sea lion could easily out-manoeuvre an orca underwater, so are these risk-takers mothers attempting to distract the hunters?

A few kilometers to the south there is evidence to suggest that this might be the case. Sea lions here must swim across a narrow channel in order to travel between two reefs, and orcas have recognized the potential to hijack the commuters. Lone adults whizz

Killer whale or orca riding in on the surf to snatch a sea lion pup from the beach. The huge whales are rarely left high and dry, wriggling their way back into the sea on the next big wave. Youngsters learn the technique from experienced beach-surfing adults.

PENÍNSULA VALDÉS

Península Valdés, about 1000 miles (1500 kilometers) south of Buenos Aires, is a prime site for seeing right whales, killer whales, sea lions, fur seals, elephant seals and Magellanic penguins. Good bases for exploring the area are Trelew for Península Valdés, and Río Galleges for southern Patagonia.

Port Madryn, on the western shore of Golfo Nuevo, is a diving center and a convenient base from which to tour the peninsula. At Puerto Pirámide on the eastern shore, boats take tourists to see the southern right whales that congregate there each austral winter. Some boats are equipped with hydrophones that enable you to hear the constant "chatter" of sonorous moans between whales. There may be mothers with calves, groups of whales in courtship clusters and whales with their tail flukes high in the air "sailing" across the bay.

Different beaches in the area are home to specific sea mammals. Just 10 miles (16 kilometers) south of Puerto Madryn, Punta Loma has a rookery of sea lions, while Punta Norte on the northwestern edge of the peninsula is host to sea lions and killer whales. Although the beaches are closed to visitors, viewing platforms are provided where you can witness killer whales surfing up the beach to snatch young sea lions. The drama does not unfold daily, so you could be there for a week or more before seeing an attack. February and March are the best times for this spectacle. On the way to the beach, look out for a large population of wild guinea pigs that skitter about in the scrub.

In the Golfo San José, the Isla de Los Pájaros has colonies of seabirds, and to the south of Trelew is Punta Tombo, the breeding ground for 800,000 Magellanic penguins that come ashore in September.

Inland, Nahuel Huapí National Park to the west of Península Valdés has alpine scenery with snow-capped mountains and crystal-blue lakes, and Los Glaciares National Park boasts spectacular glaciers, including the Upsala and Perito Marino Glaciers. A catamaran takes tourists to see the face of the 40-mile (60-kilometer-long) Upsala Glacier. It is about 5 miles (8000 meters) wide and 260 feet (80 meters) high. The countryside away from the sea is dominated by huge sheep ranches, concentrated in the canyons to shelter flocks from the incessant wind. If you are lucky, you may spot guancaos, maras, pumas, foxes, armadillos and Geoffroy's cats. Away from the lakes, birdwatchers can expect rheas, caracaras, falcons and geese.

◄

Southern right whale breaching at Peninsula Valdés. The behavior is thought to be a form of communication.

across before the killers have time to move, but youngsters are not so fast and the orcas can pick them off with ease. So groups of sea lions travel together. The adults crowd around their offspring, forming a fast-moving, protective shield aimed at confusing the predators.

Orcas are unexpectedly fast and surprisingly well practiced. During lulls in activity, when the sea lions are away at sea, they have been seen rehearsing their beach-charging skills on steeply shelving beaches nearby. Young whales learn from their elders and, once mastered, the skill delivers 20 sea lions an hour if the hunting is good. The majority of attacks, however, are by a single, experienced animal and the food is shared by the rest of the pod. But the terror does not end there. The orcas do not eat their prey immediately. Like cats playing with mice, they use their powerful tails to cuff still-living sea lion bodies into the air.

A colony of elephants seals, the largest of the seal family, is also vulnerable to orca attack. Like the penguins, they arrive in August. Males haul out first and battle for the best sites in which to gather a harem. Snorting and bellowing, they rear up and slash each other on their thick collars of blubber. By the time the bloody contests have ended, the females appear and they gather into groups, each harem overseen by a champion "beachmaster."

In September, the first pups are born. Their mothers nurse them for 20–25 days, and because elephant seal milk is so rich, a few days later they are changing their black baby fur for a light gray coat. The peak of activity is in October, when the largest number of seals and their offspring are crowded on the beaches. They remain there for six to eight weeks before heading out to sea, where the orcas are waiting for the unwary.

By November, the adult males are leaving the colonies and returning to the ocean deeps beyond the broad continental shelf to feed and put on the weight they lost during their breeding-time fast. They spend much of their life at depths of 5000 feet (1500 meters) or more, feeding on squid and fish, and return to the surface very briefly to breathe.

Shortly afterwards, the females and their offspring also leave the beaches. Some swim north to feed off the continental shelf to the east of Uruguay and southern Brazil. Others head south, where they haul out on beaches for their annual molt. Research has shown that one of their destinations is the Falkland Islands in the South Atlantic, where the last leg of our journey begins.

coasts:
INTO THE PACIFIC

If the Southern Ocean is not the most inhospitable place on Earth, then it must be close to being so. Here, the might and power of nature are all too evident. It is a place of monstrous seas and hurricane force winds that circle the southern tip of the world unchecked by any large landmass. Storms are driven by winds with evocative names such as the 'roaring forties' and the 'furious fifties', but the romance is overshadowed by the reality of a place that was once described as 'like living in a washing machine'. Many sea mammals are part of that wash, taking advantage of the cold, food-rich seas. Come the breeding season, however, some escape the hostile higher latitudes and make for a haven off the southeastern coast of South America. This is the Falklands Islands or Islas Malvinas, a small and remote archipelago sitting on the edge of the Patagonian continental shelf.

▶

Paracas Peninsula, Peru, where the desert comes right down to the sea. The sea cliffs and offshore islands are breeding and roosting sites for an extraordinary variety of seabirds, and the rocks and beaches are haul-out sites for sea mammals such as seals and sea lions.

◀

Magellanic penguins. These are one of several species of penguins found on the coasts of South America and on the Falkland Islands (Islas Malvinas).

Migrants from the stormy south are joined here by those from the north. Southern elephant seals, for example, follow the wide continental shelf abreast of South America. While some breed on the shores of Patagonia, others haul out on the islands' sand and shingle beaches to breed and undergo their annual molt.

Following winter feeding off Patagonia, rockhopper penguins also come leaping through the waves. They spend seven months of the year on the high seas, but with the arrival of the southern spring in October they must head for land to breed.

Barreling through the surf, the penguins are visible one minute and gone the next. By 'porpoising' across the surface of the water, they minimize drag while in the air and can snatch a vital breath while traveling full tilt towards home. They too are heading for one of the many breeding colonies on the Falkland Islands, but the nesting sites of some of these colonies are probably the most inaccessible places any penguin could choose. The rockhoppers, for example, nest on Westpoint Island at the top of steep cliffs that are pounded by heavy seas. As if they were entering a surging liquid elevator, the birds catch a wave and ride it part way up the clif, jumping off to scramble up the slippery, wave-weathered rocks. Well designed 'flexible' feet and grim determination are all that keep them from being swept away. Many fail to make it the first time and are snatched back by the sea, only to be smashed against the rocks by the tumultuous waves. With a body designed to 'fly' effortlessly in the water when chasing fish and squid, the rockies are amazingly capable on land and make it to their nest sites to be reunited with their lifelong mates.

Out at sea, black-browed albatrosses skim the waves, appearing momentarily as they soar over wave crests and disappearing from view as they fly into the troughs. Like the penguins, they have been feeding on squid and other marine life, but now they head for the Falklands, to nest sites often alongside those of the rockhoppers. These albatross colonies are the largest in the world, some of them so cramped that each bird is not much more than pecking distance from its neighbors.

Land is a scarce commodity in the southern oceans, so chosen areas can be crowded with sea mammals and birds eager to breed. While rockhopper penguins and albatrosses tend to take over the more formidable coastlines, gentoo penguins select more accessible places trekking for several miles inland to nest on grassy plains. Magellanic penguins hide in burrows, shearwaters dig burrows up to 6 feet (2 meters) long in the soft tussock-peat, and Falkland kelp geese nest on the beach under overhanging skirts of tussock grass. Tussock grass grows up to 6 feet (2 meters) high and, together with the moorland vegetation of grasses, ferns, and numerous flowering plants, it is the nearest that the Falklands have to a 'jungle'. It provides animals with shelter from the relentless winds.

There are few predators living here, but those that do take advantage of the sudden seasonal abundance of eggs and chicks. Unguarded nests are plundered immediately by brown skuas, but the most fearsome raider is the rare striated caracara, a relative of the falcons which behaves like a well-armed crow. Very young rockhopper chicks left unattended are attacked mercilessly and eventually fed to the caracara mother's own offspring, for this

is one of the few chances she has to find enough food for her family to survive.

Parent penguins and albatrosses must alternate their feeding excursions, at least in the early stages, to ensure that one is always guarding the nest. Such is the frantic need to raise a family before the Antarctic's winter weather returns that the birds must leave their nests every day to collect food for their growing chicks. The three species of penguins waddle back to the stormy seas where there are yet more dangers waiting for them. Orcas are here, too. They cruise the kelp zone, ready to surprise any unwary bird. With an extraordinary turn of speed that confirms them as the fastest as well as the largest members of the dolphin family, they slam into their targets and, like their more northerly relatives, play with their prey, mothers teaching offspring how to catch gentoo penguins. Giant petrels, the vultures of the Southern Ocean, are never far away. Using a remarkable sense of smell — unusual for a bird — they locate and clean up any carcass that remains.

As if the wind, weather, tumultuous seas, and predators were not enough, the journey home is not easy either. As the rockhopper and Magellanic penguins return to their colonies, rogue bull southern sea lions are waiting for them in the surf or on the rocks and beach. They grab what they can, but penguin numbers are so great that many get through in the confusion.

▶
Rockhoppper penguins. With dangers in the form of orcas and leopard seals lurking in nearshore waters, 'rockies' are quick to enter or leave the water. Sometimes, they burst from the breakers, in their eagerness to reach dry land before the next wave sweeps them back out to sea.

The southern sea lions, like the penguins, must return to the land to breed, crowding onto selected beaches. Dominant males gather the females into harems and then guard them until they give birth from a previous year's mating. As soon as the females have dropped their pups, they are ready to mate again. The atmosphere can reach fever pitch.

The bulls will have fought for the best sites on the beach and access to the most females, but they do not have everything their own way. When a dominant male 'beachmaster' is otherwise engaged, sub-adult males attempt to take over females. Should an adult bull make a stand, newborn pups can be crushed by the bodies of the large males during the ensuing battles.

In February, the surviving rockhopper chicks fledge and leave for the sea. In March, with their offspring gone, the adults molt and gradually leave the colonies. By mid-April, young albatrosses prepare to leave. Facing into the wind, they spread their wings and soar away, traveling enormous distances to traditional feeding grounds around the Southern Ocean. Some may head for southern Chile and its heavily indented coast of fjords, narrow channels, rocky shores, and countless offshore islands.

Chile's fjordland includes an extraordinary, storm-buffeted archipelago that stretches from the Isla de Chiloé off the central Chilean coast to Tierra del Fuego, the southernmost tip of South America. With just a few human settlements between Puerto Montt and Puerto Arenas along the entire 1250-mile (2000-kilometer) fjord coast, it is one of the least explored places on Earth, haunted by myths, legends, and ghost stories.

Access is by boat and is not for the faint-hearted. This stretch of coast is racked by storms and littered with rocks; in the channels the water is unexpectedly deep. In the sheltered Straits of Magellan it is over 400 feet (120 meters) deep just a few yards from the shore. Here Pacific and Atlantic meet head on, and along with fresh water from the Andes dumped into the sea from white water rivers and spectacular rumbling glaciers, this natural coalition produces rip tides and swirling currents that stir up inshore waters.

In the Atlantic mouth of the Straits themselves the current runs at 10 miles (16 kilometers) per hour. This means that through the 3-mile (5000-meter-wide) channel at Segunda Angastura, about 2 million cubic feet (57,000 cubic meters) of seawater are passing each second – 20 times the volume flowing down the Amazon River. The height difference between high and low tide is 26 feet (7.8 meters), and there is a 50-minute period of still water twice each day when the tides turn.

Outside the main channels, much of the sea is uncharted. Vast areas are labeled simply 'foul water'. On ships, lookouts are posted and hopefully rocks and sand bars spotted before disaster strikes. Some maps are over 100 years old, and so Captain Robert FitzRoy of the *Beagle*, with whom Charles Darwin rounded Cape Horn in December 1832 and who first surveyed the Straits, probably deliberated over charts similar to those used by sailors today. Even in this age of satellite navigation and computer-assisted passage, mariners must rely on the knowledge of local fishermen in order to find safe passage and anchorage in these stormy and unpredictable waters.

Extensive ice caps on the mainland and smaller ones on the larger islands feed local weather systems, causing violent fists of katabatic winds or *williwaws* to punch their way between the islands. On the outer islands, rocks on the windward edges are rasped clean by the wind, and the rest is covered with thickets of stunted trees, deep sphagnum bogs, and tussock grass. Every week, a three-day storm with winds in excess of 70–80 knots and carrying snow and freezing rain pounds land and sea. Expedition yachts drag their anchors, masts are ripped from decks . . . and this is only spring!

Yet the wildness and remoteness are the attractions of this place. On many of the outer islands, it is unlikely that any two people have walked on the same ground, and not many will have witnessed the extraordinary wealth of undisturbed wildlife. For those brave enough to venture out here, the rewards are incredible. Early in the season albatrosses, penguins, and seals are attracted to the islands and channels to breed and feed. Some, such as the black-browed albatross, giant petrel, and southern fulmar, are visitors from sub-Antarctic islands; Hudsonian godwits, on the other hand, arrive here each summer, having flown all the way from the Arctic. Other birds actually nest here.

Near Puerto Natales, one of the few centers of human population in the deep south, Last Hope Inlet is home to thousands of blue-eyed cormorants. Their colonies are tucked into cliffs, where they are raided by the aggressive Chilean skua and have their eggs stolen by visiting snowy sheathbills. Overhead, the excited 'keear-keear-keear' calls announce the presence of the black-backed dolphin gull, a specialist scavenger that feeds on sea lion dung and penguin leftovers, and the rasping 'keek-keek' of the South American tern indicates that fish must be coming close to the surface.

Penguins chase the shoals out from the deep-water channels and up towards the surface. Albatrosses and skuas join the melee of seabirds that raid the tightly packed bait balls thrashing about at the surface. When summer comes, water spouts of humpback whales announce their arrival for the feast. They navigate through the labyrinth of narrow channels to harvest a sea teeming with shoals of sardines and other small fish. Little is known about them, even though there have been local reports from whalers for hundreds of years.

The penguins all along this coast, as far north as Isla de Chiloé, are Magellanic penguins. When their crops are full they make for rookeries on sheltered islands, heading not for the tussock grass moorlands so characteristic of the sub-Antarctic islands further south, but for the woods, scrambling up muddy tracks and over fallen branches to their nests hidden among the roots of beech trees. In the damp and dripping southern temperate rainforests, with trees festooned with mosses and the semi-parasitic 'Chinese lantern' and decorated with balls of bright orange fungus, they slip and slide over the steep slopes of rock and dirt, struggling to remain upright for the 0.3-mile (500-meter) trek from the tide-line to their nests.

If you sit quietly beside a well worn track, every time these dinner-jacketed lodgers pass in the interminable rain, the distinct patter of bare feet on mud is punctuated with a polite sneeze, and then they move on once again. Are they ridding themselves of salt or do

they actually have colds? It is certainly damp enough.

In fact, the rain in this fjord region is unusually heavy. With an annual deluge exceeding 13–16 feet (4–5 meters), some regions in the northern part – the Chonos Archipelago – are said to be the wettest places on Earth. Further south, in the Queen Adelaide Archipelago, it is windier but only slightly drier, and the storms clear more quickly. Temperatures vary little between summer and winter, and the sun rarely shines. The rain turns the forest floor into a mud bath, and penguins return to the sea by tobogganing on their bellies down long mud slides to the rocky shore.

In the sea, the steep forested slopes are matched underwater by thick forests of giant kelp or *cachiyuyo*. Throughout the length and breadth of fjordland great swathes of kelp form long natural barriers off the outer islands and narrower bands clog the inshore channels. Some beds are even marked on marine charts as permanent navigational hazards.

In water up to 65 feet (20 meters) deep, the enormous strands of algae stretch from the seabed to the surface, growing 2 feet (60 centimeters) in a day. At first they trail across the sea floor before growing towards the surface. They are taller by far than the trees on adjacent shores. Southern sea lions and orcas cruise the edges of this kelp forest, waiting for an instant penguin meal to 'fly' by. The penguins, in turn, use the forest of fronds to

▲
Group of female South American sea lions and their pups. This species is found from Northern Peru and northeastern Brazil south to Tierra del Fuego and the Falkland Islands. Females give birth from December to February, within a few days of arriving at their breeding sites on flat rock platforms or open sand or pebble beaches.

cover their escape.

Southern fur seals also find temporary shelter among the kelp. Their breeding colonies are onshore, but they chill out in the extensive kelp beds. It is a place to unwind. They turn and twist, corkscrewing slowly up and down in the water. As they dive, streams of mercurylike bubbles, from the air squeezed out of their fur, trail behind them. Do they know how good they look, and are they showing off to each other? They even blow extra bubbles through their noses and spiral through them – maybe just to impress.

The kelp (along with 350 other species of brown, red, and green seaweeds found here) is home to a community of undersea creatures, each adapted to living in a particular forest 'level' much like animals in a terrestrial forest. The base of each frond is encrusted with red coralline algae, while attached further up the stem are grayish colonies of bry-ozoans, together with molluscs, amphipods, isopods, and worms of all shapes and sizes. There are crabs that cling to the fronds and small gobies known as clingfish that have mod-ified pelvic fins as suckers with which they adhere to the seaweeds. Close to the surface, the fronds are a nursery for deep-water fish that come here from the open ocean to spawn.

When the crew of HMS *Beagle* pulled strands of kelp aboard, Darwin was awed by the diversity of life living on or around the fronds. 'On shaking the great entangled roots,' he wrote, 'a small pile of fish, shells, cuttle-fish, crabs of all orders, sea-eggs, star-fish, beau-tiful Holothuriae, Planariae, and crawling nereidous animals of a multitude of forms, all fall out together. Often as I recurred to a branch of kelp, I never failed to discover animals of new and curious structures.' Scientists today have the same experience.

Below the huge Pacific surf that crashes into the outer islands, a particularly aggres-sive starfish, *Meyenaster gelatinosus,* terrorizes the sea floor, eating just about any living thing it can catch—and catch things it does, for this sea star actually pursues its food, gliding rap-idly over the sea floor on its hundreds of tube feet. It can even eat on the move, holding on to prey with one arm while chasing and grabbing something else. Curiously, potential prey animals in areas frequented by the sea star are alert to its presence and can sense whether it is feeding or not, just as antelope in Africa can sense whether a pride of lions is hunting or simply passing by. Somehow, they seem to know when to run.

For the small snails that cling to the kelp, an octopus is a deadly predator. It kills the snails in two quite different ways. It bores into their shells with its chitinous beak and extracts the meat, but if it fails to break through and the snail survives, barnacle larvae settle in the drill holes. The snail then becomes encrusted with barnacles, which makes it less stream-lined and more liable to be dislodged and washed away by the tide.

On the shore, isolated pairs of kelp geese feed – not, as their name suggests, on kelp, but on green sea-lettuce growing in the tidal rock pools. Sporting unusually short legs and conspicuously large yellow webbed feet, they cling to the slippery rocks. They are instantly distinguishable, even from a distance, for the male is white and the female black.

There are also some eccentric ducks living here. Two species of steamer ducks may be seen escaping danger not by flying but by 'steaming' across the sea's surface in the man-

▶ Southern fur seal swimming amid a forest of kelp fronds. It feeds on a variety of sea foods, including squid, octopus, anchovies, horse mackerel, rock lobster and lobster krill.

ner of a vintage paddle steamer. In a cloud of spray, the birds scull rapidly with their feet and beat furiously with their stumpy wings before diving below the waves. They also defend their patch of coastline energetically against intruders of their own species and, when undisturbed, dive to the seabed in search of shellfish. They nest on the ground among the thick tangle of vegetation on the leeward side of offshore islands. In more open places, meanwhile, Magellanic oystercatchers lay their mottled eggs in delicate scrapes in the shingle.

Along the outer edge of the kelp beds and in the channels, pods of energetic dolphins go fishing. The soft longitudinal bands of white on their flanks, together with a torpedo-shaped body, rounded snout, and sickle-shaped dorsal fins, reveal them to be Peale's dolphins, a species confined to these waters. They hunt for fish, especially kingclip and squid, traveling at high speed in groups of eight or nine.

Further out to sea, a portion of the clockwise-flowing waters of the Antarctic Circumpolar Current is diverted northwards from the Southern Ocean to form the mighty Humboldt Current, a cold but fertile ocean flow that brushes the Pacific coast of South America. It is guided just a few miles offshore by dramatic underwater cliffs that plunge down into the Peru–Chile Trench – a yawning gash in the seabed that is deeper than the Andes are tall. Down here, the water is cold and the pressure great, and it is the hunting ground of the world's largest predator – the sperm whale.

The monsters that migrate through these parts are the large and mature bull whales, each up to 100 feet (30 meters) long. They are here to feed on the profusion of squid in the deep-sea trench. At the surface they are easily spotted by their distinct spout which squirts out at an angle of 45 degrees from the tip of their great, blunt heads. When they dive they raise their great tail flukes into the air and slide silently below the surface.

Sperm whales are really deep divers, diving deeper than any other air breathing sea mammal. In the inky darkness of the abyss, more than 4000 feet (1200 meters) down, they locate their prey using high-frequency pulses of sound, and maybe even debilitate it with especially high-intensity bursts that punch it into submission. They are one of the few creatures that feed not only on deep-sea sharks but also on the 40-foot (12-meter-long) giant squid and the other deep-sea squids that comprise 80 percent of their diet.

Only the males visit southern waters. The family schools of females and their calves remain in warmer equatorial waters many thousands of miles to the north. At the end of summer, the bulls embark on a lengthy journey northwards to rejoin them, find a partner or partners, and mate.

The Humboldt Current is only 100 miles (160 kilometers) wide, but over 2000 miles (3000 kilometers) long and moving at about 2.25 miles (3.7 kilometers) an hour. Helped by the southeast trade winds that suck air from the sub-Antarctic to the Equator, the cold water is channeled between the Peru–Chile Trench and the mainland. The winds skim off the surface waters, causing water rich in nutrients to well up from the deep to take its place. The extensive area of upwelling makes this coast one of the most fertile places in the world. Fish and squid are so abundant that huge numbers of seabirds and sea mammals converge on the coastal strip to breed and feed. Breeding time for most animals up and down the coast is from October through to February, the southern summer, when the current is closer to the shore.

One of the smaller offshore islands of the Isla de Chiloé, Puñihuil marks the most northerly reach of the Magellanic penguin and the southern limit of the very rare Humboldt penguin, recognized by its slightly larger bill. It is the only place in the world where the two species can be found together.

By the time the Humboldt Current reaches the latitude of the Isla Chañaral, about 4 degrees south of the tropics, the beech forests have given way to scrub at the southern edge of the Atacama Desert. From here northwards, a strip of land not much more than 330 feet (100 meters) wide is sandwiched between one of the hottest and driest places on Earth to the east and the world's most fertile waters to the west. It is a curious mix, but even more bizarre is the discovery that here Humboldt penguins nest on the edge of the desert or on desert islands close to the shore.

The penguins feed on the wealth of fish and squid that comes close to the coast in the cold Humboldt Current. They clamber out of the water and climb desert cliffs to reach their nests — not among tussock grass or beech trees, but under cacti alongside burrowing owls. The penguins burrow under the limbs of the cacti, and the owls have burrows in the ground nearby.

▶
Antofagasta coast, Chile. The pinkish, rolling sands of the Atacama Desert, one of the driest and most barren places on Earth, lie alongside the nutrient-rich waters of the Pacific Ocean, where the narrow coastal strip is packed with an extraordinarily large number of seabirds and sea mammals.

At places like Pan de Azúcar, meaing 'sugar loaf', and Isla Chañaral, Humboldt penguins have no set breeding season, so there can be eggs and chicks at all stages of development at almost any time. Though they are protected from most terrestrial predators by having the desert in their backyard, they must still be wary of kelp gulls and turkey vultures which will take any opportunity to attack a youngster outside the nest. The penguins, therefore, nest in burrows. Unlike other penguins, Humboldts do not have crèches for young birds, for they must stay out of the hot sun. Chicks and fledglings remain in or around their burrows, where one of their biggest problems is not from predators, but from the heat.

Temperatures here can soar to 122°F (50°C), and despite a cool wind that often blows ashore, there is a danger that the birds will overheat. They have bare patches of skin on their faces that some penguin watchers believe could be an adaptation to living in such a dry place. They also pant constantly, hold out their flippers and fluff out their feathers. The water where they swim and hunt their food, however, is cold. The temperature of the

LAGUNA SAN RAFAEL

The Laguna San Rafael National Park is deservedly one of the best-known natural wonders in the Aisén region of Chile. Situated about halfway between Punta Arenas and Puerto Montt, it is approached only by boat, and so the entire area has retained its original plants and animals virtually undisturbed. Centerpiece is undoubtedly the mouth of the startlingly neon blue-white San Rafael Glacier, one of 19 major glaciers that make up the northern Patagonia ice sheet. Occasionally, huge, translucent blue pieces break free and crash into the lake. Waves about 6–10 feet (2–3 meters) high are created by the displaced water.

The laguna is not totally enclosed, opening to the sea via a narrow tidal channel into the Golfo Elefantes, so you can see albatrosses, penguins, cormorants, steamer ducks, marine otters, sea lions, and harbor porpoises. On the shore, ashy-headed geese forage on the grass, and after heavy rains a black and white frog – yet to be identified by scientists – forages for earthworms and snails. In the surrounding forests, tiny *pudú* hide among the beech forests and avoid the predatory attentions of puma and gray fox.

▼

Laguna San Rafael. Set among the fjords and islands of Chilean Patagonia are the lake and its spectacular glacier. The creaking, popping 6-mile (9-kilometer-long) glacier is advancing constantly; 400 icebergs carve from its blue wall every day.

Humboldt Current remains at a steady 58–64°F (14.4–17.8°C) throughout its length, the result of colder waters from the deep being brought up to the surface by the offshore winds.

On the mainland at dusk, the silence of the Atacama Desert is broken by what sounds like gunshots, the sudden noise made by rocks cracking and releasing the stresses and strains exerted by the extremes of air temperature. While the day is dominated by searing heat, the nighttime temperature can plummet below zero. Yet, in this truly inhospitable terrain, something stirs.

The gray gull or *garuma* is one of the most common gulls along the Atacama Desert coast. It feeds on the locally abundant burrowing crab, and while it courts and mates on the coast, the population is quite remarkable in its choice of nest site. In order to raise their young, the birds head inland for over 50 miles (80 kilometers) to the desert where rain may not have fallen for several years.

The nests themselves are no more than scrapes in the sand arranged into loose colonies on the desert floor. They may be anything from 30 feet to 0.33 miles (10 to 500 meters) apart. Both parents tend the nest, one always remaining with the eggs or chicks. It fluffs out its feathers and droops its wings to shield them from the relentless sun. The air quivers with the heat, and dust-devils pick up the sand. The eggs have fewer pores and lose water much more slowly than the eggs of other gulls, but the incubation period is prolonged.

Chicks and adults blend in so well with their bleak surroundings that they are almost invisible. As parents returning from a day's fishing at the coast arrive in the night, they must rely on sound to locate their partners. Once reunited, they exchange greetings, and after feeding the chicks the parents swap places. Before the sun rises, the outgoing bird flies back to the coast.

Few other creatures – mostly small snakes, lizards, and scorpions – venture into this wilderness, so the nesting birds are relatively safe. This is possibly one reason why they come here, but nobody really knows. Another explanation is that, many thousands of years ago, this place was pock-marked by salt water lagoons where the birds congregated in huge breeding colonies. Today, the water has gone, but this relic population of gray gulls arrives each breeding season just as it did all that time ago. In evolutionary terms, the birds have still to catch up with the constantly rising Andes and the rapidly evolving landscape.

The long, thin strip of desert and the adjacent Humboldt Current continue northward into Peru, and the upwellings in the sea off northern Chile and Peru are greater than anywhere else in the world. The water, coming up to displace the spent surface waters, rises from depths in excess of 1000 feet (300 meters). It not only encourages rich growths of phytoplankton, but because it is cold it also causes the frequent coastal fogs that drift into the desert.

At night a light, warm breeze from the land blows towards the cold sea, and so fogs form. By day, the sea breezes blow the fogs back onto the coast. A thick mist, known in Peru as the *garúa* and in Chile as the *camanchaca*, masks the sun for long periods of the day between June and December, and its influence can be felt as far as the slopes of the Andes,

more than 60 miles (100 kilometers) inland. Temperatures are higher above the fog than they are below, so vegetation tends to thicken with height.

At low levels in Peru's Lachay National Park, drought resistant cacti and mesquite dominate the landscape, while above 650 feet (200 meters) there are islands of the fog-green loma vegetation, known as 'fog oases' or 'meadows in the desert'. They flower in August and September. The local type of gray fox has dens here. Its large ears lose heat during the day, and a thick hide keeps it warm when scavenging or hunting at night.

Desert plants rely for survival on the mists and fogs condensing on their stems and leaves. The water that drips from the vegetation to the ground is absorbed through the plant's roots or, as with the coastal sand dune bromeliads, through the leaves. Mouse-sized rodents such as leaf-eared mice, small geckos, and birds drink the tiny droplets.

In these parts, however, the focus for wildlife watchers must be the concentration of seabirds and sea mammals in Peru's Parque Nacional Paracas. Just a four-hour bus ride from Lima, the sands of the desert come right down to the water's edge, and the cold Humboldt Current brushes close to the shore. The desert drops into the sea in a series of distinct terraces that mark successive sea levels as the land rises in steps. Although the desert meets the sea along most of the length of Peru, Paracas is special because it is protected and

▶

Humboldt penguin. This species takes over from the Magellanic penguin in central and northern Chile and Peru, nesting in burrows under cacti or in caves, on desert islands, and sandy shores. Non-breeding birds may reach as far north as the Gulf of Guayquil, off southern Ecuador.

◀

Gray gull, nesting on the coastal desert of the Antofagasta province of northern Chile. Surface temperatures in the desert reach 50°C (122°F), the only relief by day being a wind that blows up from the west-south-west each afternoon.

much of it is fairly inaccessible and largely uninhabited. Small offshore islands are ideal breeding sites for seabirds, seals, and sea lions. Each year, this thin strip of coast plays host to one of the most impressive wildlife spectacles in the world.

In the southern summer, nesting sites are dominated by the so-called 'guano birds'. When conditions are favorable, they nest and roost in millions. Their nitrate-rich droppings once formed the basis of a multimillion-dollar fertilizer industry, but over-exploitation led to its collapse. Today, the exploitation continues, for guano is still considered to be the best 'natural' fertilizer available, but it is more controlled and on a much smaller scale. With no vegetation, except at high levels on some of the bigger islands, where seabirds do not nest anyway, each bird scrapes its nest from dried guano. Unappealing though it may sound, this practice has its advantages. The nest does not blow away in the wind, and the whiteness dissipates heat.

There are three main species present: the brown pelican, which starts nesting in October, and the guanay cormorant and the Peruvian booby, which nest in November. They are all fish eaters, harvesting the enormous shoals of *anchoveta*, small fish that congregate offshore, and they are totally dependent on the cold, fertile waters of the Humboldt Current. They feed in their turn on the animal plankton that migrates from mid-waters to the surface each night. The best fishing, therefore, is in the early morning, when the sea is usually calm and the *anchoveta* are closest to the surface. The cormorants fly out from their roosts in long undulating lines, skimming the wave tops until they find food, not only in the shallow inshore waters but also in the deep offshore channels. They settle on the sea and dive continually in pursuit of fish. The boobies dive-bomb the *anchoveta* shoals from a height of 70 feet (20 meters). When one bird gives a whistling signal, the entire flock drops into the ocean, each one folding its wings at the last moment before impact. It rains boobies.

The pelicans dive too, but at an angle. They pile into the huge waves breaking on the shore and, in a great splash, thrust their heads below the surface and gather fish in their enormous bills. All around, piratical gulls, intent on stealing fish from out of the pelicans' mouths, scream around their heads until their victims regurgitate their hard won catch.

The cormorants nest on deep piles of guano that have accumulated for many years on coastal promontories and offshore islands, each bird scraping together a circular crater in which to raise its latest brood. There are about three nests to 11 square feet (1 square meter), which means six adults and six chicks confined to a relatively small space. The birds will nest only where the dark rocks have been sprayed with the gray and white droppings. They are not alone: small lizards and large spiders dash in and out of the nests in search of the feather lice and ticks that infest the cormorants.

While all the guano islands are breathtaking, the most accessible to visitors are the Islas Ballestas and Islas Chinchas, the former accessible by tourist boat from the pier at Paracas. On the islands and on the Paracas mainland, the high cliffs are carved by the sea into dramatic sea arches, such as the celebrated 'La Catedral', and undermined by caverns containing turquoise-blue water in which Humboldt penguins and South American fur seals

cavort.

Sharing this coastal strip between the desert and the deep blue sea are South American sea lions. They haul out in extraordinarily large numbers, crowding together on the beaches. The bulls are the most lionl-ike of their kind, with blunt, upturned snub noses and a full mane of coarse hair. They can be seen surfing in the Pacific rollers that crash on the shore. The most impressive have fought other males and won the right to be beach-master, and are surrounded by a bevy of smaller females with their pups. Peak breeding activity is in January and February. It is a time when a few large bulls have taken to hijacking and killing fur seal pups in the area. Sea lions are much larger than fur seals, so even lone female fur seals are at risk.

Humboldt penguins have their burrows further inland. In the morning rush hour to the sea, their route is relatively congestion free, as most of the sea lions are already in the water. The local species of tern, the elegant Inca tern, dives to catch small fish between the sea lions' bobbing heads. At the end of the day, however, the penguins must run the gaunt-let of irritable sea lions. When the sea lions and penguins are ashore, black skimmers use their unusually long lower bills to 'trawl' in the shallows, and the seaside cinclodes may be seen hopping about on the wet rocks at the water's edge in search of titbits the tide may

► Breeding colony of brown pelicans on the coast of Peru. They are the world's second biggest producer of guano, after the guanay cormorants. Together, the two species are known as the 'billion dollar birds' because of the commercial value of their guano as natural fertilizer.

have left behind.

All kinds of unexpected guests might arrive at this time. A normally terrestrial species of lava lizard dashes across the rocks between waves, searching for tiny shrimp, and oasis hummingbirds have been known to forage for marine invertebrates among the seaweeds on the shore. It is one of the few occasions that hummingbird have been seen fishing. The vampire bat also attends the feast. It lives in deep caves along the coast, and in the absence of its more usual supply from donkeys, cows, and sheep, it turns to seals to obtain its nightly fill of blood. Like a refugee from a horror movie, it crawls menacingly across the beach and creeps up silently on slumbering seals and sea lions. Using its razor-sharp incisor teeth, it takes a slither of skin from a flipper and then, with a tongue equipped with special grooves, laps up the blood that flows from the wound. The bat's saliva contains a special substance that prevents the victim's blood from clotting. Sleeping seabirds are at risk, too, the bats licking blood from incisions made in their naked legs.

While the bats try their hand at night, during daylight hours Andean condors visit the breeding sites, such as those at Punta San Fernando, to the south of the Paracas National Park, and Morro Quemado within the park. They swoop down from the mountains in search of seal and sea lion afterbirth as well as dead animals. Foxes come down to the shore to scavenge, and turkey vultures are here, too. Rows of them hang on draughts of rising air, alert for anything that resembles food. Some years, however, rotting carcasses outnumber the living.

Every four to seven years, a weather system known as El Niño, meaning 'the Christ Child' because it often sets in around Christmas, has a devastating effect not only on this region, but around the entire world. Hardest hit is usually South America's west coast. The principal event is a reversal of the main ocean currents. In particular, warm water from the equator flows southwards along the South American coastline, displacing the Humboldt Current. Cold, fertile water is replaced by barren warm water. Food chains collapse, sea birds and mammals die, breeding is severely disrupted and survival is the order of the day. In 1982 and 1983, for example, an El Niño event was especially savage. The fish that parent birds would have fed to their youngsters were just not there. They had moved to colder, deeper waters far from the coast. An estimated 1 percent of normal fish stocks was all that remained. Without food, the birds had no choice: they abandoned their nests and their chicks and headed far out to sea where the effects of El Niño were less intense. Many failed to make it. Millions of dead and dying birds and fish littered Peruvian beaches. All along the South American coast, fur seal mothers abandoned their pups and about a quarter of adult fur seals and sea lions died. About 10 percent of some species survived, and millions of breeding birds were reduced to thousands in subsequent years. Scavengers, though, had a field day.

Another devastating El Niño event occured in 1997 and 1998. Two years later, seabird and sea lion populations have still to recover. At Morro Quemado, where beaches contained an estimated 30,000 sea lions during the 1996–7 season, there was virtually no breeding in 1997–8, and only a thousand animals turned up in 1998–9. Populations are

looking healthier today at Morro Quemado, but the recovery elsewhere is slow.

For people who depend on the sea for their living, El Niño years have been cata-strophic. They have caused the *anchoveta* fishery to collapse, with considerable impact on local fishing communities. It is a pattern that seems to have repeated itself many times. Studies of ice cores taken from glaciers in the Andes have revealed that two particularly dev-astating El Niño events occurred around AD 600 and AD 1100; the former coincided with the demise of the Moche civilization on the north coast of Peru, and the latter with the col-lapse of the Sican culture in the Lambayaque Valley.

Remnants of these and other ancient civilizations are scattered around the land-scape. On the coast of Paracas – which means 'wind of sand' – fishermen shelter in a cove from the strong southerly breeze that blows up at lunchtime every day. The wind is so strong that the air becomes filled with a mist of sand, the 'paracas'. Etched into the hillside is the 'candelabra', a figure resembling those on the Nazca Plains. The candelabra is thought to be relatively modern in origin, having been carved after the Spanish conquest. But littered about the region are 2000-year-old archaeological remains, including well-preserved mum-mies, skulls, ceramics, textiles, and sand drawings. They were created by people from a well-developed culture that existed here from 1300 BC until AD 200, a long time before the Incas.

► Coast of Paracas, Peru. The cold Humboldt Current comes close to shore here, bringing with it a particular fish – the anchoveta – that is food for an extraordinary number of seabirds and sea mammals.

In the past, the wildlife populations have recovered. At the end of the 1982–3 event, those creatures that had been able to change their diets lived to breed another day. Penguins in the south, for example, had switched to squid and shrimp instead of their more usual *anchovetas*. Those that had moved out of the coastal area simply lost a breeding year, returning the next to carry on where they had left off.

There is, however, a feeling that human activities worldwide, such as the influence of pollution on global warming and ozone depletion, is altering the natural El Niño cycle. The effects of El Niño seem to be more prolonged, and wildlife populations along South America's Pacific coast are not bouncing back as they once did. Some scientists are even speculating whether the seabird spectacle of Paracas will ever be seen again.

At this point on its northward journey, the Humboldt Current is deflected to the northwest by the bulge of Peru, and instead of hugging the coast it peels off into the big blue. New species of marine creatures appear. As the bull sperm whales continue on their migration and follow the current, they are accompanied by bottlenose dolphins and large shoals of pelagic fish. Green turtles appear, and the startling presence of a lizard swimming in the sea reveals the current's next and final landfall – Galápagos.

The Galápagos Archipelago is a collection of volcanic islands in the Pacific Ocean about 625 miles (1000 kilometers) west of Ecuador. They appeared seemingly from nowhere millions of years ago, and their story is much like that of the Earth itself. They began as barren volcanic rocks, rising out of the sea. Gradually they acquired life, not from some primordial soup, as the Earth had done, but from the continents. Seeds, fruits, spores, and invertebrate eggs were blown by the wind, floated in on the sea or were carried on the feet of birds. Bird migrants were blown off course and made landfall on the emerging volcanic slopes. Large spiders, centipedes, reptiles, and land mammals, clinging to driftwood and other floating debris, wafted in on the ocean currents, and quite quickly all manner of living things established themselves and began to evolve.

Those that adapted to the desert island habitats survived, while those unable to cope with the demands of the new environments were eliminated. Gradually, plants and animals evolved which were quite different from the ones that originally colonized the new island, and this is precisely what stirred the young Charles Darwin when he visited the Galápagos Islands in 1835.

Darwin's encounters with the Galápagos finches were to change scientific thinking about the evolution of life. The finches, which had progressed from a basic seed eating, finchlike bird that probably flew in from South America, evolved into all sorts of different forms, each adapted to a different way of life. Isolation on the new islands and the specific demands of each new environment in which they found themselves gave rise to diversification and divergence. Today, there are finches that eat seeds, others that drink blood, some that catch insects, and still others that use 'tools'.

There are no woodpeckers on the Galápagos, but one finch, the aptly named woodpecker finch, has taken over the vacant niche. However, being a finch and having only recently (in evolutionary terms) found its food source, it does not have the anatomical wherewithal to exploit it. Woodpeckers have long, powerful beaks with which they hammer into wood, and a specialized tongue to dislodge wood-boring grubs. The woodpecker finch has neither. Instead, it makes a tool to do the job. It first visits a cactus and breaks off a spine. Then it takes the spine to a crack or crevice in which a beetle larva is confined and uses its special tool to winkle out the food.

On the coast, there are even more surprises – cormorants that have lost the ability to fly, penguins that live at the Equator, lava lizards that fall prey to snakes hunting on the seashore, and lizards that eat seaweed and sneeze salt. As a consequence of the isolation of the Galápagos Archipelago, about 25 percent of the species found in coastal waters are endemic – that is, they are now unique to these islands.

One such creature is the lizard that swims in the sea, the marine iguana. In the absence of mammalian predators, it has been able to live here and dominate the rocky volcanic shores. It has evolved a blunt snout for grazing on seaweed, a laterally flattened tail to help it swim, and powerful limbs with strong claws to help it cling to rocks and not be dislodged by waves. Despite its name, the Galápagos marine iguana spends 95 percent of its time on land basking in the sun.

The Galápagos Islands straddle the Equator, and yet they are bathed not only by the cold waters of the Humboldt Current but also by other cold currents, and the marine iguana loses body heat rapidly when feeding. In fact, its size and the way it retains or loses heat determines its method of feeding. Small individuals, which lose heat quickly, forage on rocks at low tide and rarely enter the sea. Larger ones graze seaweeds in the shallows, some diving to 40 feet (12 meters) to avoid the competition in the tidal zone. They can stay underwater for up to 20 minutes. For the rest of the day, they bask on traditional roosting rocks raising their body temperature to 97°F (36°C) before returning to the sea to feed. More than 2000 of them can be seen sunning themselves at Punta Espinosa on the island of Fernandina. While they sit as still as statues, the island race of Galápagos mockingbirds fly down to pick off parasites and dead sloughed skin. Mating takes place in November and December, and eggs are deposited in holes dug in February to mid-March. At this time the female iguanas of the northern islands have a distinct red tinge to their skin and become unusually aggressive, while those on the southern islands develop light green backs and brownish sides.

Occasionally, an iguana will sneeze violently. It is its way of ridding itself of excess salt. The red crabs that share the rocks with them and often climb all over them are not disturbed by the repeated spraying of salt. Nearby, four-eyed blennies are carried ashore by waves and make an amphibious search of the rocks for small crabs and insects. They can be out of the water for up to two hours and will travel 100 feet (30 meters) or more from the sea.

Below the waterline is a rich mix of marine life – Galápagos sea lions and fur seals, flightless cormorants, and even a penguin – all animals more usually associated with higher latitudes but living on the Equator.

GALÁPAGOS ISLANDS

The Galápagos Archipelago is a very special place, not only for the scientist keen to work in Darwin's living laboratory, but also for the visitor who discovers a world apart, where there is still a wealth of wildlife and the animals do not run away.

There are two main seasons. The 'warm' or heavy rainy season is from December through to June, when daytime temperatures may reach the 85–100°F (30s Celsius). It is typical tropical weather, cumulus clouds forming each day and heavy rain falling. This is the time when the coast is green. The other half of the year, from July to November, is dominated by the *garua*, a mist or layer of clouds that forms over the ocean. This is an inversion layer caused when the hot sun creates a warm layer of air that traps cooler air beneath. The southeast Trades blow at this time, driving the mist onto the southern slopes of the volcanoes, so the upper parts remain wet for many months. The heavy rains can sometimes fail, but the *garua* has never failed and this keeps the highlands green. Even though this is also known as the 'cold' or dry season, the highlands receive more moisture than in the so-called wet season. Skies are cloudier and daytime temperatures slightly lower, in the middle to 70–85°F (high 20s Celsius).

On all the islands, lowland areas are covered with arid scrub, but the larger islands have high volcanoes with slopes that can be divided into distinct vegetation zones. There are mangroves on the coast, cacti and spiny bushes in the arid coastal zone, taller cacti and trees in the transitional zone above 330 feet (100 meters), the *Scalesia* forest in the humid zone, and the fern-sedge zone where the tallest plants are tree ferns. The highest volcanoes have prickly pear cactus at their peaks, since they are above the moist cloud layer. The *Scalesia* forests grow in damp, slippery clay, on uplands where a light, misty rain falls all year round. The trees are native to the Galápagos and have slender, straight trunks that burst into a crown about 33–50 feet (10–15 meters) above the ground. They are surrounded by a luxuriant growth of ferns and mosses.

Each island has its own character, and the same species of animal can be quite distinctive on different islands, a feature noticed by Darwin. Older islands are in the eastern part of the archipelago and the younger ones in the west. Their modern Ecuadorian names have replaced English names given to them at the time of the buccaneers.

Española or Hood Island is flat and without a volcanic crater. On its northeastern shore the magnificent beach at Gardner Bay plays host to sea lions and is a nesting site for green sea turtles. The two sites are about 5 miles (8 kilometers) apart. From here, a trail leads past the large waved albatross colonies to Punta Suárez on the western tip of the island, where a spectacular blow-hole squirts spray 100 feet (30 meters) into the air when a large swell is running. Waved albatrosses are present for most of the year except late January to late March. The coastal rocks are littered with marine iguanas and lava lizards, while the cliffs and sand or pebble beaches are packed with seabirds. There are also Galápagos doves, Galápagos hawks and the unusually bold Hood mockingbird.

Floreana or Charles Island is known for its Post Office Barrel, established by British whalers in about 1793 to send and receive letters from the British Isles: the tradition is continued by visiting yacht crews to this day. Visitors landing at Punta Cormorant find volcanic sand with a greenish tinge, but after walking along a short trail they'll find a

▶

Galápagos giant tortoises. They congregate in traditional mating sites on the floor of an ancient volcano during the rainy season. The females deposit their eggs on the lower slopes in the arid zone.

beach of fine white sand formed from crushed coral skeletons. Here, green sea turtles haul out to deposit their eggs. Between the two beaches, a salt lagoon attracts flamingoes, pintail ducks, and stilts. Nearby, an eroded volcanic cone called the Devil's Crown is a spectacular snorkeling and diving site and a popular roosting site for boobies, pelicans, and frigate birds. Its rocky crevices are nest sites for red-billed tropic birds.

San Cristóbal or Chatham Island has the region's capital, Puerto Baquerizo Moreno. A short bus ride past highland farms brings the visitor to El Junco, the only freshwater lake in the islands. Offshore, the flanks of an ancient tuff cone, known as Kicker Rock or Leon Dormido, is covered with roosting and nesting seabirds. At night two species of bats – the hoary bat and a local relative of the red bat – may be spotted hunting insects. They roost in the same bushes each day and may also be seen on larger islands such as Santa Cruz.

Santa Fé or Barrington Island and South Plaza islands have forests of treelike *Opuntia* cacti that provide shade and fruit for land iguanas. The smooth rocks of South Plaza are littered with about a thousand sea lions, while the cliffs offer nesting sites for tropic birds, shearwaters, and the swallow-tailed gull. The island changes color with the seasons. During the rainy season, the red *Sesuvium*, one of the *Mesembryanthemum* family, with a jointed succulent stem and tubular flowers, turns green, and the leaf-succulent *Portulaca* produces large yellow flowers which are eaten by the iguanas. South Plaza is very popular with visitors because of its easy access.

Santa Cruz or Indefatigable Island is home not only to the Charles Darwin Research Station but also to 10,000 people, the largest population in the islands. A walk from Academy Bay, through candelabra cacti,

prickly pears, and *Cryptocarpus* scrub, offers views of a cross-section of Galápagos birdlife. Yellow warblers and great blue herons even enter houses in the village in search of food. A bus ride into the highlands takes you to a reserve containing the giant tortoises or *galápagos* that give the islands their name. In the forests of slender *Scalesia* trees, geological features include giant lava tubes and two deep volcanic craters called Los Gemelos, meaning "the twins". Black Turtle Beach, on the north side of the island and accessible only by sea, has an extensive mangrove lagoon where there are sea turtles, brightly colored fish, rays, and small sharks.

On the open areas of Seymour Island, the dance of the blue-footed booby can be seen during the nesting season, and there are many magnificent frigate-birds.

The black sand beach at James Bay is a focus for visitors to James or Santiago Island. It is at the western end, where a trail along the coast passes marine iguanas basking on the rocks and sea lions lazing in tidal pools. The trail ends with a series of sea caves, deep inlets, and grottoes that are home to fur seals. At Buccaneer Cove, to the north, Galápagos martins sweep past cliffs and dark beaches, but the area has been invaded by feral goats. At Sullivan Bay, on the east coast, an area of ropey lava (so named because it resembles twisted rope) looks as fresh as it did when it flowed from an eruption in 1897.

The summit of Bartólome or Bartholomew Island offers visitors a breathtaking view of the archipelago, and at the base of a rocky pinnacle, known appropriately as Pinnacle Rock, there is a small colony of Galápagos penguins or *pingüinos*. Its yellow sand beaches are fringed by mangroves.

Rábida or Jervis Island is quite different, with its reddish cliffs, beaches, and volcanic cinder slopes. Behind a strip of green salt bush a hidden salt lagoon occasionally has nesting greater flamingoes.

There are two landing places and two trails on Genovesa or Tower Island. The first is a sandy beach at Darwin Bay, at the foot of rocky crater walls within the island's breached caldera. Thousands of great frigate birds, red-footed boobies, swallow-tailed gulls, and storm petrels nest here. The peak of frigate-bird activity is between March and June. On the shore, the trail leads away from the coral beach and runs past a series of tidal lagoons with lava gulls and yellow-crowned night herons and on to a clifftop where sea birds can be seen soaring in the updrafts.

A second trail leads from another landing at the base of cliffs. It passes through the typical brush vegetation of the island, where red-footed boobies nest in trees, and on to a cliff face where short-eared owls can be spotted during the day, hunting the thousands of wedge-rumped storm petrels that nest here.

Fernandina or Narborough Island lies on the western-most edge of the archipelago. It is the youngest of the islands and has the most active volcano, which erupts every three or four years. It is also the most pristine, with no signs yet of any animals introduced by people. Flightless cormorants and Galápagos penguins nest on the flat lava, and there are large groups of marine iguanas and blue-footed boobies.

Isabela, or Arbemarle, is the largest of the islands, made up of six volcanoes connected by extensive lava flows. A two-day trek up the Alcedo volcano will take you to one of the few remaining populations of wild tortoises. although at the time of writing the area is closed because of a goat control program.

On the southern coast, the settlement at Villamil is surrounded by the best sites in the entire archipelago – salt and brackish lagoon, rocky, and muddy shores, and long sandy beaches – for waterbirds, including many migrants.

The Galápagos National Park has drawn up a code of conduct for visitors. You are asked to keep to marked paths and not touch, feed, or disturb the animals. Clothing should be checked for seeds or insects before landing at or leaving an island, and no food should be taken to uninhabited islands in case a seed, for example from an orange, happens to germinate and grow. Visitors have to be accompanied by a licensed National Park guide.

In the cool, fish-rich water the birds and mammals are in their element, but when they are on land they have a heating problem. Compact size is one way of reducing the risk of overheating. This explains why the Galápagos fur seal is the smallest marine mammal in the world, and the Galápagos penguin the second smallest penguin. An example of Bergmann's Law, closely related animals tend to be smaller in tropical environments. It is significant, perhaps, that the emperor penguin is the largest penguin, and it lives close to the South Pole, whereas the Galápagos penguin is one of the smallest and it lives on the Equator (the exception to the rule is the flightless cormorant, which is somewhat larger than its higher-latitude relatives). The sea lions show other adaptations. They stay in the water during the heat of the day, hunt mainly by day, and sometimes mate in shallow water in places where rocks, sand, or shingle support their bodies.

The flightless cormorant has taken its family's ability to pursue fish underwater to such an extreme that it has lost the ability to fly at all. Unlike a penguin or steamer duck, it does not use its degenerate wings to flap, but holds them against its sides, employing its paddlelike feet, set well back on the body, to propel itself along. It steers with its body and feet. The loose-fitting feathers on its wings are thoroughly soaked by the end of a fishing trip. So, when a cormorant leaves the water, it stands in the sun with its wings outstretched, waiting for them to dry.

Nesting pairs have another curious habit. Every time parent birds change incubation or brooding shifts, they greet each other in a most courteous manner. The returning bird calls from the water and is answered by its mate on the nest. As it leaves the water it picks up a tuft of seaweed or a yellow sea star and, bowing deeply, presents the gift to its mate as if it were offering a bouquet of flowers or a box of chocolates. The partner receives the gift and lays it gently at the edge of the nest. After drying its wings in the traditional way, the returning partner picks up a small stick and again presents it to the bird on the nest. It is duly received and placed at the nest edge, and the two birds change places. The other parent makes for the sea, while the newly arrived one takes over brooding duties.

Nests can be made of different materials, some pairs preferring seaweeds while others collect sticks, sea urchin tests, bones, and pieces of string or rope. After El Niño events, there is a shortage of large seaweeds, and so bones are the most commonly used nest materials.

Nesting on the southerly and westerly islands of the archipelago, alongside the flightless cormorants and other seabirds, are the Galápagos penguins. They nest all year round, with a peak in activity in the latter half of the year. Eggs are deposited in nothing more than hollows in cracks and crevices, some of which are not more that 3 feet (1 meter) above the high-water mark.

There is an albatross here, too. Hood Island is home to the waved albatross. Most of the world's population breeds in a single colony here, arriving in late March and early April. Unlike many of the other seabirds, it is a seasonal breeder, its reproductive habits probably linked to seasonal changes in its food supply. It is also influenced by the strength of the wind. January and February, for instance, are the doldrum months and an albatross would find it difficult to get airborne at this time. Like all albatrosses it forages far and wide, and when not involved in reproduction it journeys hundreds of miles to the south and east to the Peruvian coast. Swallow-tailed gulls make a similar migration.

Hood is also host to a large population of masked boobies, tropical relatives of the gannet. These birds nest at the same time every year, but the breeding season varies on different islands, so masked boobies are breeding somewhere in the archipelago almost every month of the year. The nest is the site of cold-blooded murder. Two chicks hatch several days apart and the older sibling will evict the younger one. The displaced bird will either die from exposure or fall victim to gulls or frigate birds. In this way the older bird can acquire all the food.

On the island of Española, masked booby chicks are occasionally injured by delinquent males that have not acquired partners and try to mate with them. The youngsters' wounds are not allowed to heal; they are kept open by the local race of mockingbird. As well as divesting animals of parasites and dead skin, this bird has turned to drinking blood. Any booby chick with an open wound is harassed mercilessly. The mockingbird keeps the blood flowing and returns periodically to drink its fill.

On remote Wolf Island, the sharp-beaked ground finch torments adult masked

▶
Marine iguanas basking in the sun. Every so often, one will sneeze salt from its nostrils. The brightly colored crabs are Sally Lightfoots, which cling to the slippery wave-washed rocks as they scrape off algae for food.

boobies. Pecking at the base of their tail and wing feathers and, breaking the skin, it draws blood. It is thought that this technique evolved from a time when the smaller bird fed on parasitic flies and lice. While pecking at the blood-sucking lice it developed a liking for the blood itself. And if that is not enough, the ground finch breaks into abandoned masked booby eggs and extracts the contents. It is too weak to pierce the egg's shell, so it presses its beak against a rock to give it some leverage, and kicks the shell against a rock opposite until it cracks. Some ornithologists refer to the bird as the 'vampire finch'.

While vampires and scenes from murder mysteries and horror movies play out on some islands, elsewhere birds get on with breeding and feeding. Penguins drive the fish into the shallows, while brown pelicans plunge their cavernous bills into the herd of fish that their penguin 'sheepdogs' have corraled. They catch a local brand of *anchoveta* as well as thread fish, grunts, and juvenile pelagic or reef fish. Penguins and larger predatory fish attack writhing balls of bait fish from below, while boobies dive on them from above. The highly maneuvrable frigate-birds behave like aerial pirates, chasing and mugging boobies and forcing them to regurgitate their catch, which the frigate-birds then steal.

Despite their reputation as hijackers, frigate-birds are actually adept flyers and competent hunters. They swoop low over the sea's surface, grabbing flying fish and plucking squid and fish from the surface. Such is the uncertainty of success that they can be away from the nest for two or more weeks at a time in search of food.

On Galápagos, they court and nest in low scrub behind the rocky shore. The male great frigate-bird inflates a huge, bright red, balloonlike throat pouch which attracts the female. As the pair meet they exchange calls that sound like laughter from a haunted house. The male then produces a rattling sound from his throat and wags his bill from side to side. The main egg-laying period on Tower Island appears to be in the first quarter of the year, although eggs can be found in nests up until September. Another species, the magnificent frigate-bird, nests here all year round.

The Galápagos have the world's largest colony of red-footed boobies, and about 30 percent of blue-footed boobies. Blue-footed boobies are known for their comical stiff-legged dance during which they draw each other's attention to their large, blue feet. Both sexes dance, males more exuberantly than females.

With so much ocean and so little land out here, the islands are beacons, meeting places and refuges in the Pacific Ocean. Migrant birds, such as terns and waders, traveling to and from South and North America, drop in to rest and refuel, some staying for the duration of the northern winter. Activity is not only above the waves but also below.

Offshore, huge meandering schools of scalloped hammerhead sharks, surrounded by blue and yellow surgeon fish, congregate every day. Each morning, they gather in great schools that swim apparently aimlessly up and down for the rest of the day, not feeding despite the abundance of food. The schools contain mainly females, the largest sharks in the center and the smaller ones wrapped around the outside. They maintain their positions in the school by bullying their neighbors, communicating in a crude form of body language.

▶
Vampire finch. A pair of masked boobies is attacked mercilessly by this aptly named bird, otherwise known as the sharp-billed ground finch. The finch once focused its attention on blood-sucking parasites hidden among the birds' plumage, but now it breaks the quills at the base of the birds' tail feathers and feeds on blood as well.

They twist, somersault, and perform 'corkscrew' dances that might end with a larger shark biting a smaller one on the back of the neck.

In the evening, the school breaks up and each shark goes its own way to hunt. Using electromagnetic sensors in its snout, it appears to follow magnetic highways on the seabed – ancient lava flows that spread out like the spokes of a wheel from each volcanic island – to traditional feeding sites some distance away.

During the night, small groups of manta rays take their place. Each ray swoops in, turning somersaults as it feeds on the plankton swarming at the surface. Food is channeled into its mouth with the aid of paddle-shaped cephalic fins or horns on either side of its head.

Inshore by day, spectacular schools of 70 or more golden rays, each 2–3 feet (60–90 centimeters) across, brush the undersurface of the sea as they feed on plankton in the shade of a cliff. On the seabed at James Bay, red-mouthed bat fish hop along the bottom, pursued by young sea lions that play with them like toys.

On land, the most extraordinary resident is the creature that gave the islands their name – the *Galápagos* or giant tortoise. The largest numbers can be seen on Isabela Island in February. After the rains, their guttural groans can be heard emanating from a volcanic crater where they congregate to mate. They clamber determinedly up the volcano's higher

◀

Patrolling school of mostly female hammerhead sharks accompanied by surgeon fish. The school forms during the day but splits up at night when each shark goes its own way to hunt.

slopes, and for creatures that normally sleep for 16 hours a day and move very little, the climb is quite a challenge.

Nevertheless, the tortoises arrive in the rain soaked crater, the 450-pound (200-kilogram) males looking for a receptive female. When a likely candidate is found, the male bumps the female with his shell and nips at her legs. Eventually, she gives in and he rather clumsily mounts her, the union helped by his concave underside. Eggs are laid in June on the sunny lower slopes. The female digs a hole, deposits about 10 eggs and covers them with soil. She then moistens the soil with urine, flattens it with the underside of her shell and moves off. The soil bakes in the sun to form a hard lid. About six months later, the youngsters hatch and must excavate their way out of the pit.

The shape of a tortoise's shell or carapace varies from island to island. On the drier islands, where they browse on cacti and bushes, the tortoises have arched or saddleback carapaces, while those living on the higher and damper islands, where there is plenty of ground vegetation, have rounded or dome shaped ones.

The larger tortoises, resembling huge mobile bolders over 4 feet (1.2 meters) long, have become lookout perches for juvenile Galápagos hawks. A hawk will swoop down and land on the smooth, domed shell, standing there unperturbed as its host lumbers slowly through the undergrowth.

Massive male land iguanas fight ferociously during the breeding season. Males compete for the sites most likely to be visited by females, and each one defends his patch rigorously. If an intruder should venture too close, the resident male nods his head in warning. If the challenger fails to back down, the lizards come to blows, each trying to grab the other's mouth or snout. When first blood is drawn, they back off, the resident either deposed or venerated.

Despite the presence of these unique plants and animals, the Galápagos Islands have a surprisingly low diversity compared to the mainland. There are, for example, just 500 native plant species present, whereas there are over 10,000 in Ecuador, 625 miles (1000 kilometers) to the east. The islands are young, geologically speaking, having risen over a volcanically active hot spot in the Earth's crust between 3 and 5 million years ago. They are still being formed, the most recent islands currently lying over the hot spot and the older, submerged ones having been transported away to the east by continental drift. The normally arid climate is slow to break down the volcanic rocks and slow to be colonized by plants – Fernandina, the youngest of the islands, has only about 10 percent of its surface cloaked with vegetation. There are few habitats to colonize, so the coastline is generally bleak and rocky.

The newness of Galápagos also reduces the number of times wayward plants and animals might have chanced upon the islands. It has been estimated that only a few hundred migrations have taken place since the islands were formed. About 400 arrivals are thought to have given rise to the present flora, meaning that one species is established every 12,000 years or so.

Golden or mustard rays. These are the smallest members of the cow-nose ray family, with a 'wingspan' of up to 60 centimeters (2 feet). They feed on molluscs in near-shore waters and lagoons.

There has been, however, an evolutionary conundrum in the Galápagos. While the land-based finches, and many of the plants could have evolved into their present forms in a relatively short period of geological time (it has been determined that the finches could have developed in less than a million years). The same cannot be said for the marine and land iguanas. In order to evolve into their present forms, they would have had to arrive in Galápagos about 15 million years ago. The islands, however, are less than 5 million years old.

The answer to the dilemma was discovered in 1992, when a sea floor survey by researchers from Oregon State University chanced upon features on the seabed to the east of the present archipelago. They found seamounts – underwater mountains – with signs of wave erosion, such as rounded pebbles and wave cut terraces, suggesting that these were drowned volcanic islands. It must have been to these islands that a common form of iguana somehow rafted in from mainland South America.

The mix of waters around the Galápagos is a far cry from the kelp forests and southern fjords. Here, the trade winds that dragged the Humboldt Current northwards and westwards give way to the balmy, eddying Doldrums – the Intertropical Convergence Zone where the Humboldt begins to lose its power.

It is also journey's end for the bull sperm whales. They come here to breed. Some individuals will have made this epic journey between the Southern Ocean and the Galápagos Islands 40 or 50 times before, usually traveling alone. The females and their calves remain in the tropics and subtropics throughout the year. They live in herds, each group led by an old matriarch, and they are joined by the bulls during the southern winter.

The males are not the gentle giants that we once thought whales to be. They fight violently for the right to escort a bevy of females, head-butting and rasping their prominent teeth along their opponents' bodies in order to be top whale. The bulls might remain with a group for a few hours, or a day at the most, and then move on to other groups.

For the bulls and their newly acquired but temporary families, Galápagos marks a new beginning, but for the Humboldt Current, which they have followed unerringly northward, it is the end of the line. At the northwestern corner of the archipelago a natural arch of rock, known appropriately as Darwin's Arch, marks its limit.

It is also the most northerly point along the South American coast reached by the *Beagle* before it took Charles Darwin on to Fiji, New Zealand, and Australia all those years ago. His observations on the wildlife of the Pacific coast of South America, especially on Galápagos, were to revolutionize our understanding of the world in which we live. Today the discoveries being made here continue to throw light not only on how our planet works, but also on how we are treating it.

▶

Galápagos land iguana on the rim of the active, 3300-feet-deep (1000-meters) caldera on Fernandina Island in the Galápagos Archipelago. The volcano is a basaltic shield volcano shaped like a turtle's back. It erupted violently in 1995.

GAZETTEER

South America is a land of extremes. Stunning extremes of habitat, extraordinary extremes of animals, and fascinating extremes of culture. But not all extremes are quite so welcome to the eco-tourist – there are extremes of climate, making choosing what to take a difficult task; extremes of infrastructure, meaning that in some countries traveling by road is not an option; extremes of service, since many countries are only getting their first tourists; and extremes of safety that are worth bearing in mind. Yet if South America was as easy to travel in as Europe or the USA, much of its charm would be lost.

WHERE TO GO?

Each country has its appeal, so deciding where to go is a tough decision. Bear in mind how much time you have. It is impossible to do justice to Brazil in even three weeks, whereas you could race around Uruguay in half that time. This gazetteer, which has drawn advice from a great many well-traveled sources, including the team that brought you *Wild South America*, is aimed at helping the internet-using eco-tourist decide where to go. Yet what exactly is eco-tourism? On the surface it may appear easy – tourism that conserves the natural environment while enlightening visitors. However, the reality is not as clear-cut. For instance, is a lodge that destroys 1.5 sq. miles (400 hectares) of primary rainforest during the construction of its buildings and walkways, but then preserves everything within its borders, ecologically friendly? And what if it recycles a proportion of its profits back into the indigenous communities? It's a tough call.

Douglas Trent, who runs Focus Tours (a company that every eco-tourism business should try to emulate), recommends that as a concerned tourist you should ask a company why it considers itself to be an eco-tour business. If their answer includes details such as a portion of the profits going into conservation projects, waste recycling, and to carrying out scientific research, then you have likely hit upon an eco-friendly lodge.

In making your choice, consider asking the following questions:

▶ **Who are your guides, and what are their qualifications?** Look for professional naturalist qualifications, rather than assuming that someone who has lived in the area all their life will know the natural history of the region. Many national guides have degrees in tourism rather than biology.

▶ **What equipment do your guides use?** Binoculars will be used by all professional guides. Binoculars will allow you to see animals well. Spotlights are necessary for night and twilight wildlife viewing. Appropriate bird and mammal field guides should be on hand. Check that your guide will carry a first-aid kit.

▶ **What equipment is available to visitors?** Very good businesses should provide visitors with equipment that is not too bulky to carry, including rubber boots, water bottles, camera tripods, and guidebooks.

▶ **What on-the-ground travel companies are booked by the major tour operators?** Travel companies have had much time to evaluate eco-tourism destinations. If an established operator is not used by any big tour companies there must be a reason.

▶ **Is there a bird and mammal checklist for the area?** There should be a tour checklist already prepared with English and Latin names.

Always keep a reserve location in mind. Also check on the exact location of the lodge you are planning to visit. For instance, in the rainforest, the further you travel from the nearest significant town the better (3 hours by boat is not considered far!).

Ecotour.org has already asked many companies these questions and via its website you can locate eco-friendly lodges all over the world, including every South American country. See: http://www.ecotour.org/service/service.htm. Both the *World Eco-tourism Directory* at http://www.green-travel.com/GTECOLIN.HTM#SOUTH or *Exploring Eco-tourism in the Americas* at http://www.greenbuilder.com/mader/ecotravel/etour.html offer similar advice. Http://www.planeta.com is useful for eco-travel in South America. Conservation International is also involved in eco-tourism. Together with indigenous communities it has set up several lodges in prime locations in desperate need of conservation. To learn more about its work, visit, http://www.conservation.org.

TOUR GROUPS

Many people visit South America as part of a tour group. This takes the hassle out of traveling and most companies visit some of the most eco-friendly sites, since their reputation and future custom depend on it. Before booking, determine what you want to get out of your trip. For some people the mere atmosphere of walking and sleeping in Amazonia, away from the city lights, is very special, while others will have a checklist of animals they want to see. For the wildlife enthusiast, the more places you visit that are mentioned in this gazetteer, the better. The best tour companies for South America include:

Explore Worldwide – http://www.explore.co.uk
Travelbag – http://www.travelbag-adventures.co.uk
Trips Worldwide – http://www.tripsworldwide.co.uk
Exodus – http://www.exodus.co.uk
Journey Latin America – http://www.journeylatinamerica.co.uk/
Earthwise Journeys for Women – http://www.teleport.com/~earthwyz/women.htm

*Guerb*a – http://www.guerba.co.uk
GAP – http://www.gap.ca/world/br_01_it.htm
OAT – http://oattravel.com
Dragoman – http://www.peregrine.net.au
Encounter Overland – http://www.encounter.co.uk
Nature Trek – http://www.naturetrek.co.uk
Wildland Adventures – http://www.wildland.com
Exito – http://www.wonderlink.com/exito

The following will organize tailor-made trips:

Focus Tours – http://www.focustours.com
Last Frontiers – http://www.lastfrontiers.co.uk
Hayes & Jarvis – http://www.TravelEShop.com/holidays/limh.shtml
Ladatco Tours – http://www.ladatco.com
South American Experience – sax@mcmail.com

For the completely independent traveler, it is worth bearing in mind that many South American owned businesses change hands frequently. Not only the contact details but also the level of service may alter. You should confirm how long a company has been established.

WHAT TO TAKE?

Since South America is a land of extremes, packing is tricky. Essentials for all destinations are sunglasses, sunscreen, hat, water bottle, and purifiers, rain gear, and walking shoes or shoes that you do not mind getting ruined. Photographers should take a range of film speeds from 50ASA for the saltpans and Andes to 400 or even 800ASA for the rainforest. It is very hard to take good pictures in the rainforest – it is dark, your lens will steam over, and animals are quick. Manual focus SLRs rarely capture things well. Many people take portable tape-recorders or mini-discs to record the buzz of the cicadas, the screech of macaws, the wolf whistles of screaming pihas, and the splashing of the rains. Of

Laguna Verde, a turquoise jewel amid the stark black and white peaks and volcanoes of the Bolivian Andes.

course, camcorders will do this too.

WHAT TO EXPECT?

It is worth remembering two things. First, this is not Africa. There are no vast plains with herds of animals that you are virtually guaranteed to see (other than Brazil's Pantanal). You could go to the most diverse rainforest in the world and see very few mammals. Second, do not expect to see everything that you have seen in the BBC series. *Wild South America* was over 3 years in the making. Camera crews stayed for 8 weeks at places that you may visit for 4 days. Nevertheless, if you go to the right places at the right time, you should see some amazing things.

THE REST

Prior to departure, check out the Latin American Travel Advisor,

which contains detailed information about current scams, safety, health, weather, economics, and politics. See http://www.amerispan.com/latc/

Much of South America is at altitudes of over 10,000 feet (3000 metres), which means that you will be affected by altitude sickness, the symptoms of which should not be ignored. It is essential that you plan to take time off to acclimatize. For symptoms and solutions to altitude sickness see '*Altitude Info*' on http://hypoxia.uchsc.edu:8080/

Malaria is common in the Amazon delta, so start taking antimalarial medication two weeks before you enter the area (and continue until the end of the recommended course – even if that is six weeks after your return). Mosquitoes are particularly problematic in the rainy season, so always use insect

repellent and carry your own mosquito net.

As well as web and e-mail addresses, some telephone and fax numbers are quoted in this gazetteer (all addresses are correct at time of publication). The international dialling codes for South American countries are:

Argentina	++54
Bolivia	++591
Brazil	++55
Chile	++56
Colombia	++57
Ecuador	++593
French Guiana	++594
Guyana	++592
Paraguay	++595
Peru	++51
Suriname	++597
Uruguay	++598
Venezuela	++58

FURTHER READING

Guidebooks such as *Lonely Planet*, *Footprints Handbooks* and *Bradt Guides* will tell you about all the non-eco-attractions as well as tips on where to stay and how to get there. In addition, to get more out of your trip, it may be worth reading a selection of the following excellent books:
Amazon Insects – A Photo Guide by James L. Castner, Feline Press, Florida 2000
The Amazon Rainforest: An Exploration of Countries, Cultures & Creatures by James L. Castner, Feline Press
The Annotated Lost World by Sir Arthur Conan Doyle, Gasogene Books, Dubuque, USA, 1996
Beneath the Canopy: Wildlife of the Latin American Rain Forest by Kevin Schafer (photographer) & Downs Matthews, Chronicle Books, San Francisco, 1999
A Field Guide to the Families and Genera of Woody Plants of Northwest South America (Colombia, Ecuador, Peru), with supplementary notes by Alwyn H. Gentry & Adrian G. Foryth, Chicago University Press, Chicago 1993
A Guide to the Birds and Mammals of Coastal Patagonia by Graham Harris (illustrator) & William Conway, Princeton University Press
A Guide to the Birds of Colombia by Steven L. Hilty & William L. Brown, Princeton University Press,

Princeton, 1996
Insight Guides Amazon Wildlife, Langenscheidt Publishers, New York, 1998
Mammals of the Neotropics: The Northern Neotropics: Panama, Columbia, Venezuela, Guyana, Suriname, French Guiana by John F. Eisenberg & Sigrid J. Bonner (illustrator), University of Chicago Press, Chicago 1989
Mammals of the Neotropics: The Southern Cone, Chile, Argentina, Uruguay, Paraguay by Kent H. Redford & John F. Eisenberg (contributor), University of Chicago Press, Chicago, 1992
A Neotropical Companion: An Introduction to the Animals, Plants, and Ecosystems of the New World Tropics by John C. Kricher & Mark Plotkin. Princeton University Press, Princeton, 1997
Neotropical Rainforest Mammals: A Field Guide by Louise H. Emmons & François Feer (illustrator), University of Chicago Press, Chicago 1989
Tropical Nature by Adrian Forsyth, Kenneth Miyata & Sarah Landry (illustrator), Prentice-Hall, Old Tappen, 1984
The Tropical Rain Forest: An Ecological Study by Paul W. Richards, R. P. D. Walsh, I. C. Baillie & P. Greig-Smith, Cambridge University Press, Cambridge, 1996
Where to Watch Birds in South America by Nigel Wheatley, Princeton University Press, Princeton, 1994

ACKNOWLEDGEMENTS

This gazetteer could not have been accomplished without the help of many highly experienced people who could recommend tour companies, suggest places we had neglected to include, and correct draft manuscripts. Any mistakes are entirely our own. We would like to thank: David Bonnardeau, Rob Clay of Guyra Paraguay, Richard Day, Andy Drumm of Tropic Ecological Adventures, Oliver Hillel of Conservation International, Rob Pople, and Douglas Trent of Focus Tours.

ARGENTINA

South America's second-largest country. The geography varies tremendously and covers a great variety of different habitats with a huge diversity of flora and fauna. The climate ranges from subtropical in the northeast, to cold temperate in Tierra del Fuego. Summer (November–February) is the best time to visit the south, although the autumn colors in late April are spectacular in the Lake District.

TOP WEBSITES

There is much useful information about Argentina on the internet. Try

The Leisure Planet Travel Guide – http://leisureplanet.com/TravelGuides/
The Buenos Aires Herald – http://www.buenosairesherald.com/
Official Argentine Tourism Site – http://www.sectur.gov.ar/g/menu.htm
Travel Notes for Argentina – http://www.travelnotes.org/LatinAmerica/Argentina/
Latin American Escapes – http://www.latinamericanescapes.com/
Eco Travels in Argentina – http://www.greenbuilder.com/mader/ecotravel/south/argentina/argentina1.html
Weather Underground: Argentina – http://www.wunderground.com/cgi-bin/findweather/getForecast?query=Argentina

TOURS

Argentina has enough tour companies to suit every traveler. These are the most consistently recommended, but there are many more, so shop around.
Equitours – http://www.ridingtours.com/argentina.htm

Sunny Land Tours – http://www.sunny-land-tours.com/latamer/argentin.htm
Tucano Tours – http://www.tucano.com.ar/
Databay Travel – http://www.databay.com/escorted/South_American_Tours/
Argentina Tours – http://www.inkas.com/argentina_tours/00_argentina_tours.html
Austral Tours – http://www.australtours.com/argentin.html
Zeus Tours – http://www.dontcryforme.com/index.html
Jungle Jensen Nature Tours – http://www.mother.com/junglejensen/argentina_bird.html
Andes Tours – http://www.andestours.com/argentina.htm
Hotels and Travel in Argentina – http://www.hotelstravel.com/argentina.html
Path tours – http://www.pathtours.com/
Speciality Travel – http://www.specialtytravel.com/destinations/frames.html

Argentina's Best

THE ANDES

The Andes run the length of Argentina, forming a natural border with Chile to the west and descending into the South Atlantic in the south. The highest and most visited peak is Aconcagua, but there are many fascinating regions where fewer people visit and wildlife is plentiful. Some of the most beautiful are mentioned below.

1. Parque Nacional El Rey

Three parks protect the strip of subtropical montane forest that extends from the border with Bolivia almost to the Catamarca province in the south. Habitats range from cloudforest to semi-desert, providing ample niches for an abundance of wildlife (particularly insects). Famous for endangered and threatened animals, including pumas, spider monkeys, and little spotted cats. Parque Nacional Baritú in the north is equally impressive but accessible only through Bolivia.

Getting there: No public transport, though group tours can be arranged from Salta. Road to the entrance passable in the dry season (June–September). Basic campsite and one hostel (closed in 1999 but may now be open again). See http://www.tecomnet.com.ar/altasierra/elrey/rey2.html for further information.

2. Parque Nacional Calilegua

Also protecting the area of peaks and subtropical valleys found in northwestern Argentina, this park is famous for its unusual birdlife. Species include the rare red-faced guan and the black and chestnut eagle. Best place for birdwatching is the northern boundary. Tracks of tapir, puma, and Andean deer are all seen regularly.

Getting there: A truck runs from Ledesma, a small town 30 miles (50km) north of San Pedro (Chile), early on Tuesday and Thursday, returning on Thursday and Sunday. Camping facilities in the park. Take warm clothes and plenty of insect repellent. Accommodation in Ledesma is basic and can be busy.

3. Parque Nacional Talampaya

This and Ischigualasto in northwestern Argentina are renowned for their amazing lunar landscapes, characterized by spectacular rock formations with overhanging ledges and deep canyons. The area is so dry that the only wildlife you are likely to see during the day are raptors such as condors and turkey vultures.

Getting there: Private vehicles may not be used in the park. Tours from San Juan and San Agustín; some include accommodation in Pagancillo. Otherwise, there are reasonable hotels in San Juan or

KEY TO MAP

1 Parque Nacional El Rey
2 Parque Nacional Calilegua
3 Parque Nacional Talampaya
4 Parque Nacional Lanín
5 Parque Nacional Chaco
6 Iguazú Falls
7 The Iberá Marshes
8 Parque Nacional El Palmar
9 Parque Nacional Lihué Calel
10 Parque Nacional Los Glaciares
11 Parque Nacional Nahuel Huapi
12 Península Valdés
13 Punta Tombo
14 Reserva Natural Ría Deseado
15 Aconcagua
16 Parque Nacional Baritú
17 Parque Nacional Ischigualasto
18 Ushuaia in Tierra del Fuego

0   500km

San Agustín. No accommodation in the park itself. For tours, try:

Eco-Tourism – http://www.wam. com.ar/tourism/agencias/foxtour/ eco/g/eco.htm
Equestrian Safaris – http://www.safaririding.com/ argentina.html

4. Parque Nacional Lanín
Running along the Chilean border and extending 100 miles (150km) from Lago Norquinco in the north to Parque Nacional Nahuel Huapi in the south. Created in 1937, the park protects beautiful lakes, wooded valleys, and the extinct Lanín volcano. Ancient forests made up of southern beech, lenga, coihue, and fantastic monkey puzzle trees.

Getting there: Regular buses from San Martín to Lago Huechulafquen and Lago Lolog. Good campsites in the park and hotels in San Martín.

THE NORTHEASTERN PLAINS

5. Parque Nacional Chaco
Northeastern Argentina comprises a vast alluvial lowland covered in thorny scrub and palm savannah. This is the Gran Chaco. It can neatly be divided into two parts – the Humid Chaco in the east where rainfall is high, and the Arid Chaco in the west, where irrigation is necessary for livestock. Parque Nacional Chaco protects a small corner of the Humid Chaco as well as some different habitat ranging from marsh and palm savannah to denser gallery forest. Notable trees are axe-breaker, algarrobo, and lapacho, which can reach over 70ft (20m). Birds commonly seen on the open savannah include rhea, roseate spoonbill, and jabiru stork.

Getting there: Buses several times a day from Resistencia. Camping in the park. Nearest accommodation at Capitán Solari, 4 miles (6km) from park entrance.

6. Iguazú Falls
In the far northeast of Argentina on the border with Brazil lies this spectacular series of waterfalls, described on page 24.

Getting there: By bus from Puerto Canoas to the Devil's Throat. On the Brazilian side, by air to Foz de Iguaçu. Accommodation abundant in Puerto Iguazú, 4 miles (6km) from the falls. Nearest camping at Puerto Canoas.

7. The Iberá Marshes
Similar to the Pantanal in Brazil, a huge area of marshy wetland in the far northeast of Argentina. If you are patient you may catch a glimpse of a maned wolf, marsh deer, or broad-nosed caiman. More likely are brocket deer, capybara, and red howler monkeys.

Getting there: Bus from Mercedesto Colonia Pellegrini (the best place to view the marshes). Tours from Mercedes or Buenos Aires (including accommodation) through Estancia Capi-Vari (Tel: 03773 420180) and Posada Aguape (Tel: 0376 4929759). A few hostels and a campsite in Colonia Pellegrini.

8. Parque Nacional El Palmar
On the border with Uruguay, this park contains one of the last remaining stands of the palm savannah that once typified this region of northeastern Argentina. The yatay palm grows up to 60ft (18m) in height and can live for over 200 years. Wildlife thrives – excellent for waterbirds such as egrets, cormorants, and kingfishers. Viscachas can frequently be seen scampering across the more open grassland or hurriedly retreating into holes in the ground, and there are many fascinating plants.

Getting there: Buses from Colón every 40 minutes. Good campsite 'Los Loros' (Tel: 03447 493031). Hotels in Colón or Concordia.

THE PAMPAS

A vast, monotonous landscape of open grassland, the Pampas covers much of central Argentina and includes Buenos Aires. It can be split into the fertile humid Pampas and the arid Pampas, which relies on irrigation for much of the year. The vegetation for both consists of small bushes and grass; the only native tree to the area, the ombu, is in fact a big bush. Wildlife is focused in the wooded valleys and around the salt lakes.

Young southern elephant seal, the world's largest seal. On the Patagonian coast there are 50,000 on Peninsula Valdés alone.

9. Parque Nacional Lihué Calel
Habitats that include forested hills, extensive grasslands, and salt lakes filled with flamingoes. Other wildlife is sparse but if you are fortunate you may see guanacos, lesser rheas, crested caracara, Patagonian hares, Geoffroy's cat, and viscacha.

Getting there: Campsite in the park; nearest accommodation at Puelches, 20 miles (35km) away. Buses to the park are not regular, but a bus going to Santa Rosa will drop you off on the way past the park entrance. Tours with:
La Pampa – http://www.sectur. gov.ar/g/reg5/reg5.htm
Kallpa Tours – http://www. kallpatour.com/irc-bsas.htm

THE LAKES

10. Parque Nacional Los Glaciares
A Natural World Heritage site and one of South America's most beautiful destinations. Famous for Lago Argentino, the country's largest lake, and the spectacular 2 miles-wide (5km) Moreno Glacier, the park also includes pristine sub-Antarctic Patagonian forest and Patagonian steppe.

Beech trees, winter's bark and Guaytecas Islands cypress abound in the forests above the lakes. Above 3300ft (1000m), the landscape is largely semi-desert scattered with hardy plants such as xerophytic cushion grasses. There is an isolated population of southern Andean huemuls, an extremely rare species of deer. More commonly seen are Argentine gray fox, guanaco and hog-nosed skunk. Two interesting birds found in the park are the torrent duck and black-throated finch.

Getting there: Regular buses and tours from Río Gallegos to El Calafate (the gateway to the park). Most tours visit several attractions; all go to Moreno Glacier. Hotels and hostels in El Calafate. Book ahead in January and February, when Argentineans take their main summer holidays.

For further information, see:
The Natural World Heritage Site http://www.wcmc.org.uk/protected_ areas/data/wh/glaciare.html and *The Living Edens, Patagonia Los Glaciares* http://pbs.bilkent.edu. tr/edens/patagonia/glaciares.htm.

Patagonian gray fox. This species of fox lives on the plains, pampas and lower mountainous areas from Ecuador to Tierra del Fuego.

TIERRA DEL FUEGO

Teetering on the end of South America, Tierra del Fuego is divided between Chile and Argentina. For more information, see under Chile.

Getting there: Flights from most major towns (including Trelew) to Ushuaia. Alternatively fly to Punta Arenas in Chile and continue by bus. Lots of travel agencies in Ushuaia, but it is advisable to book hotels or hostels in advance.

FURTHER READING

Aconcagua: A Climbing Guide (2nd ed) by R. J. Secor & Ralph Lee Hopkins, Mountaineers Books, Seattle, 1999
Argentina: The Great Estancias by Cesar Aira, Juan Pablo Queiroz (contributor), Tomas De Elia (editor) & Bonifacio Del Carril (introduction), Rizzoli Bookstore, New York, 1995
Argentina's Lost Patrol: Armed Struggle 1969–1979 by Maria Jose Moyano, Yale University Press, London, 1995
The Cloud Forest: A Chronicle of the South American Wilderness by Peter Matthiessen, Penguin USA, New York, 1987
Evita: The Real Life of Eva Peron by Nicholas Fraser, W. W. Norton, New York, 1996
In Patagonia by Bruce Chatwin, Penguin USA, New York, 1998
Natural Patagonia: Natural Argentina & Chile by Marcelo D. Beccaceci, Pangaea Publishing, Saint Paul, USA, 1998
Wine Routes of Argentina: The Wine Grapes and Wine Makers by Augusto Foix & Richard Mayson, Wine Appreciation Guild, San Francisco, 1998

11. Parque Nacional Nahuel Huapi

Argentina's oldest and most popular park, covering an area of 2900 sq. miles (750,000 hectares). Beautiful snow-capped mountains, clear mountain rivers, and rapids, lush green valleys, and deep blue lakes. Excellent for flocks of black-neck swans, geese, and ducks.

Getting there: Bus to Bariloche from most major towns in Argentina as well as from Santiago in Chile. Plentiful accommodation.

THE COAST

12. Península Valdés

A World Heritage site because of its significance to the conservation of certain marine mammals, described on page 142 .

Getting there: Regular buses from Trelew, which is accessible by bus from most major towns in Argentina. Guided tours recommended. Plenty of companies offer wildlife tours, including whale watching. Most begin from Puerto Madryn and Puerto Pirámidese, both of which have hotels and campsites.

International Expeditions –
http://www.ietravel.com/destsouthpatahome.html

Peninsula Valdes Tour –
http://www.facomar.com.ar/valdez.htm

13. Punta Tombo

One of the most important areas for birds on the Patagonian coast and home to the largest colony of Magellanic penguins in Patagonia. Other species include the kelp gull, rock cormorant, steamer duck, blackish oystercatcher, and European oystercatcher. Efforts have been made recently by environmental groups to conserve the wildlife and natural resources of the area. For more information see:
Punta Tombo –
http://reality.sgi.com/omar/personal/viaje/pvaldes/index_e.html
The Patagonian Atlantic –
http://www.sectur.gov.ar/g/menu.htm

Getting there: Book a tour in Trelew (see 'Getting There' section for Península Valdés, above). Best time to see penguins: September–March.

Tours that can be booked before you go include:
Patagonian Reisen Brokers Eco-tours – E-mail:
ReisenBrokers@starmedia.com
Tel/Fax: 054 965 29344.
Península Valdés Tours –
http://www.travelvantage.com/arg_t_val.html

14. Reserva Natural Ría Deseado

Protects a submerged estuary that is home to thousands of Magellanic penguins and other marine birdlife. Also the breeding ground of Commerson's dolphin. The islands around Puerto Deseado are a haven for wildlife; 20 miles (30km) offshore and expensive to get to, the Isla de los Pingüinos has nesting elephant seals. Easier to visit are the nesting terns on the Isla de los Pájaros and the two species of cormorant on Banco Cormorán. Tours available through local companies, some including accommodation. Visit also the petrified forest at Monumento Natural Bosques Petrificados, produced 140 million years ago when the blast from a volcano flattened a forest of Proaraucaria and buried the fallen trees in ash.

Getting there: Buses and planes to Puerto Deseado from Comodoro Rivadavia; planes to San Julián. Puerto Deseado has a good mix of hotels and hostels. Camping available.

Southwind adventures –
http://www.southwindadventures.com/ca_patag.htm

BOLIVIA

The undiscovered delight of South America, boasting some of the best scenery and wildlife accompanied by few tourists and an incredible diversity of unspoiled habitats within a small area. Unspoiled because the government declared an 'Ecological Pause' in August 1990, since when they have organized and created 11 national parks and sanctuaries. Sadly the country's infrastructure is poor (only cities have paved roads), and reaching some of the parks is difficult. Be warned, also, that Bolivia is at high altitude – La Paz, the capital is at 11,800ft (3600m). It is essential that you plan to take the first few days to acclimatize.

TOP WEBSITES

Try the following, some of which are run by tour companies that offer a variety of hassle-free tours of the country:

Lonely Planet – Bolivia – http://www.lonelyplanet.com.au/dest/sam/bolivia.htm

My Travel Guide.com – http://www.mytravelguide.com/countries/bolivia/

Bolivia Web – http://www.boliviaweb.com/

GORP Guide to Bolivia – http://www.gorp.com/gorp/location/latamer/bolivia/basic_b.htm

Hotels and Travels in Bolivia – http://www.hotelstravel.com/bolivia.html

Travel to Bolivia – http://poorbuthappy.com/bolivia/new/

TOURS

Bolivia.com – http://www.bolivia.com/agencias.htm
Kontiki Tours – http://kontiki.cc/bolivia/index.html
Crillon Tours – http://www.titicaca.com/
Magic of Bolivia Ltd – http://www.bolivia.co.uk/
Fremen Tours – http://www.andes-amazonia.com
TCA Tours – http://latinwide.com/farm-tour/
Explore Bolivia – http://www.explorebolivia.com/links.htm

Bolivia's Best

THE RAINFOREST

1. Parque Nacional Madidi

It is thought that there are more plant and animal species gracing this new park than any other preserve in South America. This is partly because of its size – almost 7700 sq. miles (2 million hectares), including habitats as varied as glaciers and tropical rainforest. Much of the mountainous region is currently inaccessible – a great shame considering that it contains more cloudforest than the rest of Central America put together. What is accessible is the rainforest, which rivals Manu of Peru in quality and may contain 10% of all the species in the world – otters, dolphins, tapirs, jaguars, spider monkeys, anteaters, ocelots, macaws, parrots, cotingas... Yet the government which has been so ecologically concerned up to now plans to jeopardize the park by building a massive hydroelectric dam in the park. Conservation International was heavily involved in the park's conception and will need much support to help conserve it.

Explore the park from the town of Rurrenabaque. Avoid the road safari and opt for a river trip. The Río Tuichi has great wildlife and the Río Yacuma offers even better because it is a completely different, more open habitat known as pampas heath: flat, marshy plains with the odd piece of forest. Capybara, sloths, armadillos, tapirs, otters, squirrel monkeys, anacondas, and a great diversity of birds, particularly tiger herons, ibises, and flamingoes, exist in incredible diversity. Check out the nearby lakes such as Lago Brave and the splendid Lago Rogagua for birds in abundance.

Getting there: By plane from La Paz and regular buses from La Paz (18–20 hours), Riberalta (12 hours) and Trinidad. Several lodges offer a variety of packages to the rainforest, the Pampas or both. Few companies are on the internet – organize everything when you arrive with companies such as *Hotel de la Pampa* or *Agencia Fluvial*. Or see the eco-friendly *Chalalán Lodge* http://www.ecotour.org/destin/places/chalalan.htm (run by Conservation International).

2. Parque Nacional Amboró

Covers at least three different ecological zones – rainforest, cloudforest, and highland plains – and boasts more than 50 mammal species and more than 700 birds. During an extended stay you may see a plethora of butterflies, macaws, hoatzins, and hummingbirds, as well as the rarer quetzal and the highly endangered blue-horned curassow. Also healthy populations of white-fronted capuchins, brown capuchins, red howlers, emperor tamarins, tapir, capybara, peccaries, even a chance of seeing spectacled bear. This park is also great for those who have only one day to spare, since it is three hours from Santa Cruz. For further information and tours, see http://www.gorp.com/gorp/location/latamer/bolivia/amboro.htm

Getting there: Bus from Santa Cruz (itself worth a visit to see the sloths that live in the Plaza 24 de Septiembre) to Buena Vista at the park's entrance (3 hours). Accommodation in Buena Vista; camping and some lodgings in the park itself. Best time to visit: in the dry season, May to October. Tour companies in Santa Cruz and guides in Buena Vista.

KEY TO MAP

1	Parque Nacional Madidi
2	Parque Nacional Amboró
3	Parque Nacional Noel Kempff
4	Apa Apa Ecological Park
5	Lake Titicaca
6	Salar de Uyuni
7	Parque Nacional Sajama
8	Parque Nacional Torotoro
9	Puerto Suárez
10	Rurrenabaque
11	Copacabana

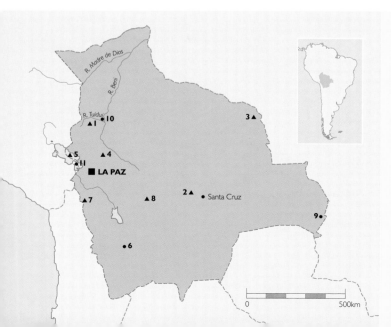

3. Parque Nacional Noel Kempff

Well worth seeing, but difficult to visit because of its remoteness. *Terra firme* forest, flooded forest, thornscrub forest, and Pantanal. More than 620 species of birds – some of them highly endangered – and a great place to see tapir, brocket deer, jaguar, spider monkey, capybara, maned wolves, giant anteaters, river dolphins, and more, if you are willing to put in the time.

Getting there: Roads and landing strips change frequently; for accurate information contact International Expeditions Incorporated (e-mail nature@ietravel.com or tel. 1-800-633-4734).

THE YUNGAS

A separate mountain range from the Andes, the Yungas have a variety of forest systems on their slopes, from wet lowland through cloud to line elfin forest, characterized by ferns, lichens, mosses, and bamboo. This has led to a great variety of flora and fauna, but only one accessible place has not suffered damage from logging or hunting.

4. Apa Apa Ecological Park

The dwarf of Bolivia's reserves at a mere 3.8 sq. miles (1000 hectares). Sadly this is all that remains of the original subtropical forest. However, you should see tamarins, night monkeys, squirrel monkeys, and many hummingbirds. Sometimes spectacled bears are around, having migrated through the valley to the reserve.

Getting there: By bus from La Paz to Chulumani on the beautiful road to Coroico. From Chulumani hire a private taxi to take you to the house owned by the reserve's managers Ramón and Tildi Portugal.

THE ALTIPLANO

5. Lake Titicaca

Lake Titicaca is beautiful. Nestled in between snow-capped mountains, the highest navigable lake in the world has a feeling of the Mediterranean but with llamas, flamingoes, and weird toads lurking nearby. Numerous islands

worth visiting – the floating islands on the Peru side are bizarre but very touristy; in Bolivia, Isla de la Sol is a must simply to experience a Greek island at 13,000ft (4000m)! Birdlife ranges from flamingoes to rare Andean ducks; and the lake proliferates with fish. As for flora, the 'totora' (a kind of cat-tail), used as a food and building material, abounds.

Getting there: From Peru: fly to Juliaca from Lima, Arequipa, or Cusco; or take a train to Puno, then a boat or a bus to Copacabana on the Bolivian side.
From Bolivia: fly to La Paz, where there are daily buses to Copacabana and Puno. Small boats run a daily service to Taquile, Amantani, and Isla de la Sol from Puno and Copacabana.

Take the necessary precautions concerning altitude. The sun is also dangerously fierce – bring strong sunscreen and use it liberally.

6. Salar de Uyuni

One of the real highlights of South America. Located in the southwest of Bolivia, it is the starting point for a 4-day tour that takes you to scenery you did not know existed. Tours begin by crossing the world's largest salt lake where the contrast between the deep blue sky and the never ending glare of white is awesome, particularly in July (sunglasses are essential). Small hills jut out like islands and are a haven for small mammals and birds – particularly birds of prey, which thrive among the giant cacti. Slowly the habitat changes as the tours climb into the volcanic deserts. Lakes of bright red and green populated by hundreds of flamingoes, rock statues carved by the wind, geysers at 16,000ft (5000m), millennia-old mosses; vicuñas, guanacos, Andean foxes, pumas, rheas, and more can be seen along the way.

See Uyuni Travel guide http://poorbuthappy.com/bolivia/new/uyuni.html for more information.

You do not need to book a tour in advance. In Uyuni 30 companies run tours for 4–6 people in Toyota Landcruisers. The standard varies

little; accommodation ranges from 6-bed rooms to 24-bed dormitories at Laguna Colorado (where space is limited). A tour booked in La Paz will cost at least double.

Getting there: Regular, dependable buses from anywhere in Bolivia. The journey from La Paz (14 hours) can be broken into 2 parts: to Potosí or Oruro one day and on to Uyuni the next. Avoid trains! It is very easy to travel to Chile from Uyuni: your tour operator will arrange a bus to pick you up from Laguna Verde on the third day. Expect to pay around US$15 extra.

Remember to bring sunglasses and lots of warm clothes. Acclimatize first, since part of the tour exceeds 16,000ft (5000 meters)

THE MOUNTAINS

Chilean and Argentinian safety standards for climbing are much higher, but these two places in Bolivia are well worth climbs to see their wildlife.

7. Parque Nacional Sajama

At 17,000ft (5200m) the world's highest forest, consisting mainly of the kenua tree. Although there is little wildlife living in this oxygen depleted environment, the gnarled trees and views over volcanoes are amazing.

Getting there: Bus from La Paz to Arica (Chile), but get off at Sajama (you can also visit the park from Chile). Basic accommodation in Sajama. Bring all supplies since there are frequent water and food shortages.

8. Parque Nacional Torotoro

A small village tucked in the mountains 124 miles (198km) from Cochabamba which very few tourists visit. As well as splendid scenery, gorges, and underground lakes (with blind catfish), there are dinosaur footprints all around the village.

Getting there: Bus from Cochabamba on Sunday and Thursday at 6 a.m. The stop is a challenge to find and lies between Riberatta and Avenida Republica on 8 de Octubre. Alternatively, rent a

4x4 in Cochabamba and return by plane. The owner of one of the two hotels in Torotoro will radio through to a Swiss pilot who will fly you cheaply to Cochabamba in a Cessna.

For further information, see: http://hjem.get2net.dk/futtrup/torotoro.html.

THE PANTANAL

9. Puerto Suárez

Bolivia has Pantanal of its own, but eco-tourism in it has hardly started. However a number of companies in this border town arrange tours to Brazil's beautiful Pantanal.

Getting there: From any Bolivian airport to Puerto Suárez; or bus from Santa Cruz; or train to nearby Quijarro. For tour operators in Puerto Suárez, visit the Plaza de Armas and Calle Vanguardia.

FURTHER READING

As well as the common guidebooks and the flora and fauna guides to the Amazon, try:
Bolivia: The Evolution of a Multi-Ethnic Society by Herbert S. Klein, Oxford University Press, Oxford, 1992
Culture Shock!: Bolivia by Mark Cramer, Graphic Arts Center, Publishing Company. Portland, USA 1996
Gods & Vampires: Return to Chipaya by Nathan Wachtel & Carol Volk (translator), University of Chicago Press, Chicago, 1994

BRAZIL

Fantastic landscapes ranging from semi-desert to grand canyons to some of the richest rainforest on the planet. The trouble with Brazil is its size. Given 3 months for your visit you might be able to do it justice. Nevertheless, this chapter is designed for short-term visitors. Under each habitat, the first location either has the best to offer or is a recommended compromise of wildlife against travel time.

TOP WEBSITES

There is a lot of information on the internet about Brazil. Visit:
BR on line Travel to Brazil – http://www.brol.com/
Go-Brazil.com – http://www.go-brazil.com/
Osinga.com – Brazil – http://www.osinga.com/page.asp?Loc=26
The Wonders of Brazil – http://www.vivabrazil.com

TOURS

Field Guides Incorporated Bird Adventures – http://www.fieldguides.com/tourssamer.html
Brazil Tours in the Amazon and Pantanal – http://www.amazonadventures.com/brazil.htm
Brazil Tours – http://www.braziltours.com
Brazil Travel, Holidays and Tours – http://kontiki.cc/brazil/
Discover Brazil Tours – http://www.discoverbraziltours.com/
Brazil–US Friendship Tours – http://www.mind.net/Brazil/
Brazil Gem Tours – http://www.sonee.com/glw/bgtours.htm
Imbassai Brazilian Tourist Centre – http://www.imbassai.com/
Amazon Travel.com – http://www.amazontravel.com/
Brazil Travel – http://www.brtravel.com/
Blumar Turismo – http://www.blumar.com.br/
Ouro Preto Tourism – http://www.ouropretotour.com/
Focus Tours – http://www.focustours.com
Brazil Vacation – http://www.brazilvacation.net/brazil.htm
Trendsetter Travel and Tours – http://www.trendsetterstours.com/

Brazil's Best

THE PANTANAL

1. Parque Nacional do Pantanal Matogrossense

The plains of the Pantanal make for easy viewing, and animal life is abundant. October is the best time to go. Birds are particularly abundant, and it is not unusual to see dozens of scarlet ibises, hundreds of macaws, and thousands of egrets in a single day, as well as jabiru storks, woodrails, toucans, kites, finches, parakeets, rheas, and more. In addition you will see many yacare caiman, anacondas, and capybara, and given a stay of a few days you may see jaguar, ocelot, giant anteaters, swamp deer, giant river otter, and black and gold howler monkeys.

For further information, see – http://www.alanet.com.br/ms/pantanal/welcome.html

Getting there: Regular flights to both Cuiabá and Campo Grande, the two entrance points to the park. Many tour companies and freelance guides. Most excel at finding wildlife but their English can be poor. Avoid the cheapest deals, meet your guide prior to payment, go in a group no bigger than 8 and check out the quality of your vehicle. Doing some of your safari on foot will enable you to get much closer to the wildlife. Try camping at night and spend as much time as possible on the plain –

particularly at dawn and dusk (also go on a night safari). Finally, try to arrange a trip in a Cessna (which all ranches have) since seeing the Pantanal from the air is wonderful.

Independent travelers may prefer to fly to Cuiabá since it is easy and very worthwhile to drive through the Pantanal as far as Porto Jofre. Several hotels, tour agencies, and individual guides in Cuiabá, Porto Jofre, along the road itself, and dozens of guides at the airport. Recommended are:
Joel Souza's tours – Tel: 065 983 3552
Anaconda Tours – Tel: 065 624 6242

However, most visitors head to Campo Grande since here and in Corumbá (6 hours by bus) there are more tours and lodges. If you do not want to go with one of the freelance guides, try:
Focus Tours – http://www.focustours.com or e-mail FocusTours@aol.com
Greentrack – Pantanal Walking Tours – http://travel.to/greentrack
Refugio Ecologica Caiman (where you will definitely see one of the world's rarest birds, the hyacinth macaw) – http://www.brol.com/caiman.html
Amazon Adventures – http://www.amazonadventures.com/pantanal.htm
Trans-Delgado-Tours – Tel/Fax: 067 741 7087
Pantanal Safari – http://www.pantanalsafari.com.br

2. Bonito

An advantage of being based at Campo Grande is that it is easy to make excursions to Bonito, 6 hours away by bus. Bonito is unique in that the nearby river is crystal clear (very rare for South America). Many tour companies offer fantastic snorkeling trips; hundreds of fish, turtles, kingfishers, and herons can be seen. As well as the above companies, try:
Baia Bonita Tours – Tel/Fax: 067 255 1193
Hapakany Eco-tourism – Tel/Fax: 067 255 1315
Ambiental Expedições – E-mail: ambiental.tur@originet.com.br
Ygarape Tour – Tel: 067 255 1733

KEY TO MAP

1 Parque Nacional do Pantanal Matogrossense
2 Bonito
3 Reserva Biológica do Guaporé
4 Parque Nacional das Emas
5 Parque Nacional da Serra do Cipó
6 Manaus
7 Mamirauá Sustainable Development Reserve
8 Parque Nacional de Pacaás Novas
9 Parque Natural do Caraça
10 Parque Nacional de Aparados da Serra
11 Parque Nacional da Chapada dos Veadeiros
12 Parque Nacional Marinho dos Abrolhos
13 Fernando de Noronha
14 Parque Nacional de Monte Pascoal
15 The Santa Catarina Coast
16 Parque Nacional do Cabo Orange
17 Parque Nacional do Superagui
18 Foz do Iguaçu
19 Parque Nacional da Chapada dos Guimarães
20 Corumbá
21 Florianópolis

3. Reserva Biológica do Guaporé

The advantage of this reserve is that while its flora and fauna are like the Pantanal, it is near Manaus, where tourists flock to see the Amazon rainforest. Hence it is a good opportunity to get an impression of what Pantanal is like without making the diversion needed to see the real thing.

Getting there: Fly or drive from Porto Velho to Costa Marques (500 miles/750km – flying recommended) before taking a 4–6 hour boat ride to Pau d'Oleo. Accommodation and camping within the reserve.

THE CERRADO

4. Parque Nacional das Emas

A highlight of Brazil, described on page 114

Getting there: Hard to reach. Air taxi can be arranged from most towns or ranches. There are two entrance points to the park: it is better to use the southern entrance of Chapado do Ceu. Several guides available. Margie Piexoto and Nadir García are frequently recommended. Accommodation at the park headquarters; camping permitted.

5. Parque Nacional da Serra do Cipó

Consists of *cerrado* as well as dense forests around river edges. An extended stay should reward you with macaws, toucans, hummingbirds, maned wolf, various marmosets, capuchins, tamanduas, maybe even a jaguar – and some great waterfalls.

Getting there: Not easy. Bus from Belo to Lagoa Santa and then on to Conceição do Mato Dentro. Get off at the park entrance along the route or at the nearest town, Cardeal Mota. You can camp anywhere within the park.

THE RAINFOREST

6. Manaus

The prime spot for tourists, actually on the Rio Negro. Classic tropical rainforest – hot, humid, dense, and diverse. Expect to see something different every day, whether it is new species of beetle or a primate you have not yet encountered.

Countless tours available, from booked to spontaneous, from luxury to makeshift, from 1 day to 3 months, from fixed to flexible and from 1 person to 30. You can experience the jungle with all conveniences or you can buy a canoe and paddle downstream. Maybe 20% of visitors to Manaus return disappointed, therefore choosing a tour is of vital importance. It is worth remembering:

▶ The companies that meet you at the airport all have glossy brochures with a list of what you will see. If the list includes jaguars, pumas, woolly spider monkeys, and hyacinth macaws, they are lying.
▶ The fewer people you go with the quieter you will be (and animals won't run away before you have a chance to see them).
▶ Spend as long as you can in the rainforest each day. Some lodges offer only 3 hours a day.
▶ The further you are from Manaus the more likely it is that hunting and logging have not occurred. Likewise, the smaller the rivers you canoe up, the harder the access is for hunters and loggers.
▶ Guides who have qualifications in biology will keep you interested if the wildlife fails to materialize. EMAMTUR registered guides must pass exams and are continually assessed.
▶ The majority of the action in a rainforest occurs in the canopy. Some lodges have canopy harnesses or walkways where you will be in for a treat.
▶ Another excellent location for wildlife is a floodplain lake. Make sure your trip visits one. Do not fish for piranha since hooks are easily bitten off and could cause serious injury to giant river otters.

If you want to book in advance, try:
Amazon Nut Safaris – http://www.netzanstalt.com/amazon-safaris/
Ariau Towers – http://www.ariautowers.com.br/
Acajatuba Jungle Lodge – http://www.iis.com.br/~thequest/acajatub.htm
Amazon Clipper Cruise – http://www.brol.com/amazon_clipper.html
Amazon Lodge – http://www.amazontravel.com/amazon.html

Swallows and Amazons – http://www.overlookinn.com/swallows.html
Jaguar Adventure Tours – http://www.objetivonet.com.br/jaguartours/
Also, see: *Hotels de Selva* – http://www.fontur.com.br/portugues/hoteis.htm

If you return to Manaus disappointed with your jungle wildlife, visit the Parque Municipal do Mindu on the outskirts of the town (catch the Parque Dez bus from the center), home to one of the last remaining populations of pied bare-face tamarins. The Amazon Eco-park, 30 minutes by boat, rehabilitates injured animals.

For Manaus information, see: http://darkwing.uoregon.edu/~sergiok/brasil/manaus.html

7. Mamirauá Sustainable Development Reserve

Eco-tourism is only just beginning here, but it is one of the best rainforest destinations on the continent. It is described on page 76.

Getting there: Located at the confluence of the rivers Solimões, Japurá, and Auati-Paraná, in the state of Amazonas. Easily accessible from Tefé, 1 hour by air from Manaus. At present there is space for only 20 or so visitors. Book in advance via its website – http://www.cnpq.br/mamiraua/mamiraua2.htm – or through:

Sociedade Civil Mamirauá – Tel/Fax: 55 092 743 2736. E-mail: Ecomami@pop-tefe.rnp.br or http://www.pop-tefe.rnp.br/

8. Parque Nacional de Pacaás Novas

Diverse habitats mean a high number of species, with a mixture of jungle and plains animals from tapirs to deer, primates, to anteaters. Birds also diverse and abundant. Very difficult to visit, but this is likely to change. Check IBAMA (http://www.ibama.gov.br/) for progress.

Getting there: Fly to Porto Velho and then drive 220 miles (350km) to the park via Ariquemes. Half of the road is unsealed. Permission

must be sought from IBAMA in Porto Velho (Tel: 223 3607).

THE OTHER FORESTS

Mata Atlântica

The 60-million-year-old Atlantic forest is located mainly in the mountainous areas close to the sea, but is also found in spaces in the interior. More than 50% of its trees are endemic and are located nowhere else.

9. Parque Natural do Caraça

Perhaps the best remaining Atlantic forest, combined with a wonderful mountainous setting. Look out for howler monkeys, marmosets, spider monkeys, paca, and harpy eagles. The highlight, however, is the old monastery (now a guesthouse) because every night maned wolves are attracted by the promise of food. A guaranteed sighting of one of South America's least seen mammals.

Getting there: By train or plane to Santa Bárbara. From there take a taxi to the park entrance at Hospedaria do Colegio Caraça (the maned wolf guesthouse – Tel: 031 837 2698). Guides and accommodation in the park.

Parque Nacional de Monte Pascoal See 'Coast' section, opposite.

Mata de Araucaria

Growing up to 160ft (50m) tall, the prehistoric looking parana pine tree or araucaria is certainly impressive. Forests of them once spanned much of southern Brazil, but have been decimated by the timber trade. Wildlife in the remaining forest is rare due to hunting pressures. Nevertheless, there remains one good place to view it:

10. Parque Nacional de Aparados da Serra

Scenically beautiful and should be visited just to see the narrow 2300ft-deep (700m) Canyon do Itaimbezinho. Wildlife includes armadillos, tamanduas, and a whole host of birds.

Getting there: Bus to Cambara do Sul from Porto Alegre, Torres, or São Francisco. Camping in the park and hotels in Cambara do Sul.

Wine-palm forest
There is one place to see whole stands of palms, reminiscent of the classic oasis, where wildlife also abounds:

11. Parque Nacional da Chapada dos Veadeiros
In addition to wine-palm stands, a chance of seeing maned wolves, tamanduas, armadillos, marmosets, tapirs, rheas, macaws (which frequently breed there), toucans, and guans. Close by is the Vale da Luna with its peculiar moonscape.

Getting there: Bus from Goiânia or Brasília to Alto Paraíso (6 hours), then local bus to São Jorge. Camping near the park entrance and hotels in São Jorge. You must hire an IBAMA guide at the park entrance.

Caatinga forest
Characterized by a semi-arid climate with irregular rains, but when the first rains begin, the thorny vegetation takes new form and the Caatinga turns a verdant green. Sadly, the surviving 2 percent that has been protected is too difficult to try to get to. Check with IBAMA, since this situation may change.
(http://www.ibama.gov.br/)

THE COAST

Along Brazil's huge coastline there are several places worth visiting for diving, whale watching, mangrove swamps, and birding.

12. Parque Nacional Marinho dos Abrolhos
An archipelago of five islands lying 60 miles (100km) from the coastal town of Caravelas. A bird reserve, home to a great number of frigates, petrels, and other marine birds, the islands are surrounded by coral reef. Visibility can reach 100ft (30m) and the diversity of fish (including four species of shark) and healthy coral is good. Between March and September there is a good chance of seeing turtles (green and loggerhead) while snorkeling or diving. The turtles also nest on some of the islands' beaches. July–November it is possible to arrange to dive with humpback whales with calves.

Getting there: Trips, from 1 day to 1 week, available from good tour operators in Caravelas and Alcobaça. More dive companies in Alcobaça, otherwise both towns offer similar trips.

For Brazilian dive companies, see the website of *Three Routes Diving Directory for Brazil* – http://www.3routes.com/scuba/sa/braz/index.html
Whale-watching in Brazil – http://www.dive-info.com/antarctica/wwa.htm

13. Fernando de Noronha
An archipelago some 200 miles (320km) off the coast and a haven for the marine enthusiast. Underwater visibility can be as much as 130ft (40m), which makes viewing the turtles, 250 fish species, and many coral species a real pleasure. Local dive and snorkel tour operators know the best spots. Spectacular viewing of spinner dolphins in Mirante dos Golfinhos, best September–October.

There are many dive operators on the islands and tour operators in Recife and Natal, all of which have good reputations. Goods are expensive, so take plenty of film, sunscreen, insect repellent, and food with you.

Getting there: Fly from Natal or Recife.

14. Parque Nacional de Monte Pascoal
A coastal national park with a fine reef system, Monte Pascoal also offers Atlantic forest, mangrove, and swamps. Diverse fauna includes armadillos, capuchins, sloths, capybara, spider monkeys, marine birds, parrots, and toucans. Underwater visibility can reach 50ft (15m).

Getting there: Boat from Corumbau or Caraiva, or private transport to the park along Highway BR 101. At the park headquarters you can pick up a guide.

15. The Santa Catarina Coast
Several good places to see marine wildlife can be reached easily by public bus and hired boats. There is no need to use tour operators:

▶ *Anhatomirim Island* – Just off the coast near Florianópolis (hire a boat), this island is made up of Atlantic forest but in its bays live a large group of rare tucuxi dolphins.
▶ *Arvoredo Marine Biological Reserve* – 4 miles (7km) off the coast of Florianópolis, home to hundreds of marine birds including frigates and terns.
▶ *Lobos Island Ecological Reserve* – 1 mile (2km) off the coast of Torres, home to hundreds of southern fur seals.
▶ *Laguna* – South of Florianópolis, offering the spectacle of bottlenose dolphins helping fishermen by herding the mullet schools towards the fishermen and making body movements (such as head-slapping) which the fishermen recognize as a signal to throw their nets. Best mid-May.

Between May and November southern right whales can be seen within 80ft (25m) of several beaches. Try Rosa, Ibiraquera, and Luz Beach, Imbituba. For more information see *IWC Right Whale Project* – http://www.via-rs.com.br/iwcbr/frafrai.html.

16. Parque Nacional do Cabo Orange
A massive national park hugging the coast, mostly lush mangroves. Look out for species that you may not have seen before including manatees, crab-eating raccoons, coatis, armadillos, and turtles which nest on the beach. Southern right whales off the coast in the right season.

Getting there: Hire an air taxi or get a bus to Macapá, then a combination of jeep and boat. The owners of the boat will also act as guides.

17. Parque Nacional do Superagui
A marine park made up of the Pecas Islands as well as the island after which the park is named. Superagui includes some excellent mangroves where you should look out for manatees, capuchins, and coatis. You pass through the mangrove area on the boat when you arrive or make excursions to other islands. Snorkeling around the islands is reasonable, and the birdlife on Ilha dos Currais is highly rated.

Getting there: Bus or boat from Paranaguá to Guaraqueçaba from where you hop on a supply boat to Superagui.

FURTHER READING

After the Trees: Living on the Transamazon Highway by Douglas Ian Stewart, University of Texas Press, Austin, USA, 1994
Amazon Journal: Dispatches from a Vanishing Frontier by Geoffrey O'Connor, Plume, New York, 1992
The Amazon: Past, Present and Future (Discoveries Series) by Alain Gheerbrant., Harry N. Abrams (Pap), New York, 1992
The Amazon River Forest: A Natural History of Plants, Animals, and People by Nigel J. H. Smith, Oxford University Press, Oxford, 1999
Brazilian Adventure by Peter Fleming, Northwestern University Press, Evanston, USA, 1999
The Burning Season: The Murder of Chico Mendes and the Fight for the Amazon Rain Forest by Andrew Revkin, Plume, New York 1996
Floods of Fortune: Ecology and Economy Along the Amazon by Michael Goulding, Nigel J. H. Smith (contributor) & Dennis J. Mahar (contributor), Columbia University Press, New York, 1996
Through Amazonian Eyes: The Human Ecology of Amazonian Populations by Emilio F. Moran, University of Iowa Press, Iowa City, 1993

CHILE

A land of extremes because of its unique shape that allows visitors to explore arid deserts, lonely *altiplano*, dramatic coastline, frozen volcanoes, ancient forest, and icy glaciers in an area only slightly larger than Texas. Chile's fauna and flora are no way near as diverse as that of Amazonian countries, but what it does have, it usually has in abundance.

Traveling in Chile is easy, as the country has an excellent infrastructure (where nature allows), many English speakers, and many tour companies.

TOP WEBSITES

Away.com – Chile – http://away.com/chile/index.adp
Chile Travel Search – http://www.ciudadnet.com/
Chile Information Project Travel Guide – http://www.chiptravel.cl/
Chile's Tourism – http://www.segegob.cl/sernatur/respaldo/inicio3.html
Guide to Chilean Patagonia – http://www.chileaustral.com/

TOURS

Many well-established Chilean tour companies on line. Some of the most consistently recommended are:
Discover Chile – http://www.discover-chile.com/chile/index.html
Chile Tour Packages – http://www.cocha.com/inhome_receptivo.htm
Tours and Adventure Travel in Patagonia – http://www.io.com/~jmc12/chile.html
Freegate Tourism – Chile – http://www.freegatetours.com/chile.htm

Lost World Adventures – Chile – http://www.lostworldadventures.com/chile.htm
Chile Travel.com – http://www.chile-travel.com/
Patagonia Vacations – http://www.chiletravel.com/patagonia/tourism/dwav/english.htm
Del Inca Travel – http://www.delincatravel.cl/
Lanchile (National Airline offering great on-line discounts) – http://www.lanchile.cl/english/
Birding Alto Andino Nature Tours – http://www.birdingaltoandino.com/guide.htm
Azimut 360 – http://www.azimut.cl

Chile's Best

THE COAST & ISLANDS

Chile's coast varies tremendously. Much of the northern coast is barren, while the southern carved fjords are astounding.

1. Parque Nacional Pan de Azúcar

Just north of Chañaral and home to Humboldt penguins as well as over 100 species of other birds, South American fur seals, and South American sea lions. The penguins are only to be found on the offshore island of Isla Pan de Azúcar.

Getting there: Daily bus from Chañaral, leaving at around 7 a.m. from the library and returning some 12 hours later. To get to the island, you can charter a fishing boat.

Permission must be sought from CONAF (the National Park authority) in Caleta Pan de Azúcar.

2. Reserva Nacional Pingüino de Humboldt

Just offshore from Caleta Chañaral is Isla Chañaral, home to penguins, seals, sea lions, and a great variety of seabirds including shearwaters and petrels.

Getting there: Cannot be reached by public transport. Tours from Vallenar or La Serena. Or turn off the Pan American highway at Domeyko, head on the dirt road to Caleta Chañaral and ask to charter a boat in the port.

Permission from CONAF in Caleta Choros must be obtained in advance – remind tour operators of this fact.

3. Cruises via Puerto Montt

Starting point for some excellent cruises of Fjordland, which has, at the northern end, many steeply carved islands where the glaciers have retreated, allowing temperate rainforest to dominate the vegetation; and towards the south, carving glaciers still at work. Trips to, among others, Puerto Natales, Laguna San Rafael, Puerto Aguirre, or Puerto Edén are the highlight of many people's visit. The further south you go, the better, so allocate at least seven days for such a cruise. Look out for Humboldt penguins, Magellan penguins, dolphins, South American fur seals, kingfishers, and a variety of sea birds.

Most tours are available only from late October to early April. Many companies operate tours from Puerto Montt and all are worthwhile but expensive. Remember that the less you pay, the more people brought on the trip to make a profit – sleeping will be very 'cosy' in economy class. This is particularly true for the Navimag's ferry, the *Puerto Edén*. If you get seasick avoid economy class, which is often located next to the engine room. Bring very warm clothes so that you can spend as much time on deck as possible.

Cruises like this are also available from Puerto Natales, Punta Arenas, and Ushuaia (in Argentina). From Ushuaia, trips to Antarctica can also be arranged via cruise companies or the navy. Check out the following websites:
Navimag – http://www.navimag.com/
Skorpios I and II – via http://travelvantage.com/chi_cru_skorpios2.html

KEY TO MAP

1 Parque Nacional Pan de Azúcar
2 Reserva Nacional Pinguino de Humboldt
3 Cruises via Puerto Montt
4 Parque Nacional Chiloé
5 Parque Nacional Laguna San Rafael
6 Isla Magdelena
7 Parque Nacional Tierra del Fuego
8 The Beagle Channel
9 Parque Nacional Lauca
10 Parque Nacional La Campana
11 Parque Nacional Laguna de Laja
12 Parque Nacional Conguillo
13 Reserva Nacional Lago Jeinmeni
14 Parque Nacional Torres del Paine
15 Monumento Natural Salar de Surire
16 San Pedro de Atacama
17 La Serena
18 Punta Arenas
19 Puerto Natales
20 Arica

Austral adventures – http://www.
austral-adventures.com/
Victory Cruises – http://www.
victory-cruises.com/
Cruce de Lagos – http://www.
crucedelagos.cl/english.htm
Chile-tourism-Patagonia –
http://www.australis.com
*Laguna San Rafael Tourism
Vacations and cruises* –
http://www.chiletravel.com/laguna_
san_rafael/tourism/dwav/english.htm
Laguna San Rafael Tours –
http://www.chileaustral.com/
lmpatagonia/sanrafael.htm
Patagonian Connection –
info@patagoniaconnex.cl

4. Parque Nacional Chiloé
Located just south of Puerto Montt
on Isla del Chiloé and home to a
splendid evergreen forest and a
diversity of reptiles and birds
including cormorants, flightless
ducks, and South American terns.
Look out for one of the world's
smallest deer, the pudú, and
Darwin's fox, so named after one
was killed by the great naturalist's
rock hammer. Excursions can also
be made to Isla Punihuil – the only
site in the world where Humboldt
and Magellanic penguins cohabit
(see http://www.australadventures.
com/penguin1.htm).

Getting there: Ferry from Puerto
Montt to Ancud, then bus to any of
the island's tourist destinations.

5. Parque Nacional Laguna San Rafael
One of Chile's real gems, whose
incredible scenery culminates in a
dazzling glacier. Described on
page 156.

Getting there: By air taxi or boat.
You can charter planes in
Coyhaique or Puerto Aisén – make
sure your pilot is willing to land,
since some prefer only to fly over
the glacier and then return. To
arrive by sea, see the companies
listed under Puerto Montt, above.

6. Isla Magdelena
Although penguins can be seen all
along Chile's coast, no site can
rival that of Monumento Natural
Los Pingüinos on Isla Magdelena.
Between November and January
over 150,000 penguins come ashore
to breed.

Getting there: 15 miles (25km)
northeast of Punta Arenas. Turismo
Compaña runs a boat service every
Tuesday, Thursday, and Saturday at
8 a.m., 2 hours each way with 2
hours on the island (Tel: 241437.
Fax: 247514).

7. Parque Nacional Tierra del Fuego
As the southernmost tip of the
continent lies one of its most
protected national parks; visitors
are restricted to a few trails through
beech forest, sphagnum peat bogs,
and along the shore. Look out for
insectivorous plants including many
species of pitcher plant, many birds
(especially along Lapataia Bay), as
well as some introduced mammals
such as muskrats and beavers.

Getting there: Regular buses from
Ushuaia which is also home to a
number of good tour companies.

8. The Beagle Channel
South America's most southerly
marine destination, named after
Darwin's ship. As well as admiring
the southern beech forest on shore,
keep your eyes peeled for the
world's largest woodpecker,
magellanic penguins, gentoo
penguins, imperial cormorants,
rock cormorants, kelp gulls,
dolphin gulls, South American
terns, and Chilean skuas. Several
species of marine mammal breed
here, so keep your eyes peeled for
blow-hole signatures.

Getting there: All tour agencies in
Ushuaia offer trips along the
Beagle Channel as well as to nearby
islands which are home to penguin
colonies, South American fur seal
colonies, and southern elephant
seal breeding sites. Note that the
channel can be rough.

THE ANDES

9. Parque Nacional Lauca
In the northernmost part of Chile
lies a real gem – not only easy to
reach, but also quite beautiful.
Lauca National Park is 530 sq. miles
(138,000 hectares) of utter
remoteness with snowy volcanoes,
multicolored lakes, lava fields, and
few tourists. It is also renowned for
its birdlife (see http://www.
birdingaltoandino.com – Birds seen
above) and is one of the best places

Rhea, a large, flightless bird about 1.5 meters (5 feet) tall.

to see viscachas, Andean foxes,
vicuñas, and even pumas. Be warned
that the park is high: Lago Chungara
– a must for its views over four
volcanoes – is over 15,000ft (4500m).

Getting there: Daily buses from
Arica to Putre, 10 miles (15km)
outside the park (4 hours). Tour
companies in Putre. Birding
AltoAndino is recommended for
eco-tourists. Several tour
companies in Arica will arrange
1–3 day trips. Good
accommodation in Putre. It can be
hard to reach the park between
December and March and in
August when rain and snow
respectively may close the road.

10. Parque Nacional La Campana
The best place to see forests of the
peculiar Chilean palm with their
bottlelike appearance caused by
swollen mid-trunks. No altitude
problems.

Getting there: Bus from Limache to
the entrance at Granizo. If you
have your own transport, turn off
the Pan American highway between
Hijuelas and Llaillay on to a dirt
road signposted to Palmar de Ocoa.

11. Parque Nacional Laguna de Laja
The highlight is the barren
landscape sculptured by lava from
the still active Antuco volcano.
Frequent sightings of viscachas,
foxes, and more than 50 species of
bird, including the Andean condor
and black-necked swans. The long
ago eruption also dammed part of
the Río Laja to create the large lake.

Getting there: Bus from Los
Angeles to Abanico, then a 1-hour
walk to the entrance.

12. Parque Nacional Conguillo
Home to active volcanoes,
aquamarine lakes, and some great
forests. Best place in Chile to see
ancient monkey puzzle forest
which once dominated much of the
landscape. Amid these dinosaurian
trees (some of which are over 2000
years old) you can see orchids,
pudú, pumas, foxes, and parrots.

Getting there: Open November–
June. Buses from Vilcún and from
Curacautín. Alternatively hire a car
in Temuco. If you do this, you
should also drive to Lago Budi –
the only saltwater lake in Chile
where more than 140 waterbird

Snow-capped Parinacota volcano in the Lauca National Park, Chile. The young cone with its 985-feet-diameter (300-meter) crater formed about 13,500 years ago after the major cone collapsed, obstructing drainage in the area. This resulted in the formation of Lake Chungara.

species, including black-necked swans, can be seen. Camping facilities in the park and various hotels just outside. CONAF run guided walks.

13. Reserva Nacional Lago Jeinmeni

Boasting lakes, waterfalls, glaciers, and beautiful forest, the best place in the world to see the endangered national emblem of Chile, the huemul. You may also see pumas, foxes, condors, and large numbers of flamingoes.

Getting there: Difficult without your own transport. Try asking for a lift in the CONAF office in Chile Chico or hitching on a timber truck. Camping is allowed but bring all your own supplies and make sure that you have a good map.

14. Parque Nacional Torres del Paine

Justifiably regarded as one of the most spectacular wilderness areas in the world. Described on page 53. Pack for all eventualities, as the weather can change in minutes.

Getting there: Daily buses or car hire from Puerto Natales. Many tours available in Puerto Natales (consistently recommended is *Casa Cecilia* – redcecilia@entelchile.net) and Punta Arenas. Several places to stay within the park but book in advance in high season (for bus tickets too!). Puerto Natales is also the starting point for access to Argentina's Parque Nacional Los Glaciares.

THE ALTIPLANO

Chile has some of the best *altiplano* in the continent, home to a variety of wildlife including guanacos and vicuñas, short-tailed chinchillas, mountain viscachas, flamingoes, rheas, cacti, and lichen. Moreover, the scenery is extraordinary.

15. Monumento Natural Salar de Surire

Although the scenery is not as impressive as other *altiplano*, Surire, a drying salt lake, has a resident population of three species of flamingo, numbering around 14,000 individuals. Nesting

season January–March. You should also be able to see Andean goose and rhea.

Getting there: Not easy. You can hitch a ride on one of the mining trucks on the Arica–La Paz road but these are few and far between. 90 miles (140km) to the north, the town of Putre is the starting point for tours to Parque Nacional Lauca. Putre is popular with tourists and you may be able to club together to rent a car or organize a tour to Surire. Beds and cooking facilities are available but you will not be allowed to use them without prior consent from CONAF in Arica.

16. San Pedro de Atacama

Located in the Atacama Desert, the driest place on earth, San Pedro may not appear to offer much at first. But outside the town there are at least five sites that are worth a visit:

▶ *El Tatio*: 20 miles (30km) east, set between volcanoes, the site of the highest geyser in the world and easily the most impressive in South America. Best in the early morning.

▶ *Valle de la Luna*: 8 miles (12km) west, a bizarre lunar landscape, particularly remarkable at dawn and dusk.

▶ *Salar de Atacama*: 60 miles (100km) southeast. The world's third largest saltpan. Flying pink flamingoes contrast wonderfully with the never ending whiteness.

▶ *Toconao*: 23 miles (37km) south. Splendid stands of pepper trees in which you should find rheas and maybe Austral pygmy owls.

▶ *Laguna Miscanti and Laguna Lejía*: South of Toconao, these high-altitude lakes are situated in the Reserva Nacional de Los Flamencos. All year round, three species of flamingo abound. On the way look out for herds of llama and guanaco.

Getting there: Fly to Calama, or take a bus (22 hours from Santiago, 6 from Antofagasta). From Calama a bus will take you the 60 miles (100km) or so to San Pedro. You can drive yourself, but gas is costly.

In San Pedro, there are many tour companies. Avoid the cheapest and try to find an English-speaking guide. Most tours visit the five sites, but they are also very flexible and should you wish to arrange to

climb a volcano or visit some extraordinary sites in Bolivia, they will accommodate you:

Cascada Expediciones – info@cascada-expediciones.com Tel. (562) 234 2274
Cosmo Andino Expediciones – cosmoandino@entelchile.net
Turismo Cocha – http://www. cocha.com/chile/tours/sanpedro/pac kage/atacama.htm

Note: From San Pedro you can enter Bolivia. Your tour company can arrange transportation to Laguna Verde and then into Bolivia—Perhaps the most beautiful border crossing in the world. (See Uyuni under Bolivia, above.)

FURTHER READING

As well as any of the common guidebooks, look out for:
A Guide to the Birds and Mammals of Coastal Patagonia by Graham Harris (illustrator) & William Conway. Princeton University Press. ISBN: 0 69105 831 8
Natural Patagonia: Natural Argentina & Chile by Marcelo D. Beccaceci. Pangaea Publications. ISBN: 0 96301 803 5
Travels in a Thin Country: A Journey Through Chile by Sara Wheeler, Modern Library, New York, 1999
Voyage of the Beagle: Journal of Researches into the Natural History and Geology of the Countries Visited During the Voyage of H.M.S. Beagle by Charles Darwin, John Clare & J. W. Tibble, Wordsworth Editions, Ware, England, 1997

COLOMBIA

Colombia provides maximum variety within one country, a fascinating mixture of different habitats resulting in a diverse flora and fauna, including more bird species (over 1800) than any other country. Due to its small size you can combine whale watching, mountain biking, and forest exploration in the same day. From the wettest region in South America (El Chocó) to the crystal clear waters of the Caribbean coast to the snow-capped Nevados mountains, Colombia is an eco-tourist's paradise.

It is, of course, notorious for its violence. But as a tourist you could visit and never realize there was a problem. Keep away from the no-go zones deep in the jungle and within some cities, and you should be fine. The tourist police in Colombia are very good, and in many places an armed guard will automatically accompany you.

TOP WEBSITES

The following are good starting points and particularly important for updates on the areas to avoid.

The Lonely Planet for Colombia – http://www.lonelyplanet.com.au/dest/sam/col.htm

Viajes Chapinero – http://www.viajeschapinero.com.co/colombia.htm

My Travel Guide.com – http://www.mytravelguide.com/countries/colombia/

The World Travel Guide – http://www.wtgonline.com/data/col/col.asp

Travel Spots – http://www.travelspots.com/colombia.htm

Colombia Hotspots – http://www.camacdonald.com/birding/sacolombia.htm

TOURS

Colombia Hotels – http://www.infortur.com.co/

Hotelstravel.com – http://www.hotelstravel.com/colombia.html

Ladatco Tours – http://www.ladatco.com/e-col.htm

Path Tours – http://www.pathtours.com/

Amazon River Tours – http://www.infohub.com/TRAVEL/SIT/sit_pages/Colombia.html

Birding Colombia – http://www.proaxis.com/~salaman/birding_colombia/

Nature Guides – http://www.natureguides.com/Colombia.html

Colombia's Best

THE HIGHLANDS

The Andes split into 3 mountain ranges when they enter Colombia – the Cordillera Eastern, Central, and Western – and each runs all the way to the Caribbean lowlands. A separate range is the Sierra Nevada de Santa Marta.

1. Parque Nacional Los Nevados
Breathtaking views from Nevado del Ruíz and Nevado de Tolima. In the cloudforest lush vegetation including giant ferns, orchids, and bromeliads provides food for rare animals such as spectacled bear, pudú, and Andean fox.

The high Andes, characterized by the extremely tall grass *Espeletia*, are good for hummingbirds, Andean coot, and Andean teal. Two notable raptors are the red-backed hawk and the mountain caracara.

Getting there: Buses to the park and organized tours are easily booked from Manizales. Good range of accommodation, though it is expensive and busy in January. Alternatively Ibagué has plenty of hotels and tour agents who will arrange trips into the park for groups on foot or on horseback. For further information and tours, see:
Los Nevados National Park – http://www.viajeschapinero.com.co/nevados.htm

2. Parque Nacional Sierra Nevada del Cocuy
In the Eastern Cordillera. Awesome views, beautiful lakes, and fascinating flora and fauna, especially the club mosses and chuquiraguas found around the waterfalls. Some unusual species of hummingbird, notably the black-tailed trainbearer, found at high altitudes.

Getting there: Stay at El Cocuy or Güicán, both of which have a regular bus service to Bogotá and Capitanejo. Plenty of hotels and it is easy to arrange organized hikes and tours of the mountains.

3. The Sierra Nevada de Santa Marta
The highest coastal mountain range in the world, rising from the Caribbean coast to 19,000ft (5800m) in just 30 miles (45km). Much of the higher ground is desolate rocky scree and *páramo*, but the lower slopes are richly

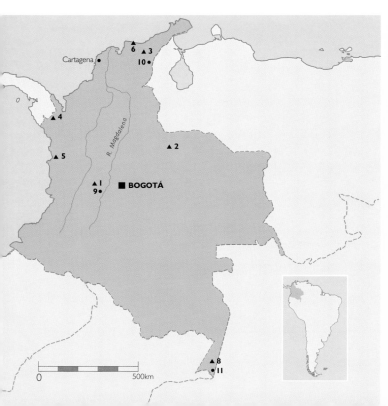

KEY TO MAP

1	Parque Nacional Los Nevados
2	Parque Nacional Sierra Nevada del Cocuy
3	The Sierra Nevada de Santa Marta
4	Parque Nacional Los Katíos
5	Parque Nacional Ensenada de Utría
6	Parque Nacional Tayrona
7	The San Andrés and Providencia Archipelago
8	Parque Nacional Amacayacú
9	Ibagué
10	Valledupar
11	Leticia

forested with lianas, bromeliads, and euphorbia. Poison-dart frogs, butterflies, and tree vipers are prevalent in the canopy.

Getting there: It is not possible to hike deep in the Sierra due to complaints by the indigenous people, but there are guided day trips of the forested valleys. Stay in Valledupar where you can hire local guides. Valledupar is a big town with plenty of accommodation, an airport, and regular buses to most major towns in Colombia.
For further information, see:
Sierra de Marta National Park – http://www.viajeschapinero.com.co/sierra.htm
Nature Guides – http://home.earthlink.net/~natureguides/Colombia.html

THE COAST

Colombia's coast is 2000 miles (3000km) long. To the west lies the Pacific, to the north the Caribbean.

The Pacific Coast

4. Parque Nacional Los Katíos
Stretching between the Cordillera Occidental and the Pacific coast lies the Chocó forest, one of South America's most pristine and among the most biodiverse reserves in the world. Very wet, so visit during the 'dry season', December–March. The fascinating national park runs right up to the border with Panama, but is unfortunately a center for guerrilla activity and not recommended at the time of writing.

Getting there: Buses to Chocó from Medellín and Pereira most days, a spectacular 8–10 hour journey over the Cordillera Occidental. Hotels in the nearby town of Quibdó.

5. Parque Nacional Ensenada de Utría
Beautiful white sandy beaches and lush tropical rainforest; known locally as 'the tanager coast' because birdlife is so prolific. Also good for marine life – dolphins can be spotted all year round and humpback whales June–October.

Getting there: Organized day trip from El Valle or Nuquí. Both towns offer accommodation and are well served by local buses.

The Caribbean Coast
This vast area of swampy lowland has some interesting places to visit.

6. Parque Nacional Tayrona
A remote region near the town of Santa Marta, with pristine deserted beaches, untouched coastal forests, and abundant wildlife. If you are lucky you will see red howler monkeys, hummingbirds, iguanas, and a huge diversity of insects. The Ciénaga de Santa Marta lagoon – teeming with bird and plant life, frogs, and toads – can be seen on most organized trips to the park.

Getting there: Santa Marta is best reached by bus from Barranquilla and has a good range of hotels and hostels. From there, catch a minibus from the market or ask at hotels for organized excursions. Ciénaga de Santa Marta lies on the road from Barranquilla to the national park.

7. The San Andrés and Providencia Archipelago
The reefs off these small islands nearly 300 miles (500km) north of the coast are famous for their crystal clear waters and abundance of marine life. Diving is excellent: look out for hawksbill turtles crunching on sponges and gray reef sharks hiding under coral ledges.

Getting there: San Andrés is connected by air to most major Colombian cities. Tour boats and cruises take 4 days and leave from Cartagena. Providencia is reached by air from San Andrés in about 25 minutes. Boats take 8 hours but are not regular. Plenty of places to stay on San Andrés, though it is expensive. Providencia offers less choice; most of the decent accommodation is at Playa Agua Dulce.

THE RAINFOREST

More than 30% of Colombia is covered by Amazon rainforest of very high quality.

8. Parque Nacional Amacayacú
Situated in the Department of Amazonas and covers 11,000 sq. miles (28,000 sq. km). Look out for the thick buttress roots of the axe-breaker tree, the rubber tree and the strangling fig. Mammals

Tropical hummingbird.

include the three-toed sloth, the tamandua, the white-eared opossum, and cotton-top tamarin.

There is a visitors' center with lodging for 40 people, a museum, an auditorium, and a research center. Four platforms in the rainforest allow you to observe flora and fauna, and have refuges in which to stay overnight. You can also visit two Tikuna Indian groups within the park. Ask your guide if it is possible to visit any of the ox-bow lakes and waterways where manatees and spectacled caiman and hoatzins can be found.

Getting there: Leticia is a good base, with flights from Bogotá most days. The park is 40 miles (60km) upstream at the mouth of the Matamata Creek. Boats leave daily and take about 2 hours. Alternatively, several tour operators arrange a wide range of tours from 2–10 days. Independent guides and touts for tour companies can be found in Leticia and on the riverfront. The Yavari river trips are consistently recommended. Plenty of accommodation in Leticia.

FURTHER READING

As well as the usual country guidebooks and field guides, try any of the following before departure:
Alta Colombia: The Splendor of the Mountains by Juan Pablo Ruíz, Carlos Mauricio Vega & Cristobal Von Rothkirch (photographer), St Martin's Press, New York, 1997
Colombia: The Genocidal Democracy by Javier Giraldo, Common Courage Press, Monroe, 1996
Love in the Time of Cholera by Gabriel García Márquez, Penguin USA, New York, 1989
One Hundred Years of Solitude by Gabriel García Márquez, Harperperennial Library, Bogota, 1998
Panoramic Colombia by Enrique Pulecio Marino & Miguel Salazar Aparicio (photographer). Villegas Editores. ISBN: 9 58939 338 1
Tropic: The Nature of Columbia by Aldo Brando (photographer) & Arturo Guerrero, Villegas Editores, Bogota, 1998

ECUADOR

One of the most popular tourist destinations within South America as people are attracted to a seemingly insignificant group of 19 islands lying around 625 miles (1000km) off the coast. The Galápagos are, however, far from trivial. They led to the most important biological revolution of all time – the theory of evolution by natural selection, published in *Origin of Species* by Charles Darwin. People come to experience the atmosphere that generated this theory and to revel in the islands' unique and incredibly tame wildlife – so tame that you must remember to pack your macro lens as well as your zoom.

The rest of Ecuador has been quick to learn that the majority of its visitors are interested in wildlife – other eco-tourism activities abound.

TOP WEBSITES

Many good sites. Try:

Ecuador Explorer – http://www.ecuadorexplorer.com/
Ecuador – http://www.ecuador.org/index.html
The Funky Fish Ecuador Guide – http://www.qni.com/~mj/
Ecuador Eco-tourism – http://www.ecuador.org/ecotouri.htm

TOURS

There are numerous tour operators on the Internet. Here is a selection:

Ecuador – Tour operators – http://www.travel.com/country/ecu/to.htm
Birds of Ecuador (tours specifically for 'twitchers') – http://www.qni.com/~mj/boe/boe.html
Travel Ecuador – http://www.travelecuador.net/
Latin Tours of Ecuador – http://www.galapagos-tours.com/
Galápagos Dive Land – http://www.galapagosdiveland.com/html/ecuador.html

Inca Holidays – http://www.incaholidays.com/
Adventure Discoveries International – http://www.abstravel.com/discover.shtml
Tropical Ecological Adventures – http://www.tropiceco.com

There are some eco-tourism companies that are out to make a quick buck. Such enterprises do not have experienced guides, do not go to the best locations and can be damaging to the environment. As a result Ecuador has set up an 'eco-tourism watchdog'. If you want to confirm the reliability of your chosen operator e-mail Raul García on Etransturi@uio.satnet.net.

Ecuador's best

THE COAST AND ISLANDS

1. The Galápagos
Home to iguanas, penguins, fur seals, boobies, frigates, giant tortoises, lava cacti, finches, and a plethora of marine life including sperm whales, the Galápagos are a must, but do not come cheap. Expect to pay US$900 for a 6-day tour on the most basic boat. Prices are set high to limit the number of tourists and thus ensure that the park will be worth visiting for years to come. Remember, in the interests of conservation, do not touch any animals, be careful not to transfer sand from one island to the next and take all your litter with you!

There are 45 different docking points around the islands, and from each landing stage there are several trails. All of the trails are excellent and will provide you with very close encounters with birds, reptiles, and mammals. In addition, diving is superb with an excellent diversity of hard and soft coral, tropical fish, and invertebrates. There is a great variety of dive sites. You can tour the Galápagos on a dive boat or arrange day trips from the dive schools on the islands. Currently no dive guidebook to the Galápagos exists, but all companies are experienced (and safe) and will take you to the best places. Underwater visibility best January–March.

Getting there: Daily flights from Quito and Guayaquil to Baltra and Puerto Baquerizo Moreno. If your tour does not include the flight, make sure you fly to the correct destination.

All boats are required to have a park-trained guide on board – make sure that your boat's guide is trained to naturalist level III: This means that he or she will have an excellent knowledge of the flora and fauna and will be fluent in English, Spanish, and one other language.

Organize a tour before you arrive on the islands; if you have already invested the money for your flight, tour operators know that they can charge through the nose since having got there you are unlikely to turn back.

The following are consistently recommended but be warned that when a boat's crew changes, its recommendation may no longer be valid. Get up-to-date information via the Internet.
International Expeditions – http://www.ietravel.com

KEY TO MAP

1 The Galápagos
2 Isla de la Plata
3 Cuyabeno Wildlife Reserve
4 Parque Nacional Yasuní
5 Parque Nacional Podocarpus
6 Maquipucuna Reserve
7 Parque Nacional Sangay
8 Baltra
9 Puerto Baquerizo Moreno
10 Puerto Lopez
11 Coca

0   200km

QUITO

R. Cuyabeno
R. Napo
R. Tiputini

0   200km

Andean condor. The symbol of the Andes may be graceful in the air, but it is singularly unattractive on the ground. Its naked head is an adaptation to rooting round in carcasses.

Explorama Diving – http://www. exploratur.com/scuba.htm
Galápagos Classic Cruises – E-mail – Galapagoscruises@ compuserve.com
*Galápagos Adventure Tour*s – http://www.galapagos.co.uk
Galacruises Expeditions – http://www.galapagosseaman.com.ec
Quasar Nautica – http://www. quasarnautica.com
Galápagos Tours – http://www. galapagos-tours.com
Galasam Galápagos Tours – http://www.galasam.com.ec
Scuba Iguana – E-mail – scubaigu@ayora.ecua.net.ec

There is a cheaper way of seeing the Galápagos, by going over on the supply boat. This does not sail all that regularly, however, and is certainly not a good way of seeing the islands. Occasionally a group of tourists will club together and hire a large vessel to take them there. Look for news on hostel noticeboards, particularly in Guayaquil. Expect to pay around US$100 to get there (a saving of US$250 on the flight).

2. Isla de la Plata
Known as the poor man's Galápagos, this is a superb alternative for travelers on a budget, reached via the coastal town of Puerto López. 15 miles (24km) offshore, Isla de la Plata's many trails will take you past the same species as the Galápagos with the exception of tortoises and iguanas. To compensate, some say that the viewing of albatross courting is better. The snorkeling is also excellent. May–October there is a very good chance of seeing humpback whales on their migration. These whales tend to stick closer to the shore and are very rarely seen at the Galápagos. A day's excursion including guide, lunch and park entry fee should cost no more than US$50.

Getting there: Regular buses from Quito and Guayaquil to Puerto López. Nearest airport is Portoviejo, 1 hour to the north. The reserve can be toured within a day but if you need to stay in Puerto López, there are plenty of (low-quality) hotels.

THE RAINFOREST

Pockets of rainforest all over Ecuador are open to tourists. Enthusiasts should head to the vast area known as the Oriente where there are lodges, guides, and many destinations to choose from. New ones, which may or may not contain fantastic wildlife, emerge every year. Ask around in tour agencies, and ask to read references, since any photos they show could have been taken anywhere. Two established and recommended destinations are:

3. Cuyabeno Wildlife Reserve
With more than 500 species of birds, 250 fish, and 100 mammals, including river dolphins and an incredible 15 species of primate, this is a superb example of the Amazon's tropical richness and beauty. Lodges differ in the quality of their accommodation and guides as well as of the excursions they make. Birdwatchers should ask to be taken to Imuya Lake or Inapari Lake. The following companies are good:

Ecuador Explorer Tours – http:// www.ecuadorexplorer.com/html/ body_rainforest_people_cuyabeno. html
Neotropic Tours and The Grand Cuyabeno Lake Lodge – http://www.ecuadorexplorer.com/ neotropic
Siecoya Treks – http://www. travelecuador.net/cuyabeno.html
Neuvo Mundo and The Cuyabeno River Lodge – http://www. tourworld.ab.ca/nmundo/amazon. htm
Flotel Orellana (a floating hotel) – http://www.discoveramazonia.com/ ecuador/flotel.htm

It is worth booking trips before you arrive since you will not be able to lower prices on arrival and you run the risk of lodges being full.

Getting there: Fly to Lago Agrio (from Quito) and then get a boat on the Río Aguarico to the appropriate lodge on the Río Cuyabeno.

4. Parque Nacional Yasuní
This huge park is explored out of Coca along the Río Napo. To reach the pristine forest requires a long boat ride – hence, trips of less than 3 days are not worthwhile. Expect to be inundated with howler monkeys, capuchins, emperor tamarins, squirrel monkeys, hoatzins, toucans, and macaws. You may also see tapirs and even jaguars. If you have time, rent a boat with a guide to take you along the Río Tiputini, one of the most beautiful and animal abundant river trips in the Amazon which no regular tours visit. Many people are attracted to this area to see one of the last indigenous peoples, the Huaorani. Allow at least 5 days for such a trip and insist upon seeing your guide's documentation, since few guides are allowed to visit their territory.

Along the Río Napo, there are many award-winning lodges. Look out for those with butterfly farms, tree platforms, and excursions to clay-licks. La Selva Jungle Lodge was a winner in the 1999 eco-tourism awards. The following are consistently recommended:
La Selva Jungle Lodge – http://www.discoveramazonia.com/ ecuador/laselva.htm
or tel. (561) 334 0489

Sacha Lodge – http://www.
sachalodge.com/
Yuturi Forest Lodge – E-mail:
yuturilodge@yahoo.com

Getting there: Daily flights from
Quito where you will be met by an
array of tour operators and private
guides. The lodges are then
reached by river.

THE CLOUD FOREST

5. Parque Nacional Podocarpus
Located in the southernmost
Andes of Ecuador and ranging in
altitude from 3100–12,100ft
(950–3700m), the park is divided
into two halves – the upper
permontane and lower subtropical
section. With a diversity of natural
habitats from upper tropical
rainforest to alpine páramo, its
estimated 600 or so bird species
include the threatened golden-
plumed parakeet, mountain toucan,
cock-of-the-rock, red-faced parrot,
bearded guan, and bay-vented
cotinga. The park also supports
populations of mountain tapir,
northern pudú, and spectacled
bear.

Getting there: To reach the upper
section, take the Vilcabamba bus
from Loja for 20 minutes, then
hike for 5 miles (8km) to the guard
station. Or get a taxi from Loja all
the way.

For the lower section, take a taxi
from Zamora to the entrance and
then walk 1/2 mile (1km) to the
guard station. Camping is the only
option in the lower section; in the
upper there are rooms available at
the guards' station – book in Loja
before arrival (Tel: 571534). But
due to its ease of access, most
visitors who want an extended stay
simply make several return day
trips from Loja or Zamora.

Few tour groups include
Podocarpus on their itinerary, but
try *Madre Tierra* –
http://www.ecuadorexplorer.com/
madretierra/html/activities.html

6. Maquipucana Reserve
With few visitors, this large private
reserve makes a welcome break
from certain lodges in the Oriente.
It is described on page 44.

Wire-tailed manakin. A male prepares to perform his unique display on a branch in Yasuni National Park, Ecuador.

Getting there: A 2-hour drive from
Quito via Nanagalito. 4x4 vehicles
are advisable. The one lodge in the
reserve is highly recommended:
Maquipucana Lodge –
http://www.rainforest.org.uk/html/
expmaq.html

THE HIGHLANDS

7. Parque Nacional Sangay
Situated some 125 miles (200km)
south of Quito, this huge reserve
encompasses several magnificent
volcanoes before plunging down to
the eastern base of the Cordillera.
It contains tundra, *páramo*, stunted
elfin forest, cloudforest, montane
forest, and subtropical rainforest.
Mountain tapir, spectacled bear
(which you may hear howling at
night), and various primate species
may all be seen. Views of Sangay
volcano, giant ferns, towering old
palms, and large animal tracks
make this a memorable experience.
All walks are somewhat strenuous.
Serious climbers wanting to
organize their own treks should talk
to the South American Explorers'
Club in Quito for advice on when to
go, what to take, and which guides
are reliable (see http://www.

samexplo.org/opening.htm).

Getting there: Taxi from Riobamba
to the park's entrance near Alao or
go with one of the many tour
companies – be sure to ask which
tour each company recommends
for wildlife:
Andisimo Tours – http://www.
andisimo.com/exped.html
Tropical Ecological Adventures –
http://www.tropiceco.com/html/
climbing.html
Classical Andean Journeys –
http://www4.ecotrek.com.ec/andian.
htm
Sierra Nevada Expeditions –
http://www.aha.ru/~sierra/en_hike.
htm

FURTHER READING

As well as guidebooks and
Amazonian books, look out for:
*Ecuador and its Galápagos Islands:
The Ecotravelers' Wildlife Guide*
by David Pearson (editor) & Les
Beletsky, Academic Press, London,
2000
*Ecuador in Focus: A Guide to the
People, Politics and Culture* by
Wilma Roos & Omer Van
Renterghem, Interlink Publishing
Group, New York, 1997
The Fishes of the Galápagos Islands
by Robert J. Lavenberg
(contributor), Jack Stein Grove &
Jean-Michel Cousteau, Stanford
University Press, Stanford, 1997
Flowering Plants of the Galápagos
by Conley K. McMullen, Cornell
University Press, New York, 1999
Galápagos by Michael Jackson,
University of Calgary Press,
Calgary, 1997
*A Guide to the Birds of the
Galápagos* by Isabel Castro &
Antonia Phillips (illustrator),
Christopher Helm, London, 1996
*The New Key to Ecuador and the
Galápagos* by David L. Pearson,
David W. Middleton & Doug
McCarthy (illustrator), Ulysses
Press, Berkeley, 1999
*The Traveler's Guide to the
Galápagos Islands* by Barry Boyce,
Hunter Publications, Edison, USA,
1998

FRENCH GUIANA

An intriguing mix of a country, this overseas department of France has an array of prisons – most of which now stand empty – some great beaches, a variety of interesting habitats, and Kourou, South America's answer to Cape Canaveral. Eco-tourism is an adventure which is worth the effort since 90% of the country is primary tropical rainforest.

TOP WEBSITES

Internet services are poor, unless you read French. Try:
Escape Amazonie (French) – http://www.espace-amazonie.com/
My Travel Guide – French Guiana – http://www.mytravelguide.com/countries/french_guiana/
Lonely Planet – French Guiana – http://www.lonelyplanet.com/dest/sam/fgu.htm
A Personal Guide (French) – http://www.multimania.com/toucan/framefr1.htm
La Guyane (French) – http://laguyane.free.fr/French.htm

TOURS

Escape Amazonie (see above) offers a variety of tours along with much background information. Also try any of the following:
JAL Voyages, 1 Ave. des Plages, Montjoly. Tel: 31 68 20
Takari Tour, Colline du Montabo. Tel: 31 19 60
Guyane Excursions, Centre Commercial Simarouba, Kourou. Tel: 32 05 41
Somarig, 32 Us Rue. Tel: 30 29 80

French Guiana's Best

THE COAST

Beautiful, and best between April and August.

1. Les Hattes

The beach is a nesting site for leatherback turtles. Nesting peaks in May and June, hatchling emergence in July and August. Since the turtles emerge at night, bring mosquito repellent. Keep at least 16ft (5m) from the turtles and do not shine flashlights directly at them. Most importantly, never pick up hatchlings, even if they appear to be going the wrong way. They will imprint on your body odor and never return to their natal beach to lay eggs. You will effectively be sterilizing them.

Getting there: Regular buses from the capital Cayenne to Aouara. From Aouara, no public transportation, but most cars on the road will act as your 'taxi'. Or rent a car in Cayenne and drive yourself. Nearest accommodation in Mana, 25 miles (40 km) away.

2. Iles du Salat

Expenal colony with a small turtle beach, plus capuchins, squirrel monkeys, agoutis, hummingbirds, and macaws in the island's secondary forest.

Getting there: Two boats a day from Kourou, which is serviced regularly by buses from all over the country.

3. Kaw

A mere 40 miles (60km) from Cayenne, the Kaw Marshes are bound by rivers, mountains and the Atlantic and consist of a vast herbaceous marsh beyond a wide muddy area covered mainly by mangrove and forest swamps, inhabited by one of the last big populations of black caimans. There is also a great diversity of waterbirds.

Getting there: By road via Roura in the mountains, or by dug-out canoe from the Cayenne Road as the road leaves the coast and begins to head towards the hills.

THE RAINFOREST

The adventurous may rent a boat and hire a guide and head off into the smaller rivers. Otherwise, try:

4. Saül

Virtually in the middle of French Guiana and surrounded by rainforest, Saül was once a remote gold mining settlement. The road remains open to scientists and tourists, and an extensive and well marked trail system takes visitors through a variety of vegetation zones. Good diversity of birds (including trogons and aracaris), butterflies, and reptiles.

Consult local guides (available in the village and at Eaux Claires – see below) for up-to-date information about trails, because their condition may change drastically even after only a few months without maintenance.

Getting there: On Monday, Wednesday, and Friday by a 45-minute Air Guyane flight over undisturbed forest for most of the distance. Rustic accommodation in the town – for the most part, visitors sleep in hammocks, and are sometimes required to use their own. Take enough food for the duration of your stay – the local shop sells only rum and sugar. 4 miles (7km) north on the Route de Bélizon is an excellent tourist facility providing sheltered hammock space and great food alongside a beautiful stream (*Les Eaux Claires*. Tel: 30 91 11, fax: 594 27 01 71). Alternatively, rent a guided boat in Mana and head up the Mana River for 9–12 days – your skipper will know where Saül is.

5. Maripasoula and the River Maroni

The town has little to offer, but is the departure point for trips along the Maroni and Inini Rivers (see Escape Amazonie website, above).The surrounding forest is beautiful. Expect to see various primate species, caiman and a multitude of birds including macaws, toucans, and jacanas. Nights are spent at the primitive camps of Saut Sonnelle and Tolenga.

Getting there: Fly to Maripasoula from Cayenne. Arriving via the River Maroni could take over 20 days.

FURTHER READING

South American guidebooks do cover French Guiana, but not in detail. The definitive guide has yet to be written. In the meantime try:
Guide to the Vascular Plants of Central French Guiana by Scott A. Mori (editor), Georges Cremers & Jean Granville, New York Botanical Garden, New York, 1997

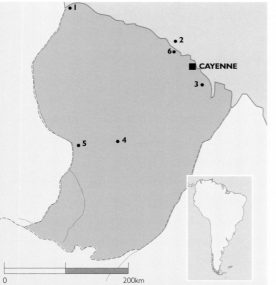

KEY TO MAP

I	Les Hattes
2	Iles du Salat
3	Kaw
4	Saül
5	Maripasoula
6	Kourou

CAYENNE

0   200km

GUYANA

An increasingly popular holiday destination, containing some beautiful beaches, pristine rainforest, one of the most beautiful waterfalls in the world, and a high density of harpy eagles. At present it is probably best to combine visiting Guyana with other countries, but as tourism is developing at such a rate, it is worth monitoring the situation via the Tourism and Hospitality Association of Guyana, 157 Waterloo Street, North Cummingsburg, Georgetown, Guyana. Tel: (2) 50807. Fax: (2) 50817. E-mail: tag@solutions2000.net http://www.interknowledge.com/guyana/

TOP WEBSITES

Guyana Guide – http://www.guyanaguide.com/
Guyana – http://www.caribbeannews.com/hot/guyana1.htm
Epinions.com – Guyana – http://www.epinions.com/./
trvl-r-Geographia:Guyanaa
IWOKRAMA – International Centre For Rain Forest Conservation And Development – http://www.sdnp.org.gy/iwokrama

TOURS

Wilderness Explorers – http://www.wilderness-explorers.com/guyana.htm
Pan Sur Guyana Tours – http://www.pan-sur.com/pan-sur/Guyana/fraguyana.htm
Wonderland Tours – 158 Waterloo St, Georgetown, Tel: 53122. Fax: 59795 (24 hrs)
Discover Tours – Hotel Tower, 74–5 Main St, Georgetown, Tel: 72011, Fax: 65691
Shell Beach Adventures – Tel: 54483/4. Fax: 60532
Rainbow River Marshall Falls – c/o Allison, Guyenterprise Agency, 234 Almond St, Tel: 2 69874. Fax 2 56959
Greenheart Tours – 36 Craig St, Campbellville, Georgetown, Tel or Fax: 58219

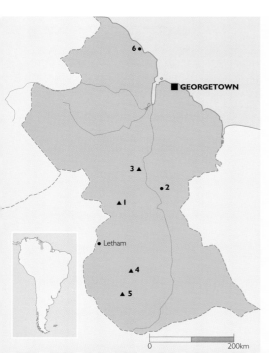

KEY TO MAP

1 Iwokrama Forest Reserve
2 Maparri Wilderness
3 Kaieteur National Park
4 The Kanuku Mountains
5 Rupununi Savannah
6 Shell Beach

Toco toucan, widely distributed in the rainforests of the Guyanas, Brazil, Paraguay, Bolivia and northern Argentina.

Guyana's Best

THE RAINFOREST

Many of the potential destinations are also home to indigenous communities who have used the rainforest for food; big animals may be scarce.

1. Iwokrama Forest Reserve
Some 200 miles (300km) south of Georgetown lie almost 1 million acres (400,000 hectares) of high quality rainforest of which half is devoted to eco-tourism and half to the sustainable use of forest products. The reserve covers several distinct land systems, including the undulating plains of the Kurupukari Sand Terraces, the steep granite of the Iwokrama Mountains, and flat *terra firme* forest. Each has its own flora, and the reserve boasts more than 450 species of birds, 120 species of reptiles and amphibians, and 150 species of mammals. A key feature is the relative abundance of jaguar, black caiman, giant river otters, giant river turtles, and harpy eagles.

Getting there: The Georgetown–Lethem road bisects the reserve. A bus from either town will take you to the park headquarters. Once in the reserve there is a multitude of rivers that you can canoe along, though you must be accompanied by a forest ranger. Good accommodation at the headquarters; camping allowed anywhere in the park. Georgetown-based tour companies will take you into the reserve or you can arrange to stay at the lodge yourself. E-mail: iwokrama@guyana.net.gy.

2. Maparri Wilderness
A tributary of the Rupununi River with a rustic camp (Maparri Wilderness Camp) set up for tourism. You should see macaws, toucans, tayras, agoutis, capuchins, and possibly even harpy eagles and ocelots.

Getting there: Only possible through a tour agency by a combination of air, jeep, and canoe.

Giant river otter. It lives in shallow creeks throughout South America, excluding Chile, Uruguay, and Argentina.

THE COAST

6. Shell Beach

Each year, between March and May, hundreds of female turtles come ashore here, on Guyana's northern Atlantic coast, to nest. At least four of the world's eight species of endangered turtles – the leatherback, green, Olive Ridley, and hawksbill – nest here at the same time each year and it is possible that a fifth – the loggerhead – also uses this beach. Certainly an extraordinary spectacle. However, Guyana's turtles suffer from poaching, since their meat is considered a delicacy. Conservation International are trying to put a stop to this through education. Financial input through eco-tourism will help a great deal. So go!

Getting there: Northwest of Georgetown via the coast road. Ask the Tourist Board where the best sites are, since they vary from year to year. E-mail: tag@solutions2000.net

FURTHER READING

Guyana's guidebooks can only improve in the next few years. In the meantime, as well as the brief sections in the well-known guides, try:
Guyana by Katherine Dunn & Alexis Rockman (illustrator), Twin Palms Publishing, Santa Fe, 1996
Guyana in Pictures (Visual Geography Series) by F. Charles, Lerner Publications, Minneapolis, 1987
Guyana: The Lost Eldorado, My Fifty Years in the Guyanese Wilds by Matthew French Young, Peepal Tree Press, Leeds, 1998

THE HIGHLANDS

Towards the Brazilian border, Guyana's rainforest begins to rise. Towering out of the undulating landscape are some beautiful mountains.

3. Kaieteur National Park

Guyana's biggest tourist attraction and one of the most impressive waterfalls in the world, five times higher than Niagara and wider than Angel Falls in Venezuela.

The park supports a unique micro-environment that includes many tank bromeliads, the largest to be found anywhere in the world. The bromeliads themselves are often home to several frogs. It is also possible to see silver foxes, armadillos, ocelots, various primates, cock-of-the-rocks, and the local swifts which each evening fly through the torrent of water to roost in the rocks behind.

Getting there: Fly from Georgetown's Ogle Airport, where you can arrange circular flights, flights that give you 2 hours at the falls and flights that take you to other falls beyond. All will be cheapest if there are four passengers. The only alternative is to go with a tour company from Georgetown, which will take you to the falls in the course of a great four-day tour via rainforest and rivers.

4. The Kanuku Mountains

A beautiful place with the highest known population of harpy eagle on the planet. Conservation International has established a reserve so that the harpy's future is all but guaranteed. They are looking to develop an eco-tourist venture within the reserve by early 2002.

Getting there: Currently inaccessible but this will change soon. For now only the lower slopes can be visited from lodges in the grassland savannahs (see below).

THE GRASSLAND

5. Rupununi Savannah

Guyana's grassland consists of two parts: the Intermediate Savannah and the Rupununi Savannah. The latter, in the very southwest of the country, offers fascinating flora, and all the lodges are close enough to the Kanuku Mountains to allow for day trips to the best forest in Guyana. Around Kanuku expect to see woolly monkeys, spider monkeys, howler monkeys, saddle-back tamarins, opossums, and many bird species.

Every year between June and August, the grassland area floods. During this time it is possible to canoe all over the southern part of Guyana, which should allow you to see black caimans, anacondas, turtles, herons, scarlet ibis, capybara, harpy eagles, ocelots, giant otters, and more.

Getting there: Bus from Georgetown to Lethem, where it is possible to rent a 4x4 vehicle. Alternatively tour operators in Georgetown will arrange transport.

Many of these lodges can be viewed on the Wilderness Explorers website. Consistently recommended is Karanambu Ranch, owned by Diane McTurk, who is famous for her work in rehabilitating orphaned giant otters.

PARAGUAY

A landlocked country divided by the Río Paraguay into the mostly uninhabited wilderness of the *chaco* to the west and the more fertile, rolling grasslands, and forest to the east, Paraguay has remained largely undiscovered by tourists. Sadly its roads are rather antiquated, so access to some national parks is very difficult. But Paraguay does have areas that will delight eco-tourists and make the effort of getting there worthwhile.

Before visiting Paraguay it is worth contacting Guyra Paraguay, an organization whose aim is to conserve endemic birds, for advice about the best places to go and who to contact about obtaining a permit:

Guyra Paraguay: Conservación de Aves, Bélgica 165 c/ Mcal. López, C.C. 714, Asunción, Paraguay. Tel/Fax: 595 21 604 768 or E-mail: guyra@highway.com.py

TOP WEBSITES

As the number of tourists visiting Paraguay begins to increase, more internet sites will spring up. For now, have a look at:

The Unofficial Homepage of Paraguay – http://www.eskimo.com/~krautm/index.html

Paraguay – http://www.pla.net.py/intertours/home.htm

Lonely Planet – Paraguay – http://www.lonelyplanet.com/dest/sam/par.htm

TOURS

Few tour companies include Paraguay on their itineraries and those that do offer little for the eco-tourist. However there are companies out there who excel in making customized tours:

Focus Tours – http://www.focustours.com/

Ladatco Tours – http://www.ladatco.com/

Design Travel and Tours – http://www.designtraveltours.com/

Ecoturs Paraguay – http://www.pla.net.py/intertours/ecoturs.htm

Latin American Escapes – http://www.latinamericanescapes.com

Blue-fronted Amazon found in Paraguay, Brazil and northern Argentina.

Paraguay's Best

None of the following is easy to get to, so it may be best to investigate the trips on offer from tour companies in Asunción. To visit the majority of national parks (and other state-protected areas) in Paraguay you need a permit which can be obtained from the National Parks Service. If you are traveling independently, make sure you do this in advance.

For National Park administration: Dirección de Parques Nacionales y Vida Silvestre, Ing. Marciano Barreto, Director, Subsecretaria de Recursos Naturales y Medio Ambiente, Kilimetro 11, San Lorenzo, Paraguay. E-mail: dirdpnvs@webmail.com.py

For Private Nature Reserves: Fundación Moisés Bertoni, Procer Arguello 208, entre Mcal. López y Boggiani, C.C. 714, Asunción, Paraguay. Tel: 595 21 608 741 or E-mail: moises@sce.cnc.una.py

You could also try e-mailing the director of the National Park Service, Marciano Barreto, on dirdpnvs@webmail.com.py. He is more likely to reply if correspondence is in Spanish.

THE FOREST

1. Parque Nacional Defensores del Chaco

Paraguay's largest national park – an impressive 3000 sq. miles (780,000 hectares) – one of the hardest to get to, since much of the 520-mile (830km) road from Asunción is impassable after rain. Amid the impressively thorny stands of quebraco, algarrobo, palo santo, and various cacti, there is a chance of seeing rare mammals such as jaguar, puma, Geoffroy's cat, giant Chacoan peccary, maned wolf, and giant anteater.

Getting there: No public

KEY TO MAP

1 Parque Nacional Defensores del Chaco
2 Parque Nacional Ybycuí
3 Reserva Natural del Bosque Mbaracayú
4 Parque Nacional Cerro Corà
5 Lago Ypoá
6 Parque Nacional Tifunqué
7 Parque Nacional Estero Milagro
8 Filidelfia

Giant anteater with domestic cattle.

6. Parque Nacional Tifunqué

Consisting of meandering rivers and lakes surrounded by gallery forest, this is a breeding refuge for several threatened species such as rhea, caiman, turtle and jaguar. It also supports a relative abundance of capybara and probably marsh deer, giant armadillos, and maned wolf. Birds are abundant in species and number since the site is along the migratory route.

Getting there: Rent a 4x4 vehicle and drive south from Asunción along Route 9 as far as Pozo Colorado, where you head west for another 40 miles (60km) or so (it is signposted). Alternatively book a tour in Asunción.

7. Parque Nacional Estero Milagro

Natural grasslands, low forests, wooded savannahs, and small marshes with a great diversity of plant species. Migratory birds include greater yellowlegs, ospreys, and common nighthawks. There is potential to see rare species such as the broad-snouted caiman, giant otters, and crested eagles.

Getting there: Located in central Paraguay along the Río Paraguay. Drive (in a 4x4) to Puerto Ybapobó, some 10 miles (15km) to the south of the park. From there, ask for directions. Alternatively trips can be arranged by tour companies in Asunción.

FURTHER READING

The usual guidebooks do not cover Paraguay well and there is no real alternative. For fun, try finding: *All About Paraguay* by Friedhelm Angersbach, Friedhelm Angersbach & Westfalehaus, Germany, 1999 *Land Without Evil* by Matthew J. Pallamary, Charles Publishing Company, Oceanside, California, 2000 *Status, Distribution and Biogeography of the Birds of Paraguay* (Monographs in Field Ornithology, No. 1) by Floyd E. Hayes, American Birding Association Sales, Colorado Springs, 1995

---

transportation. Rent a 4x4 vehicle in Asunción and drive north through Filidelfia to Fortín Medrojon, keeping your eyes open for good birding spots by lakes and riverbanks (storks, ibis, herons, egrets, and more). The last 125 miles (200km) of the road, after Fortín Teniente Martinez, is of particularly poor quality, so leave early enough to return to Fortín Teniente Martinez in case the road is impassable – it is also advisable to take plenty of water.

For a permit to visit the park, telephone the Fundación para el Desarrollo Sustentable del Chaco near Filidelfia on: (595 918) 2235 or contact fdschaco@telemail.com.py or fdschaco@telesurf.com.py.

2. Parque Nacional Ybycuí

One of the last remaining stands of Paraguay's subtropical rainforest also offers some good waterfalls. Patience is essential (except for the botanist) because the vegetation is so dense that viewing fauna can be very hard indeed. Nevertheless, if you give yourself plenty of time, you may see deer, peccaries, toucans, parakeets, and a good diversity of butterflies.

Getting there: The most accessible of Paraguay's national parks, lying only 94 miles (151km) from Asunción. Get a bus to Acahay, then another to Ybycuí. From Ybycuí buses for the park entrance leave at 6 a.m. and noon every day, returning at 7 a.m. and 2 p.m. You can camp at the park headquarters.

3. Reserva Natural del Bosque Mbaracayú

25 miles (40km) north of Curuguaty, Mbaracayú, is the largest remaining Atlantic forest in Paraguay. Although illegal logging, hunting, and marijuana cultivation are still problems, the park remains a good place to see jaguar, Brazilian tapir, black howler monkeys, and 420 bird species, including the rare black-fronted piping-guan, white-winged nightjar, and bare-throated bellbird.

Getting there: Around 200 miles (300km) northeast of Asunción is the town of Curuguaty. From here take a private taxi to the reserve entrance. Be sure to arrange a pick-up time. To visit this reserve you must contact the Fundación Moisés Bertoni (see above).

4. Parque Nacional Cerro Corá

Perhaps the most scenic of Paraguay's parks, made up of rolling subtropical forest and *cerrado* (palm savannah) interspersed with isolated near vertical mountain peaks. The lower slopes of the mountains are good for bird-watching, with more than 200 species so far recorded.

Getting there: The park is 12 miles (20km) west of Pedro Juan Caballero, some 300 miles (500km) northeast of Asunción on the Brazilian border. From Pedro Juan Caballero many buses make the 12-hour trip to the park daily. If driving yourself go via Porto Colorado and Concepción. There are hotels in Pedro Juan Caballero or camping facilities in the park itself.

THE LOWLAND PLAINS

5. Lago Ypoá

This area of extensive, shallow, clustered lakes with floating mats of vegetation is considered one of the most important aquatic environments in the country. Several threatened species inhabit the area; in addition you may see giant anteaters, black howler monkeys, and greater rheas. The site is also an important migration route for birds including ospreys and Mississippi kites.

Getting there: Only 100 miles (150km) south of Asunción on Route 1, but buses do not stop and there are no towns nearby. Rent a car or take a tour from Asunción.

PERU

Some 84 of the world's 103 known ecological zones and 28 different climates occur in Peru, which places it among the top five countries in the world for biological diversity. With tropical coastline, high sierra, and Amazonian jungle, it is difficult for the eco-tourist to know where to start.

TOP WEBSITES

These offer general information about Peru, its national parks, top tourist destinations, and weather, plus maps:

Peru Traveler Guide – www.geocities.com/TheTropics/Cabana/6110/index.htm
Peru Explorer – www.peru-explorer.com
Amazon Andes Inkanatura Travel – www.inkanatura.com/
Eco Travels in Peru – www2.planeta.com/mader/ecotravel/south/peru/peru1.html

TOURS

The following offer flexible tours:

Lost World Adventures – info@lostworldadventures.com
Peruvian Andean Treks – http://www.cbc.org.pe/pat/patinde2.htm
Aracari Tours – http://www.aracari.com
Alegria Tours – http://www.nazcaperu.com
Tambo Tours – http://www.tambotours.com
Hada Tours – E-mail: saleprom@hadatours.com.pe
Servicios Aereos S. A. E-mail: aqpsa-lima@mail.interplace.com.pe
Ideal Travels – E-mail: idealperu@mail.interplace.com.pe
Manu Expeditions – http://manuexpeditions.com
Explorandes – http://www.explorandes.com/iti17.htm
Kontiki Tours – http://www.kontikitours.com/arequipa_canyon.html
Peru Expeditions – http://www.peru-expeditions.com/route1-i.htm

You can even tour Peru on the back of a Harley-Davidson with *Inca-Moto Adventures* – http://www.peru-info.com/master/incamoto/welcome.html

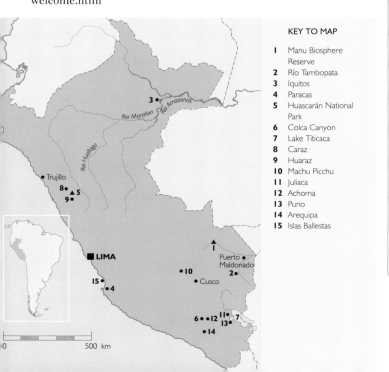

KEY TO MAP

1	Manu Biosphere Reserve
2	Río Tambopata
3	Iquitos
4	Paracas
5	Huascarán National Park
6	Colca Canyon
7	Lake Titicaca
8	Caraz
9	Huaraz
10	Machu Picchu
11	Juliaca
12	Achoma
13	Puno
14	Arequipa
15	Islas Ballestas

Peru's Best

RAINFOREST

There are three sites to which people head in order to experience the diverse rainforests of Peru. Each has its own special wildlife community. Everywhere expect to see caiman, parrots, toucans, bamboo rats, and a hoard of interesting insects.

1. Manu Biosphere Reserve
With more than 850 species of bird and 13 species of primate, the Manu Biosphere Reserve is world famous (see page 100).

Getting there: A 35-minute flight from Cusco to the Manu River followed by a 90-minute boat ride on the Madre de Dios. The cheaper option of boat and bus may take up to 10 hours. The following lodges are recommended:
Manu Lodge – http://www.ekeko.rcp.net.pe/manu
Manu Wildlife Centre – http://manuexpeditions.com
Pantiacolla Lodge – http://www.pantiacolla.com/
One advantage of going to Manu by bus is that you travel through fantastic cloudforest. Try to stop for a couple of nights at one of the lodges on the way, since you should be able to see Peru's gorgeous national bird, the cock-of-the-rock, as well as woolly monkeys and even spectacled bears.
Peruvian Fieldguides – E-mail: guides@peruvianfieldguides.com
Cock of the Rock Lodge – http://www.inkanatura.com/cockrock.htm
Manu Cloud Forest Lodge – E-mail: mnt@amanta.rcp.net.pe
The Inca Trail is also good for cloudforest – hummingbirds are particularly abundant. Arrange a tour in Cusco, where there are lots of companies. Ask where you will camp, how many in a group, what the food will be like and the price. Do not go with tours that are under US$45. It is best to arrive at Machu Picchu on a Thursday or Monday when fewer tour groups arrive.

2. Tambopata Candamo Reserve
Possibly the most biodiverse area in the world, containing up to 10 million species of insect and more than 605 bird species and 1200 butterflies. An extended stay should also reward you with sightings of brown capuchins, saddle-back tamarins, giant otters, and spectacled caiman, as well as macaws, Spix's guans, and tinamous. If you venture into the forest at night, you could see night monkeys, olingos, and kinkajous. Some 8 hours upstream from the airport, at the Tambopata Research Centre, is the world's biggest clay lick – a ½ mile (500m) long cliff-face where every morning hundreds of macaws and twelve species of parrot flock to eat the clay. Most lodges will organize a camping trip nearby, or you can stay at the research center.

Standards of lodges vary tremendously, but these are consistently recommended:
Lago Sandoval Lodge – http://www.inkanatura.com/sandoval.htm
Tambopata Research Centre – http://www.perunature.com.
Pasados Amazonas' website: http://www.perunature.com.

Getting there: Daily flights from Cusco and Lima to Puerto Maldonado. Then a boat to one of the many lodges. If you are a hardened traveler with time to spare, you can also travel by truck. The breathtaking scenery you pass through as you climb over the Andes and descend into the Amazon Basin via mysterious cloudforest is worth every bruise of your 100-hour journey. From Cusco take a bus to Urcos, where trucks leave every afternoon. Take food, warm clothes, and plastic sheets to use as shelter from the sun or rain. Never undertake this trip in the wet season (September–March), as it can take up to a month.

3. Iquitos
Similar flora and fauna to Tambopata plus river dolphins, both botos, and tucuxis.

Getting there: Daily flights from Lima to Iquitos, followed by boats from town into the forest. It is not advisable to arrive by road since

there have been bus-jackings in the northeast of Peru. There are a great variety of lodges and again the standards vary considerably. The following are frequently recommended:

Explorama – http://www.explorama.com.
The Green Tracks Amazon River Boat – http://www.greentracks.com
Yacumama Lodge – http://www.gorp.com/yacumama/

THE COAST

4. Paracas National Reserve
147 miles (235km) south of Lima, this is a must for bird lovers. Commonly seen species include Humboldt penguin, Peruvian booby, Peruvian brown pelican, Chilean flamingo, Guanay cormorant, and even Andean condor. Mammals include sea lions, sea otters, dolphins, and various whale species (depending on the season). Excursions by boat and glider to the Ballestas Islands, where even more wildlife can be seen.

Getting there: Just off the Pan American highway near Pisco, 4 hours south of Lima, Paracas is easy to get to by bus and has a good selection of hotels. No public transport to the reserve, which is 6 miles (10km) out of town. The offices of the tour agencies are in the town center, in Plaza de Armas. Many tours take visitors by motorized launch to the Ballestas Islands in the morning and then by bus to the reserve itself in the afternoon .

THE MOUNTAINS

5. Huascaran National Park
Vast area in the central Andes, great for hiking and wildlife such as condors, viscachas, and even pumas. Get a permit from the park office in Huaraz where you should

Jaguar. Manu National Park in Peru is one of the few places where you might encounter a jaguar in the open.

enquire about trail conditions and the current political situation. Many of the spectacular peaks of the Cordillera Blanca are well over 20,000ft (6000m) above sea level. Acclimatization is essential. In May, look for the spectacular flowers of the Puya raymondi bromeliads, which grow up to 40ft (12m) high and live for about 40 years. Some areas, such as the Lakes of Llanganuco and the snowy peak of Pastoruri, can be visited by road.

Getting there: Daily buses to Huaraz, from Lima (250 miles/400km, 7 hours) and from Trujillo (350 miles/570km, 10 hours).
A selection of 1–3 star accommodation in Huaraz and Caraz, but only camping inside the park. Easy to visit without the aid of a tour company.

6. Colca Canyon
The deepest gorge in the world and the best place in South America to see condors. Day trips, organized treks, or horse-riding tours that can last up to a week and descend 10,000ft (3000m) to the river floor can be arranged.

Getting there: Daily flights from Lima, Cusco and Juliaca to Arequipa; bus on the Pan American Highway from all major towns; or trains from Cusco to Juliaca and from Juliaca to Arequipa. From Arequipa to the Colca Canyon takes 5–6 hours by gravel road. No public transportation – only tours and private vehicles. Several hotels in Arequipa. Basic lodging near the canyon in villages such as Achoma. Only camping in the canyon itself.

7. Loma de Lachay National Reserve
In the foothills of the Andes, 12 miles (20km) from the coast. *Loma* is a rare cold and damp habitat made up of 'fog vegetation', produced when the fog caused by the Humboldt current drifts inland on to the lower slopes of the Andes, whereupon it condenses. The unique flora is accompanied by

unusual fauna, particularly birds such as the thick-billed miner, South American pochard, and golden-plumed conure.

Getting there: Not easy. Around 60 miles (100km) north of Lima on the Pan American Highway is the junction for Sayán. ½ mile (1km) north of this junction, turn right for the park, whose entrance is 2 miles (3km) along this road. Public transport is not advised. Even arranging a tour in Lima may be tricky since this park is not often visited by tourists. Your best bet is to rent a 4x4 in Lima and make your own way there.

8. Lake Titicaca
Can be visited on a day trip. See under Bolivia, above.

FURTHER READING

As well as the usual guidebooks, try:
Dance of the Four Winds: Secrets of the Inca Medicine Wheel by Alberto Villoldo & Erik Jendresen, Inner Traditions International Ltd., Richester, USA, 1994
A Guide to the Birds of Peru: An Annotated Checklist by James F. Clements, Ibis Publishing Company, Vista, USA, 2000
The Hidden Amazon: The Greatest Voyage in Natural History by Dick Lutz, Dimi Press, Salem, Oregon, 1998
Inca Kola by Matthew Parris, Phoenix Press, London, 1993
Manu: The Biodiversity of Southeastern Peru by Don E. Wilson & Abelardo Sandoval (editors), Smithsonian Institute Press, Washington DC, 1996
Warriors of the Clouds: A Lost Civilization in the Upper Amazon of Peru by Keith Muscutt, University of New Mexico Press, Albuquerque, 1998

SURINAME

Over 90% of Suriname is rainforest. The rest is pristine coastline and settlements of diverse cultural origin. Despite this, Suriname is among the least visited countries of South America and not well geared up for tourism. But this is likely to change and information is already becoming more available to the Internet user.

TOP WEBSITES

Movement for Eco-tourism in Suriname – http://www.metsresorts.com/index-en.html
Home page for Suriname – http://www.sr.net/srnet/InfoSurinam/welcome.html
Suriname tourism foundation – http://www.parbo.com/tourism/
Conservation International – Suriname – http://www.conservation.org/WEB/FIELDACT/REGIONS/GUIANREG/Suriname.htm
Srnana Connection – http://www.nickerie.com/sranan/
Ecotour.org – http://www.ecotour.org

TOURS

Jungle Tours – http://www.netview.nl/tour/index.htm
Suriname Safari Tours (Dutch) – http://www.cq-link.sr/sst/Index.html
Pangaea Exotic Tours – http://www6.bcity.com/indosuriname/

For companies that are not on the Internet but have offices in Suriname, see http://www.parbo.com/tourism/address2.htm#tour

Suriname's Best

THE RAINFOREST

For an idea of what fauna to expect, visit the Rainforest of Surinam site: http://www.euronet.nl/users/mbleeker/suriname/suri-eng.html

1. Central Suriname Nature Reserve
Conservation International has negotiated with the government to establish an impressively large national park of 6177 sq. miles (1.6 million hectares), linking the three most important protected areas in central Suriname – the Raleighvallen, Tafelberg, and Eilerts de Haan Gebergte Nature Reserves – and protecting the entire upper Coppename River watershed. The new reserve is home to all eight species of Suriname's primates, more than 400 bird species, impressive mammals such as jaguar, giant armadillos, and giant river otters, and yapok, an amphibious nocturnal opossum.

This park promises much and it is hoped that the first eco-friendly lodges will be constructed by October 2001. Both *Ecotour.org* and *Conservation International*'s websites will keep you informed.

2. Palumeu Reserve
High on the River Tapanahony, in prime hilly rainforest, this reserve offers everything from tiny streams encroached by jungle on both sides to wide rivers, and from gently undulating forest to sudden vertical peaks. Great diversity of birds (particularly parrots) and mammals, notably red howler monkeys and squirrel monkeys.

Getting there: Fly from Paramaribo to Palumeu. At the airport there are a variety of tour representatives – most are reliable, but it is best to avoid the very cheap ones. A 4-day trip is recommended.

3. Awarradam Reserve
Just outside the Central Suriname Nature Reserve and offering a good diversity of animals, Awarradam also gives the opportunity to encounter tribal peoples, in this case the largest Maroon population in Suriname.

Getting there: Fly from Paramaribo to Kuyana, then head upstream in a motorized dug-out. Tour representatives at the airport.

THE HIGHLANDS

4. Mount Kasikasima
Amidst the flat *terra firme* forest, twelve granite peaks erupt. The highest, Kasikasima, is 2355ft (718m). This area is not visited often, so animals are fearful of humans. Nevertheless, you should see various primates, caiman, capybara, and a whole host of birds.

Getting there: Quite an adventure. Fly to Palameu and then work your way upriver in a motorized dug out canoe, getting out to walk whenever there are rapids. This has to be done in a tour group, of which there are many in Palumeu.

THE COAST

5. Galibi Reserve
Between April and September each year, many leatherback, green, and Olive Ridley turtles can be seen at night, whether it be females arriving to lay or hatchlings escaping to the sea (see under French Guyana, above, for guidance on appropriate behavior).

Visiting the turtle beaches is best done independently, but real enthusiasts can volunteer for a turtle conservation working vacation. See http://away.com/xnet/one-product.tcl?product_id=101030

Getting there: Head to Albina, a small village on the Marowijne River. The coastal road is very good, as are bus services from Paramaribo. From Albina, Carib Indians will take you to the reserve by canoe.

6. Bigi Pan and the Coastal Mudflats
Extensive mudflats resulting from the mud thrown out by the Amazon and local rivers are revealed at low tide, when a veritable feast of small fish and crustaceans are also exposed to herons, ibises, and many small waders. The highlight is the red subspecies of the American white ibis, but you should also see golden plover, ruddy turnstone, and whimbrel.

Getting there: Drive yourself, or take a bus and get off wherever the birding looks good. The mangroves around the town of Bigi Pan (120 miles/180km west of Paramaribo) have been recommended and can be reached by bus or rent car on the main coastal road.

FURTHER READING

Guide books for Suriname are currently not all that useful. Expect that to change as the number of tourists increases. In the meantime, try:
The Boni Maroon Wars in Suriname by Wim S. M. Hoogbergen, Brill Academic Publishers, Leiden, Netherlands, 1999
The Freshwater Ecosystems of Suriname by Paul E. Ouboter (editor), Kluwer Academic Publishers, Dordrecht, Netherlands, 1993
Suriname by Noelle Blackmer Beatty, Chelsea House, Leiden, Netherlands, 1990

KEY TO MAP

PARAMARIBO

R. Coppename
R. Tapanahony

1 Central Suriname Nature Reserve
2 Palumeu Reserve
3 Awarradam Reserve
4 Mount Kasikasima
5 Galibi Reserve
6 Bigi Pan and the coastal mudflats

0   200km

URUGUAY

The smallest country in Hispanic South America, wedged between enormous Brazil and Argentina, Uruguay offers a beautiful coastline (including some of the best beaches in South America), charming colonial atmosphere and the hustle and bustle of Montevideo. But there is little to offer the wildlife enthusiast, since most of the rolling, fertile countryside is used for sheep and cattle farming. This section suggests some worthwhile wildlife watching day trips from the coast or Montevideo.

TOP WEBSITES

Lonely Planet Uruguay – http://www.lonelyplanet.com.au/dest/sam/uru.htm
Infohub Uruguay – www.infohub.com/TravelGuide/TRAVELER/SOUTH_AMERICA/uruguay.html
Escape Artist – http://www.escapeartist.com/uruguay/travel.htm
Uruguay – http://www.turismo.gub.uy/

TOURS

Lost World Adventures – http://www.lostworldadventures.com/uruguay.htm
Maxim Tours Ltd – http://www.gorp.com/maximsa/uruguay.htm
Vantage Adventures – http://travelvantage.com/tou_uru.html
Pan Tours – http://www.reduy.com/empresas/pantours/
Adventure Associates – http://www.adventureassociates.com/southamerica/uruguay.htm

Uruguay's Best

THE COAST

Southern sea lions are the attraction at various places along the coast. The two best are:

1. Dunas de Cabo Polonio

An impressive sea lion colony set among magnficent sand dunes.

Getting there: Stop at kilometer 264 on Ruta 10 (east of La Paloma, 150 miles/250km northeast of Montevideo). From here it is a tough 6-mile (10km) hike through sand dunes to the coast. A number of guides will offer to drive you there in 4x4s, or you can arrange a day trip from La Paloma which will not cost much more.

Throughout South America, sunset presents the familiar sight of egrets, herons, and jabiru gathering in trees close to lakes, ponds and rivers.

2. Punta del Este

A popular holiday resort, so expect it to be crowded. Lying offshore is Isla de Lobos, home to thousands of sea lions.

Getting there: Daily excursions from the harbor. Accommodation is plentiful in the harbor town.

INLAND

3. Laguna de Rocha

Ecological reserve 6 miles (10km) west of La Paloma. Expect to see a surprising diversity of waterbirds including black-necked swans, storks, and waterfowl.

Getting there: Taxi to the reserve headquarters from La Paloma. Be sure to arrange a return taxi since the phone in the office is unreliable. Stay in La Paloma.

4. Parque Nacional Santa Teresa

Do not be put off by references to the fact that the park is more of a historical attraction than an ecological one, for within its boundaries lie the splendid Laguna Negra and the marshes of the Banado de Santa Teresa. Sightings from a day's visit should include ibises, terns, herons, and many kingfishers.

Getting there: Taxi from Chuy, 25 miles (35km) to the north. You should be able to haggle the driver down to a very reasonable price. Simple camping facilities, a restaurant, and a supermarket of sorts at the park headquarters.

5. Parque Salas

One of the few places where rheas can still be seen in the wild. The walk through some great scenery is worth it even if the giant birds prove elusive.

Getting there: 5 miles (8km) south of Minas (80 miles/120km northeast of Montevideo). Take the town bus marked 'Cerveceria Salas' to the Salas brewery, make your way to the bottling plant 1 mile (2km) away, then enjoy the 3-hour walk back to Minas.

Rheas can sometimes be seen at various points along the Río Uruguay. Write to the Ministry of Tourism near your departure date to find out when and where recent sightings have been.

FURTHER READING

The common guidebooks do not cover Uruguay in much detail. However there are no good alternatives. Try looking at:
Heroes on Horseback: A Life and Times of the Last Gaucho Caudillos (Dialogos) by John Charles Chasteen, University of New Mexico Press, Albuquerque, 1995
Ornithological Gazetteer of Uruguay by Raymond A. Paynter Jr, Museum of Comparative Zoology, Cambridge, USA, 1994
The Tree of Red Stars by Tessa Bridal, Milkweed Editions, Minneapolis, USA, 1997

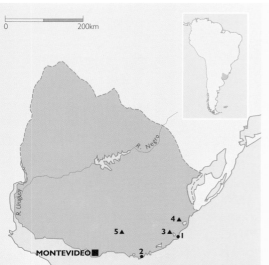

0   200km

KEY TO MAP

1 Dunas de Cabo Polonio
2 Punta del Este
3 Laguna de Rocha
4 Parque Nacional Santa Teresa
5 Parque Salas

MONTEVIDEO

VENEZUELA

A country of superlatives. Angel Falls is the world's highest waterfall and the Orinoco is its third longest river. Lago de Maracaibo is a vast inlet of the Caribbean Sea. For an eco-tourist it is a paradise; the beautiful Caribbean beaches of the northern coast are only a day's drive away from the fascinating forests in the Orinoco delta or the Guayana Highlands.

Much of the north coast is still recovering from the devastating floods and mudslides of December 1999. Caracas and the regions of Zulia, Vargas, and Miranda were the worst hit, with an estimated 150,000 left homeless. Before visiting any of these areas check what the situation is via the Internet.

TOP WEBSITES

Venezuela has many good websites. Before booking check the 'latest information' site, as this gives updates on everything from weather to poor-quality hotels and tour companies.
Think Venezuela – http://think-venezuela.net/
Latest Travel Information – http://www.lastfrontiers.co.uk/info_venezuela.htm
Wildlife Venezuela – http://www.members.tripod.com/~wildlife_vzla/birdwatch.htm
Venezuelan Embassy – http://www.embavenez-us.org/
Travelers Tips for Venezuela – http://www.travel.com.hk/venezuel.htm
Lonely Planet to Venezuela – http://www.lonelyplanet.com/dest/sam/ven.htm
Escape Magazine – http://www.escape.com.ve/
National Parks of Venezuela – http://www.embavenez-sofia.bg/av/parks.htm

TOURS

Eco-Voyager – http://www.ecovoyager.com/tripitin.htm
Lost World Adventures – http://www.lostworldadventures.com/venez.htm
Geodyssey Tours – http://www.geodyssey.co.uk/
Bum-Bum Tours – http://jvm.com/bumbum/index.htm

Path Tours – http://www.pathtours.com/
Speciality Travel – Lost World – http://www.specialtytravel.com/destinations/frames.html
Amazing Tours – http://www.amazingtours.com/

Venezuela's Best

THE MOUNTAINS

1. Parque Nacional Sierra Nevada de Mérida
In Venezuela the Andes divide into two ridges split by a deep valley. The snowy peaks of the Sierra Nevada de Mérida mark the end of the southern ridge and offer a fascinating array of flora and fauna. The *páramo*, with its unique high-altitude grasses, is best seen in November and December at the end of the rainy season, when the *frailejon* have a glorious yellow bloom which attracts hummingbirds and a huge array of insect life. The park includes the world's highest and longest cable-car.

Getting there: Several buses daily from Caracas. The park entrance is a few miles before the road from Valera meets the road from Barinas. Good free campsite; two hotels at Laguna Mucubaji (next to the park entrance) and many hotels in Mérida. Several tour companies in Mérida of which *Bum Bum Tours* (Tel: 524 075) and *Guamanchi Tours* (Tel: 522 080) are recommended.
The world's most diverse ice cream shop, La Heladeria Coromoto, is located in Mérida and offers more than 600 flavors including 'beer' and 'meat and potatoes'.

For further information, see *The Andes Network* – http://www.andes.net/english/

2. Parque Nacional Canaima and Angel Falls
The upland area to the south of the Orinoco with its awesome flat-topped mountains (tepuis) is known as La Gran Sabana. The Parque Nacional Canaima, one of the six largest parks in the world, is characterized by these tepuis as well as beautiful waterfalls – the most famous being Angel Falls. Each isolated tepui has evolved independently, resulting in a characteristic flora. Over 900 species of plant are endemic. Particularly interesting is the huge diversity of carnivorous plants, including *Heliamphora spp.*, *Drosera roraima* and *Utricularia humboldtii*.
The park is also home to a huge variety of animals: 118 mammals, 550 birds, 72 reptiles, and 55 amphibians have been recorded, including such very rare species as the giant anteater, giant armadillo, giant otter, bush dog, little spotted cat, and margay. You are also likely to see nine-banded armadillos, capybara, agouti, three-toed sloths, toucans, macaws, parrots, parakeets, cock-of-the-rock, bananaquit, and hummingbirds.

Getting there: Fly to Canaima from Caracas or Ciudad Bolívar. In the dry season you can reach the falls by boat from Ciudad Bolívar. Many tour companies and individual guides take group excursions to the falls and surrounding areas (try *La Gran Sabana Tours* – http://www.venezuelatuya.com/gransabana/eng.htm). Book at the airport or in Canaima. Scenic flights are expensive and can be bumpy. In the rainy season (June–November) the falls are often shrouded in cloud.

For further information, see *Natural World Heritage* – http://www.wcmc.org.uk/protected_areas/data/wh/canaima.html

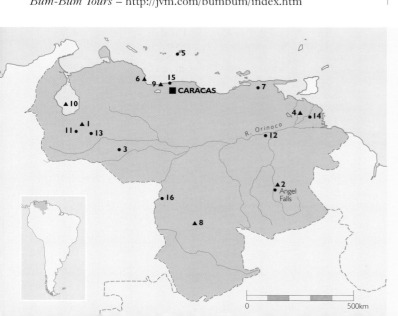

KEY TO MAP

1. Parque Nacional Sierra Nevada de Mérida
2. Parque Nacional Canaima and Angel Falls
3. Los Llanos
4. The Guayana Lowlands
5. Islas Los Roques
6. Parque Nacional Morrocoy
7. Cueva del Guácharo
8. Amazonas
9. Henri Pittier National Park
10. Lago de Maracaibo
11. Mérida
12. Ciudad Bolívar
13. Barinas
14. Tucupita
15. Maiquetia
16. Puerto Ayacucho

0   500km

THE LOWLAND PLAINS

3. Los Llanos

Vast grasslands between the Andes and the Orinoco, home to the majority of Venezuela's cattle. In October and November the plains are still partially flooded, and huge groups of capybara, as well as anacondas, river dolphins, and scarlet ibis, can be seen. Hunting and pollution threaten the future of this park.

Getting there: The best base is Barinas, which can be reached by bus from every major city. If you have a 4x4, the road to Barinas from Apartaderos in Sierra Nevada de Mérida is beautiful. Accommodation in Barinas; lodges in Los Llanos. Tours can be arranged in Barinas or see *Think Venezuela*'s webpage (see above) about Los Llanos.

4. The Guayana Lowlands

The Orinoco delta is a wild and beautiful place, rich in natural resources. Mangrove merges gently into rainforest and cerrado, providing a variety of habitats. Excellent for howler monkeys, capuchins, tamarins, macaws, and hoatzins. On a tour of the delta, a good guide should find manatees and river dolphins.

Getting there: Tours start from Tucupita, which can be reached from most major cities and has basic hotels. All-inclusive 2- or 4-day trips are strongly recommended since independent travel is very difficult. The following tour companies are often recommended: *Tucupita Expeditions* – http://orinocodelta.com/
Jakera Tours – http://www.jakera.com/

THE COASTS

Venezuela has some of South America's most beautiful coastline. Designated areas have been made into marine parks which provide protection for turtles, birds, and coral reef.

5. Islas Los Roques

An archipelago to the north of Caracas with over 10 miles (15km) of coral reef and an abundance of marine life. Snorkeling and scuba diving are excellent. More than 80 species of bird have been recorded

here – look out for boobies, gulls, pelicans, Louisiana herons, frigate-birds, great blue herons, and reddish egrets. There are also four species of turtle (green, Olive Ridley, hawksbill, and leatherback) which nest April–September. The Marine Biological Station on the island of Dos Mosquises Sur rears marine turtles from eggs until they are large enough to be released back into the wild.

Getting there: Flights to Gran Roque on Los Roques leave daily from Maiquetia. One-day tours can be arranged from the airport, although it is more relaxing and economical to stay longer and travel independently. On the islands, fishermen will gladly ferry you from site to site for a fee. Diving is best organized on Gran Roque – ask around for the best companies. Gran Roque has a range of accommodation. It is also an excellent place to camp – pick up a free permit at the Inparques office. Watch out for the scavenging crabs that will relieve you of anything you don't nail down.

Cumaco Tours – http://www.gis.net/~jcharth/index.html
Trotamundas International – http://www.trotamundos.com/beaches.htm Roques
Geodyssey – http://www.geodyssey.co.uk/pages/special/scuba.htm

6. Parque Nacional Morrocoy

A string of islets surrounded by coral reefs. Cayo Borracho and Playuela are the least spoiled – the latter has a particularly good mangrove for snorkeling. Unfortunately much of the coral has been killed by oil leaks from a nearby refinery, so it is not worth diving. On the edge of the park is the Cuare Wildlife Sanctuary, where mangroves provide a nesting area for scarlet ibis, flamingos, cormorants, ducks, pelicans, and herons.

Getting there: Well serviced by boats from Tucacas in the south and Chichiriviche in the north. Camping permitted on the islands of Sal, Sombrero, Muerto, and Paiclás.

7. Cueva del Guácharo

This string of caves was first discovered by Humboldt and is home to a fascinating variety of

wildlife, notably 17,000 oilbirds. The cave is also home to blind mice, ants, and plants; fish and crabs can be seen in the stream. All live off the birds' dropped scraps.

Getting There: Regular bus service from Caripe, Cumaná and Carúpano. Cave open 8.30 a.m.–5 p.m.; guide compulsory. The population of birds reaches its peak during the wet season (August–December). Accommodation in any of the nearby towns, but if you camp alongside the cave's entrance you will see the birds leave the cave to forage for fruit at dusk and return just before dawn. *Geodyssey Tours* has been recommended – http://www.geodyssey.co.uk/pages/special/birdsenthusiastsfortnight.htm

THE RAINFOREST

8. Amazonas

Covered in a thick carpet of tropical forest in the Orinoco drainage basin and less uniform than other parts of the Amazon Basin because of the tepuis that scatter the landscape. Towards the border with Brazil is the Serrania de la Neblina or Misty Mountain. The canyon that divides La Neblina is believed to be one of the world's deepest and although the area has hardly been explored it is thought to have more endemic plant species than anywhere else in the world.

Some 250 mammal and 30,000 insect species have been recorded in Venezuela. Most are found in the rainforest, including pacarana, red-bellied tamarins, the rare white-faced saki monkey and spider monkeys. Also look out for black caiman – this is one of the few remaining strongholds for this member of the alligator family.

Getting there: Head for Puerto Ayacucho by air from Caracas or bus from most major towns. Once there, ask around for recommended tours. Three-day trips up the Sipapo and Autana Rivers are popular. It is virtually impossible to travel into the forest independently. Plenty of basic hotels in Puerto Ayacucho.

9. Henri Pittier National Park

Stretches from the north of Maracay to the Caribbean and includes the dramatic coastal range of Cordillera de la Costa. Mangrove

and coconut groves at sea level slowly change into deciduous forest as you approach the foothills. Above this lies evergreen forest, which becomes cloudforest towards the park's highest point, Pico Cenizo (7970ft/2430m).

A must for ornithologists since more than 550 species of bird (over 40% of Venezuela's birdlife) have been identified within the park, including many rare and exotic species. Those interested in the birds migrating between Canada and Argentina should visit the Rancho Grande biological field station (Tel: 043 450153). The best time for migratory birds is September–November. You can also expect to see collared peccaries, common opossums, kinkajous, capuchins, and tamarin.

Getting there: Bus from Maracay to Puerto Colombia and the interior of the park. One-day tours can be arranged to the Rancho Grande from Puerto Colombia or you can stay at the station if they have vacancies. Hire a boat from the riverfront to visit any of the beautiful beaches. Both Maracay and Puerto Colombia offer a wide selection of hotels and hostels. *King Tours* are reliable – http://web31.com/consinteg/kingtours/choroni.html.

FURTHER READING

Guide to the Birds of Venezuela by Radlophe Meyer De Schauenesee & William H. Phelps, Princeton University Press, Princeton, 1978
In Trouble Again: A Journey Between the Orinoco and the Amazon by Redmond O'Hanlon, Vintage, New York, 1990
1 Day in the Tropical Rain Forest by Jean Craighead George & Gary Allen (illustrator), Ty Crowell, New York, 1990
Orchid Hunting in the Lost World (and Elsewhere in Venezuela) by G.C.K. Dunsterville & E. Dunsterville, American Orchid Society., West Palm Beach, USA, 1998
Site Guide Venezuela: A Guide to the Best Birding Locations by Dennis Rogers, Cinclus Publications, Portland USA, 1993
Venezuela in Pictures (Visual Geography Series) by Lincoln A. Boehm, Lerner Publications, Minneapolis, 1987

SPECIES LIST

The main text of this book generally uses only common names, but since many plants and animals have more than one common name, the Latin names listed here permit more definite identification.

Algarrobo *Prosopis* spp.
Algodão-do-pantanal *Ipomoea fistulosa*
Anqush *Senecio canescens*
Araucaria or Parana pine *Araucaria augustifolia*
Axe-breaker *Quebrachia lorentziihe*
Bacaiúva *Acrocomia aculeata*
Balsam-of-Peru *Myxroxylon balsamum*
Breadnut tree *Brosium alicastrum*
Buriti palm *Mauritia flexuosa*
Butternut tree *Caryocar* spp.
Calafate *Berberis* spp.
Cambúra *Voshysia divergens*
Candelabra cactus *Euphorbia lactea* or *Jasminocereus* spp.
Cannonball tree *Couroupita guianensis*
Cattail *Typha domingensis*
Caviúna-do-cerraido *Dalbergia violacea*
Chilean palm *Jubea chilensis*
Chinese lantern *Myzodendron* spp.
Climbing palm *Desmoneus* spp.
Coihue *Nothofagus dombeyi*
Coirones *Festuca & Stipa* spp.
Copaiba *Copaifera langsdorfii*
Creole willow *Salix humboldtiana*
Giant kelp *Macrocystis pyrifera & Lessonia trabeculata*
Giant puya *Puya raymondii*
Gold tree or paratudo *Tabebuia caraiba*
Guarana *Poullinia cupana*
Guaytecas Islands cypress *Pilgerodendron uviferum*
Ipê *Vochysia divergens*
Ironwood *Copaifera* spp.
Ishpingo tree *Amburana* spp.
Kapok tree see Silk cotton tree
Kenua tree *Polylepis tarapana*
Lapacho *Tabebuia ipe*
Lenga *Nothofagus pumilio*
Lobeira *Solanum lycocarpum*
Monkey puzzle tree *Araucaria araucana*
Munguba *Pseudobombax munguba*
Ombu *Phytolacca dioica*
Palo santo *Bulnesia sarmientii*
Parana pine see Araucaria
Paratudo see Gold tree
Patagonian cypress *Fitzroya cupressoides*
Piranha tree *Piranhea trifoliata*
Piuva *Tabebuia ipe*
Prickly pear *Opuntia* spp.
Puya raymondi *Pourretia gigantea*
Quebracho *Aspidosperma quebracho blanco*
Queen Victoria waterlily *Victoria amazonica*
Queñoa *Polylepsis australis*
Red fuchsia *Fuschia magellanica*

Rubber tree *Hevea brasiliensis*
Sea lettuce *Ulva* spp.
Silk cotton tree *Ceiba pentandra*
Southern beech *Nothofagus nervosa*
Strangler fig *Ficus dendrocida*
Swiss cheese plant *Monstera deliciosa*
Tall gray friar *Espeletia*
Taulli *Lupinus weverbauerii*
Trumpet or umbrella tree *Cecropia* spp
Tussock grass *Poa flabellata*
Urumbeva *Cereus peruvianus*
Water hyacinth *Eichhornia* spp
Water lettuce *Pistia* spp
Wax palm *Ceroxyton alpinus*
Winter's bark *Drimys winteri*
Wood's lady's slipper *Calceolaria biflora*
Yatay palm *Syagrus yatay*

American golden plover *Pluvialis dominica*
American white ibis *Eudocimus albus*
American yellow warbler *Dendroica petechia*
Andean avocet *Recurvirostra andina*
Andean condor *Vultur gryphus*
Andean coot *Fulica ardesiaca*
Andean flamingo *Phoenicoparrus andinus*
Andean flicker *Colaptes rupicola*
Andean goose *Chloephaga melanoptera*
Andean gull *Larus serranus*
Andean hillstar *Oreotrochilus estella*
Andean teal *Anas flavirostris*
Antpitta *Grallaria andina*
Antshrike *Thamnomanes schistogynus*
Aplomado falcon *Falco femoralis*
Aracari *Pteroglossus* spp.
Ashy-headed goose *Chloephaga poliocephala*
Audubon shearwater *Puffinus lherminieri*
Austral parakeet *Enicognathus ferrugineus*
Austral pygmy owl *Glaucidium nanum*
Bananaquit *Coereba flaveola*
Bare-throated bellbird *Procnias nudicollis*
Bay-vented cotinga *Doliornis sclateri*
Bearded guan *Penelope barbata*
Black-and-chestnut eagle *Onoaetus isidori*
Black and yellow macaw *Ara ararauna*
Black-browed albatross *Diomedea melanophris*
Black-chested buzzard eagle *Geranoaetus melanoleucus*
Black-fronted piping-guan *Pipile jacutinga*
Black-hooded sierra finch *Phrygilius atriceps*
Black-necked swan *Cygnus melanocorypha*
Black skimmer *Rynchops niger*
Black-tailed trainbearer *Lesbia victoriae*
Black-throated finch *Melanodera melanodera.*
Black-throated huet-huet *Pteroptochos tarnii*
Black vulture *Coragyps atratus*
Blackish oystercatcher *Haematopus ater*
Blue and yellow macaw *Ara ararauna*
Blue-eyed cormorant *Phalacrocorax atriceps*
Blue-footed booby *Sula nebouxii*
Blue-headed macaw *Ara couloni*

Blue-headed parrot *Pionus menstruus*
Booted racket-tail *Ocreatus underwoodii*
Brown pelican *Pelecanus occidentalis*
Brown skua *Catharacta antarctica*
Buff-necked ibis *Theristicus caudatus*
Burrowing owl *Speotyto cunicularia*
Cacique *Cacicus* spp.
Caracara *Polyborus plancus*
Carbonated sierra finch *Phrygilus carbonarius*
Chestnut-fronted macaw *Ara severa*
Chilean flamingo *Phoenicopterus chilensis*
Chilean skua *Catharacta chilensis*
Chimango caracara *Milvago chimango*
Chucao tapaclo *Scelorchilus rubecula*
Club-winged manakin *Allocotopterus deliciosus*
Cock-of-the-rock *Rupiola peruviana*
Common nighthawk *Chordeiles minor*
Crane hawk *Geranospitza caerulescens*
Crested eagle *Morphnus guianensis*
Curassow *Crax* spp.
Des Mur's wire-tail *Sylviorthorhynchus desmursii*
Diuca finch *Diuca diuca*
Dusky swift *Aerornis senex*
Dwarf tinamou *Taoniscus nanus*
Elegant crested tinamou *Eudromia elegans*
Emerald toucanet *Aulacorhynchus prasinus*
European oystercatcher *Haematopus ostralegus*
Falkland kelp goose *Chloephaga hybrida*
Flightless cormorant *Nannopterum harrisi*
Flightless grebe *Centropelma micropterum*
Flightless or steamer duck *Tachyeres leucocephalus*
Fio-fio *Elania albiceps*
Frigate birds *Fregata* spp.
Galápagos dove *Zenaida galapagoensis*
Galápagos hawk *Buteo galapagoensis*
Galápagos martin *Progne modesta*
Galápagos mockingbird *Nesomimus parvulus*
Galápagos penguin *Spheniscus mendiculus*
Garuma see Gray gull
Gentoo penguin *Pygoscelis papua*
Giant coot *Fulica gigantea*
Giant hummingbird *Patagona gigas*
Giant petrel *Macronectes giganteus*
Golden-plumed conure or parakeet *Leptosittaca branickii*
Gray gull or garuma *Larus modestus*
Gray-hooded Sierra finch *Phrygilus gayi*
Great black hawk *Buteogallus urubitinga*
Great blue heron *Ardea herodias*
Great egret *Casmerodius albus*
Great frigate bird *Fregata minor*
Great grebe *Podiceps major*
Greater flamingo *Phoenicopterus ruber*
Greater yellowleg *Tringa melanoleuca*
Green-backed firecrown *Sephanoides sephanoides*
Green heron *Burirudes virescens*
Greenish-yellow finch *Sicalis olivascens*
Ground cuckoo *Neomorphus* spp.
Ground tyrant *Muscisaxiola* spp.
Guanay cormorant *Phalacrocorax bougainvillii*
Harpy eagle *Harpia harpyja*

Helmeted manakin *Antilophia galeata*
Hoatzin *Opisthocomus hoazin*
Hood mockingbird *Nesomimus macdonaldi*
Hooded vulture *Necrosyrtes monachus*
Horned coot *Fulica cornuta*
Horned screamer *Anhima cornuta*
Hudsonian godwit *Limosa haemastica*
Humboldt penguin *Spheniscus humboldti*
Hyacinth macaw *Anodorhynchus hyacinthus*
Imperial cormorant *Phalacrocorax atriceps*
Inca tern *Larosterna inca*
Jabiru stork *Jabiru mycteria*
Jacana *Jacana jacana*
James's flamingo *Phoenicoparrus jamesi*
Kelp gull *Larus dominicanus*
Lava gull *Larus fuliginosis*
Lesser rhea *Pterocnemia pennata*
Long-wattled umbrellabird *Cephalopterus penduliger*
Louisiana heron *Egretta tricolor*
Lyre-tailed nightjar *Uropsalis lyra*
Magellanic oystercatcher *Haematopus leucopodus*
Magellanic penguin *Spheniscus magellanicus*
Magellanic woodpecker *Campephilus magellanicus*
Magnificent frigate bird *Fregata magnificens*
Masked booby *Sula dactylatra*
Mealy parrot *Amazona farinosa*
Mississippi kite *Ictinia mississippiensis*
Monk parakeet *Myiopsitta monachus*
Mountain caracara *Phalcoboenus megalopterus*
Mountain toucan *Andigena laminirostris*
Muscovy duck *Cairina moschata*
Neotropical cormorant *Phalacrocorax brasilianus*
Oasis hummingbird *Rhodopsis vesper*
Ocellated antbird *Phaenostictus mcleannani*
Oilbird *Steatornis caripensis*
Olivaceous thornbill *Chalcostigma olivaceum*
Oropendola *Psarocolius* spp.
Osprey *Pandion haliaetus*
Ovenbird *Seiurus surocapillus*
Patagonian mockingbird *Mimus patagonicus*
Patagonian yellow finch *Sicalis lebruni*
Peruvian booby *Sula variegata*
Peruvian brown pelican *Pelecanus occidentalis thagus*
Piping guan *Pipile* spp.
Plum-crowned parrot *Pionus tumultuosus*
Puna hawk *Buteo poecilochrous*
Puna plover *Charadrius alticola*
Quetzal *Pharomachrus* spp.
Red and green macaw *Ara chloroptera*
Red-backed hawk *Buteo polyosoma*
Red-bellied macaw *Ara manilata*
Red-billed tropic birds *Phaethon aethereus*
Red-faced Guan *Penelope dabbenei*
Red-faced parrot *Hapalopsittaca pyrrhops*
Red-footed booby *Sula sula*
Red-legged cormorant *Phalacrocorax gaimardi*
Reddish egret *Egretta rufescens*
Rhea or great rhea *Rhea americana*
Rock cormorant *Phalacrocorax magellanicus*

Rockhopper penguin *Eudyptes chrysocome*
Roseate spoonbill *Ajaja ajaja*
Ruddy duck *Oxyura jamaicensis*
Ruddy turnstone *Arenaria interpres*
Rufescent tiger-heron *Tigrisoma lineatum*
Rufous-collared sparrow *Zonotrichia capensis*
Savannah hawk *Heterospizias meriodionalis*
Seriemas *Cariama* spp.
Scarlet ibis *Eudocimus ruber*
Scarlet macaw *Ara macao*
Screaming piha *Lipaugus vociferans*
Seaside cinclodes *Cinclodes nigrofumosus*
Seedsnipe *Thinocorus* spp.
Shearwater *Puffinus* spp.
Short-eared owl *Asio flammeus*
Snail kite *Rostrhamus sociabilis*
Snowy egret *Egretta thula*
Snowy sheathbill *Chionis alba*
South American tern *Sterna hirundinacea*
Southern fulmar *Fulmarus glacialoides*
Southern lapwing *Vanellus chilensis*
Southern pochard *Netta erythrophthalma*
Southern screamer *Chauna torquata*
Spinetail *Synallaxinae* spp.
Spix's guan *Penelope jacquacu*
Spotted antbird *Hylophylax naevioïdes*
Steamer or flightless duck *Tachyeres leucocephalus*
Striated caracara *Phalcoboenus australis*
Sunbittern *Eurypyga helias*
Swallow-tailed gull *Creagrus furcatus*
Swallow-tailed manakin *Chiroxiphia caudata*
Sword-billed hummingbird *Ensifera ensifera*
Tanager *Tangara* spp.
Thick-billed miner *Geositta crassirostris*
Toco toucan *Raphastos toco*
Torrent duck *Merganetta armata*
Toucan barbet *Semnornis ramphastinus*
Trogon *Trogon* spp.
Trumpeter bird *Psophia* spp.
Tui parakeet *Brotogeris sanctithomae*
Turkey vulture *Cathartes aura*
Umbrella bird *Cephalopterus* spp.
Upland goose *Chloephaga picta*
Vermilion flycatcher *Pyrocephalus rubinus*
Waved albatross *Diomedea irrorata*
Wedge-rumped storm petrel *Oceanodroma tethys*
Whimbrel *Numenius phaeopus*
White-necked heron *Ardea cocoi*
White-winged nightjar *Caprimulgus candicans*
Wilson's phalarope *Steganopus tricolor*
Wire-tailed manakin *Pipra filicauda*
Woodcreeper *Camphylorhanphus* spp.
Woodpecker finch *Camarhynchus pallidus*
Wood stork *Mycteria americana*
Yellow-crowned night heron *Nyctanassa violacea*
Yellow-leg *Tringa melanoleuca & T. flavipes*
Yellow-ridged toucan *Ramphastos culminatus*

MAMMALS

Agouti *Dasyprocta leporina*
Andean deer or huemul *Hippocamelus antisensis*
Andean fox *Dusicyon culpaeus*
Andean mountain cat *Oreailurus jacobita*
Bearded saki *Chiropotes satanas*
Black and gold howler monkey *Alouatta caraya*
Black-capped capuchin *Cebus apella*
Black-handed spider monkey *Ateles geoffroyi*
Blackish spider monkey *Saimiri vanzolini*
Bottlenose dolphin *Tursiops truncatus*
Botos *Inia geoffrensis*
Brazilian tapir *Tapirus terrestris*
Brocket deer *Mazama* spp.
Brown capuchin *Cebus apella*
Bush dog *Speothos venaticus*
Capybara *Hydrochoerus hydrochaeris*
Cavy *Cavia* spp.
Chacoan peccary *Catagonus wagneri*
Chinchilla *Chinchilla brevicaudata*
Chungungo see Sea cat
Coati *Nasua* spp.
Collared peccary *Tayassu tajacu*
Colocolo *Dromiciops australis*
Commerson's dolphin *Cephalorhynchus commersonii*
Common marmoset *Callithrix jacchus*
Common opossum *Didelphis marsupialis*
Common squirrel monkey *Saimiri sciureus*
Common woolly monkey *Lagothrix lagothricha*
Coro-coro rat *Dactylomys dactylinus*
Cotton-top tamarin *Saguinus oedipus*
Crab-eating fox *Cerdocyon thous*
Culpeo fox see Andean fox
Darwin's fox *Dusicyon fulvipes*
Dusky dolphin *Lagenorhynchus obscurus*
Emperor tamarin *Saguinus imperator*
Galapagos fur seal *Arctocephalus galapagoensis*
Geoffroy's cat *Oncifelis geoffroyi*
Geoffroy's tamarin *Saguinus geoffroyi*
Giant anteater *Myrmecophaga tridactyla*
Giant armadillo *Priodontes maximus*
Giant river otter *Pteronura brasiliensis*
Goeldi's monkey *Callimico goeldii*
Golden lion tamarin *Leontopithecus rosalia*
Gray-cap squirrel monkey *Saimiri sciureus*
Gray fox *Pseudalopex* spp.
Greater hairy armadillo *Chaetophractus villosus*
Guanaco *Lama guanico*
Guiana dolphin *Sotalia guianensis*
Guiña or kodkod *Oncifelis guigna*
Harbour porpoise *Phocoena phocoena*
Hoary bat *Lasiurus cinereus*
Hog-nosed skunk *Conepatus humboldti*
Howler monkey *Alouatta* spp.
Huemul see Andean deer
Humpback dolphin *Sousa* spp.
Humpback whale *Megaptera novaeangliae*
Jaguar *Panthera onca*
Killer whale or orca *Orcinus orca*
Kinkajou *Potos flavus*

Kodkod see guiña
Leaf-eared mouse *Phyllotis* spp.
Little spotted cat *Leopardus tigrina*
Manatee *Trichechus inunguis*
Maned wolf *Chrysocyon brachyurus*
Mara see Patagonian hare
Margay *Leopardus wiedii*
Marmoset *Callithrix* spp.
Monito del monte *Dromiciops australis*
Mountain tapir *Tapirus pinchaque*
Mountain viscacha *Lagidium viscacia*
Moustached tamarin *Saguinus mystax*
Muskrat *Ondata zibethicus*
Night or owl monkey *Aotus trivirgatus*
Nine-banded armadillo *Dasypus novemcinctus*
Northern pudú *Felis pardalis*
Olingo *Bassaricyon gabbii*
Orca see Killer whale
Owl monkey see Night monkey
Paca *Agouti paca*
Pacarana *Dinomys branickii*
Pampas cat *Oncifelis colocolo*
Pampas deer *Ozotoceros bezoarticus*
Patagonian hare or mara *Dolichotis patagonum*
Peale's dolphin *Lagenorhynchus australis*
Peccary *Tayassu tajacu* & *T. pecari*
Pichi *Zaedyus pichiy*
Plains viscacha *Lagostomus maximus*
Pudú *Pudu pudu*
Puma *Felis concolor*
Pygmy marmoset *Cebuella pygmaea*
Rat or shrew possum *Rhincolestes, Caenolestes & Lestoros* spp.
Red and white uakari *Cacajao calvus*
Red bat *Lasiurus brachyotis*
Red fox *Dusicyon culpaeus*
Red howler monkey *Alouatta seniculus*
Right whale *Balaena glacialis*
Ring-tailed coatis *Nasua nasua*
River dolphin see Botos
Saddle-back tamarin *Saguinus fuscicollis*
Sea cat or chungungo *Lutra felina*
Short-tailed chinchillas *Chinchilla brevicaudata*
Silver fox *Vulpes vulpes*
Silvery marmoset *Callithrix argentata*
South American or southern fur seal *Arctocephalus australis*
South American sea lion *Otaria flavescens*
Southern Andean huemul *Hippocamelus bisulcus*
Southern anteater or tamandua *Tamandua tetradactyla*
Southern elephant seal *Mirounga leonina*
Southern right whale *Eubalaena australis*
Southern river otter *Lutra provocax*
Southern sea lion *Otaria flavescens*
Spectacled bear *Tremarctos ornatus*
Sperm whale *Physeter catodon*
Swamp or marsh deer *Blastocerus dichotomus*
Tamandua see Southern anteater
Tapir *Tapirus terrestris*
Tayra *Eira barbara*
Three-toed sloth *Bradypus tridactylus*

Tucuxi dolphin *Sotalia fluviatilis guianensis*
Two-toed sloth *Choloepus* spp.
Vicuña *Vicugna vicugna*
Water opossum *Chironectus minimus*
White-eared opossum *Didelphus albiventris*
White-faced saki *Pithecia pithecia*
White-lipped peccary *Tayassu pecari*
White-throated capuchin *Cebus capucinus*
Woolly monkey *Lagothrix lagotricha*
Woolly opossum *Caluromys* spp.
Woolly spider monkey *Brachyteles arachnoides*
Yapok *Chironectes minimus*

REPTILES

Anaconda *Eunectes murinus*
Andean smooth-throated iguana *Liolaemus multiformis*
Black caiman *Melanosuchus niger*
Boa constrictor *Boa constrictor*
Broad nosed caiman *Caiman latirostris*
Bushmaster *Lachesis muta*
Caiman lizard *Tupinambis teguixin*
Dwarf caiman *Paleosuchus* spp.
Galapagos land iguana *Conolophus subcristatus*
Galapagos marine iguana *Amblyrhynchus cristatus*
Galapagos (giant) tortoise *Geochelone elephantopus*
Giant river turtle *Podocnemis expansa*
Green turtle *Chelonia mydas*
Hawksbill turtle *Eretmochelys imbricata*
Jacaré see Pantanal caiman
Lancehead *Bothrops atrox*
Land iguana *Conolphus subcristatus*
Lava lizard *Tropidurus* spp.
Leatherback turtle *Dermochelys coriacea*
Matamata terrapin *Chelus fimbriatus*
Matuasto *Diplolaemus darwini*
Olive Ridley turtle *Lepidochelys olivacea*
Orinoco crocodile *Crocodylus intermedius*
Pantanal caiman *Caiman crocodilus yacare*
Patagonian gecko *Homonata darwini*
Smooth-fronted caiman *Paleosuchus* spp.
Spectacled caiman *Caiman crocodilus*
Teju lizard *Tupinambis teguixin*
Tree boa *Corallus* spp.
Vine snake *Chironius carinatus*
Yellow spotted sideneck turtle *Podocnemis unifilis*

AMPHIBIANS

Glass frog *Centrolenella* spp.
Lake Titicaca frog *Telmatobius culeus*
Leptodatylid frog *Eleutherodactylus* spp.
Poison dart frog *Dendrobates ventrimaculatus*
Reticulated or red-backed poison dart frog *Dendrobates reticulatus*

FISH AND OTHER MARINE CREATURES

Angel fish *Pterophyllum* spp.
Banded head-standers *Leporinus fasciatus*

Burrowing crab *Emerita analoga*
Candiru *Pygidiidae*
Cardinal tetra *Paracheirodon axelrodi*
Clingfish *Sicyases sanguineus*
Deep-bodied hatchet fish *Gasteropelecus & Carnegiella* spp.
Discus fish *Symphsodon* spp.
Electric eel *Electrophorus electricus*
Flatfish *Achirus* spp.
Four-eyed blenny *Dialomus fuscus*
Golden ray *Rhinoptera steindachneri*
Jaraqui *Semaprochilodus* spp.
Leaf fish *Monocirrhus polycanthus*
Kingclip *Genypterus blacodes*
Knife fish *Gymnotiformes*
Krill *Euphausia superba*
Manta ray *Manta hamiltoni*
Mapará *Hypophthalmus* spp.
Matrinchão (river trout) *Brycon* spp.
Needlefish *Potamorrhaphis guianensis*
Pacú *Mylossoma* spp.
Piraiba catfish *Brachyplatystoma filamentosum*
Pirarucu *Arapaima giga*
Red-bellied piranha *Pygocentrus nattereri*
Red-mouthed bat fish *Ogocephalus darwini*
Red star *Grapsus grapsus*
Sally lightfoot *Grapsus* spp.
Scalloped hammerhead shark *Sphyrna lewini*
Sea star *Meyenaster gelatinosus*
Silverfish *Thysanura* spp.
Splashing tetra *Copella arnoldi*
Squid *Loligo patagonica*
Surgeon fish *Prionurus laticlavius*
Swamp eel *Symbranchus marmoratus*
Tambaquí *Colossoma macropomum*
Tamoatá *Hoplosternum* spp.
Traíra *Hoplias malabaricus*

INSECTS

Ambush ant *Azteca lanuginosa*
Army ant *Eciton* spp.
Carpenter ant *Camponotus* spp.
Crazy ant *Paratrachina longicornis*
Fire ant *Solenopsis* spp.
Leafcutter ant *Atta* spp.
Morpho butterfly *Morpho aega*
Phorid fly *Apocephalus* spp.
Rove beetle *Staphylinidae*
Thief ant *Solenopsis* spp.
Tiger beetle *Megacephala* spp.

INDEX

S

saki 101
  bearded 101
  white-faced 101
Salar Uyuni 36, 38–9, 186
Salimóes, Rio 69
salt lakes 25, 36–40, 45
saltpans 27, 36–40, 42, 130
San Andrés and Providencia
  Archipelago 194
San Cristóbal 168
San Pedro de Atacama 192
sandbanks 79–82
Santa Catarina Coast 189
Santa Cruz 168
Santa Fé 168
Saül 198
savannah *see cerrado*
Scalesia 166, 168
scarab beetle 62–3
scorpions 88
screamer, horned 75
sea lions 139, 142, 143, 166, 168
  Galápagos 170
  South American *150*, 161–3
  southern 147–8, 151
seals 149
  fur 151, *152–3*, 161, 162, 168, 170
seaweeds 151
seedsnipe 135
Segunda Angastura 148
seriemas 21
Serra da Canastra National Park 112
Sesuvium 168
Seymour Island 168
shark, scalloped hammerhead 172–4,
  174
shearwater 146, 168
sheathbill, snowy 149
Shell Beach 200
shrimp 67
  brine 36, 45
Sican culture 163
Sillaguay mountain 40
silver dollar 73
skimmer 162
skua
  brown 146
  Chilean 149
sloths 15, 92–3, 98
  brown-throated three-toed *93*
snails 151
Sol de Mañana 35–6
Southern Ocean 144–6, 148–9, 154
Spanish conquistadors 29, 30
sparrow, rufous-collared 135
spider monkey 98, *104*, 105
spiders 79, 88, 109
spinetail 45
sponges 79
spoonbill, roseate 135

squid 154, 155
squirrel monkey 71, 101
  gray-cap 101
starfish 151
steamer duck 154
Stegolepis 11
steppe, Patagonia 20, 135–8
strangler fig *102–3*, 125–6
sulphur mines 40
sunbittern 126
surgeon fish 172, *174*
Suriname 205, *205*
swan, black-necked 52, 53, 136
swift, dusky 24
Swiss-cheese plant 88

T

'tall gray friar' 45
tamarins 101
  emperor 101
  Geoffroy's 98
  golden lion 30, *30*
  moustached 91, 101
  saddle-back 91, 101
tambaqui 74, *74*, 78
Tambopata Candamo Reserve 203
tamoatá 74, 77
tanager 18
Tapajós River 67–9
tapir 25, 44, 86, 87, 89, *89*, 106, 112
tarantula 25
El Tatio 35, *37*
tepuis 11, 12
teratorn 20–1
termites 88, 112, 114, *114*, 116–18,
  119–21
tern
  Inca 161–2
  South American 149
terror birds 21
Tertiary period 25
tetra
  cardinal 66–7
  splashing 66
thornbill, olivaceous 42
Tierra del Fuego 184
tiger beetle 71
tinamou 136
Tiputini Biodiversity Station 89
Titicaca, Lake 27, 186
toad
  black 12
  puna 40
torrent duck 18, 44, 52
Torres del Paine 51, 53, *54–5*, 192
tortoise, giant *167*, 168, 169, 175
toucan, toco *199*
toucanet, emerald 18
tour groups 180
Touro Morto River 121

toxins, rainforest trees 105
traíra 62, 130
trees
  fruit 71, 73
  Pantanal 125–6
  rainforest 86, 88–90, 92, 97, 105,
    106
tropic bird 168
trumpeter bird 86
Tungurahua 34
Tupungato 34
turtle
  giant river 79–83, *82–3*
  green sea 164, 166, 168
tussock grass 146

U

uakari, white and red *68*, 71, 76, *76*
umbrella bird 44, 73
umbrella tree 92
UNESCO 53
Upsala Glacier 142
Uruguay 206, *206*
Urumbamba Gorge 18
urumbeva 126

V

Valley of the Moon 26
Valley of the Volcanoes 25
Venezuela 12, 207–8, *207*
vicuña 25, 40–1, 42, *43*
Villamil 169
vine snake 96
viscacha, mountain *32*, 39, 42, 45
volcanoes *16–17*, 20, 34, *34*, 166, 169
vultures 63, 90
  black 63, 133
  turkey 52, 155, 162

W

Wallace, Alfred Russel 66
warbler, American yellow 168
wasps 101
  sweat 84–6
water, in rainforest canopy 94–7
water hyacinth 126
waterfalls 12, *13*, 24, *24*
waterlilies 126
  Queen Victoria 62–3, *62*
weather
  Amazon Basin 69, 82
  Andes 41–5
  Chilean fjords 149, 150
  Galápagos Islands 166
  El Niño 162–4
  Southern Ocean 144

wetlands, Pantanal 121–35
whales 139
  humpback 149
  right 139, 142, *142*
  sperm 154, 164, 178
white-water rivers 67
wire-tail, Des Mur's 57
Wolf Island 172
wolf's fruit 121
wood stork 133
woodcreeper 112
woodpecker, giant Magellanic 57
woolly monkey 89, 98, 106

X

Xingu River 67, 69, 79–83

Y

yellowlegs 133
Yungas 186

Z

zebu cattle 131, 133

215

PICTURE CREDITS

André Bärtschi 14, 43, 44, 66, 84, 87, 95, 100 bottom, 102–3, 104, 204

BBC Natural History Unit: Doug Allan 34, 38, 181, Niall Benvie 1,
Barrie Britton 199, Jim Clare 29, 47, 158, 173, Michael & Patricia Fogden 93,
194, Jeff Foott 140–1, Armin Maywald 142, Pete Oxford 19, 58, 61, 144, 155,
156, 183, 197, Francois Savigny 130, Anup Shah 30, David Welling 13,
Staffan Widstrand 10

Laurie Campbell 48–9, 53, 54–5, 184

Huw Cordey 82–3

Tui De Roy 46, 147, 150, 167, 176–7, 179

Michael & Patricia Fogden 5, 5, 24, 72, 85 and running head,
96, 145 and running head

Robert Fulton 5, 16–17, 111 and running head, 128–9

Nick Gordon 5, 11 and running head, 64, 89, 92

Rhonda Klevansky 5, 26, 33 and running head, 37

Antonio Larrea 159, 163

Luiz Claudio Marigo 31, 62, 68, 114, 116, 118, 124, 202

Minden Pictures: Tui De Roy 2, 50, 99, 110, 161, 171, 196, Gerry Ellis 107,
Frans Lanting 80–1, 100 top, 122–3, 125, 132, 200, Claus Meyer 5, 59 and
running head, 76, 120, Mark Moffett 90, Flip Nicklin 70,

Oxford Scientific Films: Doug Allan 152–3, Michael Goulding 74,
Philip Sharpe 108, Norbett Wu 174

Planet Earth Pictures: Richard Matthews 113

Tim Scoones 32, 192

South American Pictures: Kathy Jarvis 22–3, Tony Morrison 28,

Staffan Widstrand 126, 127, 138, 191, 201, 206

Mark Yates 134